SCOTLAND

ATLANTIC

OCEAN

FOULA
SHETLAND
ISLANDS
Lerwick
Sumburgh

FAIR ISLE

WESTERAY
SANDAY
ORKNEY
ISLANDS
Kirkwall
Stromness
HOY
Burwick

NORTH

Cape Wrath
Port of Ness
Barvas
LEWIS
Carloway
Aird
Stornoway
Callanish
Balallan
Tarbert
Rodel

OUTER HEBRIDES

NORTH UIST
Lochmaddy
Ulig
SOUTH UIST
Lochboisdale

BARRA

Portree
SKYE
Stormeferry
Broadford
Kyle of Lochalsh

RHUM

TIREE

MULL
Tobermory
Craignure
Fionnphort
Kilmelfort

INNER HEBRIDES

Durness
Heilam
Loxford Bridge
Tongue
Scourie
3041
Lochinver
3274
3153
Lairg
Ullapool
Torridon
3422
Dingwall
Beauly
Inverness
Fort Augustus
Invergarry
Mallaig
Spean Bridge
Fort William
4409
Ballachulish
Lochaline
Oban

Bettyhill
Halkirk
Dounreay
Thurso
Castletown
John ò Groats
Wick
Latheron
Helmsdale
Brora
Golspie
Dornoch
Tain
Bonar Bridge
Invergordon
Cromarty
Fortrose
Nairn
Forres
Elgin
Lossiemouth
Grantown - on Spey
Aviemore
4298
Ballater
3789
Dee
Pitlochry
Kirriemuir
Blairgowrie
Tay
94
E15
Perth

NORTHWEST HIGHLANDS

Moray
Firth
SEA

Portsoy
Buckie
Banff
96
Huntly
Keith
Turriff
Elion
Oldmeldrum
Inverurie
Aboyne
Banchory
Laurencekirk
Brechin
Inverbervie
Montrose
Arbroath
Carnoustie
Fraserburgh
Peterhead
ABERDEEN

SCOTLAND

GRAMPIAN
Mountains

9
82

Crianlarich
Iveraray
Callander
Arrochar
Crieff
Cupar
M85
DUNDEE
St. Andrews
M90
Kinross
Leven
Anstruther
Stirling
Kirkcaldy
Dunfermline
Firth of Forth
North Berwick

Lochgilphead
Ardlussa
Port Askaig
ISLAY
Port Ellen
Campbeltown

KINTYRE

ARRAN
Brodick

Tarbert
Greenock
Rothesay
Ardrossan
Irvine

Paisley
GLASGOW
East Kilbride
Kilmarnock
Ayr

UNITED

Dumbarton
Coatbridge
Hamilton
Lanark
Cumnock
Maybole
Thornhill
Girvan
2765
New Galloway
Newton Stewart
77
Stranraer
Wigtown
Withorn

Falkirk
M8
EDINBURGH
Haddington
Peebles
Galashiels
Biggar
Selkirk
Sanquhar
Moffat
Nith
Lochmaben
E5
Dumfries
75
Annan
Dalbeattie
KINGDOM

Eyemouth
Berwick-upon-Tweed
Lauder
Coldstream
Kelso
Jedburgh
Alnwick
1
E15
Hawick
7
ENGLAND
Morpeth
NEWCASTLE UPON TYNE
Tynemouth
Haltwhistle
Maryport
Workington

Moville
Carndonagh
Portrush
Coleraine
Ballycastle
Ballymoney
Londonderry
Ballymena
Larne
Antrim
Newtown-abbey
Bangor
Omagh

NORTHERN IRELAND

Firth of Clyde

SCOTLAND

| 0 | | 50 km |
| 0 | | 50 miles |

7

TABLE OF CONTENTS

GUIDELINES

MAP LIST

SCOTLAND:

AN INTRODUCTION

"A great many people go to Scotland in the autumn. When you have your autumn holiday in hand to dispose of it, there is nothing more aristocratic you can do than go to Scotland... To go to Scotland in August and stay there, perhaps, till the end of September, is about the most certain step you can take towards autumnal fashion."

Anthony Trollope was writing in the Victorian Age, but his words again draw a smile of recognition today: Scotland is in vogue. And with reason. Scotland has something for everyone. For nature lovers, there's the raw beauty of its landscapes, with its *bens* or mountains, wave-beaten cliffs, and wildlife. Culture vultures can seek out the sites of favorite books and movies, from Stevenson's *Kidnapped* to the films *Rob Roy* and *Braveheart*, or take the pulse of the contemporary performing arts scene at Edinburgh's summer festival. And food lovers can feast on seafood and Angus beef, while tipplers seek out a "wee dram" in the distilleries along the Malt Whisky Trail.

And all of this within a relatively small space. Measuring 30,414 square miles (78,772 sq. km) in area, the whole region is a little smaller than the state of Maine, or the country of Austria. Extending upward from England and splintering, on its northern and western sides, into islands, Scotland is almost like an island itself: nowhere is the sea more than 70 miles (112 km) away, and there are 2,300 miles (3,700 km) of coastline. And where there's no sea, there are likely to be lochs, lakes left

Preceding pages: Postcard-perfect: Eilean Donan Castle, near Skye. The Standing Stones of Callanish on Lewis (Outer Hebrides). Left: Modern Highlanders reenact the Rallying of the Clans at Glenfinnian.

like the footprints of retreating glaciers, or the crinkled ridges of high mountain ranges.

The Lie of the Land

Geographically, Scotland can be roughly divided into three areas. Southernmost are the Southern Uplands. Starting at the Cheviot Hills, one of many different borders that have been drawn between Scotland and England through the ages, the Southern Uplands includes Dumfries and Galloway, tucked away to the southwest, as well as the Borders. Here rises one of Scotland's main rivers, the Tweed, itself forming a section of the border, which snakes eastwards through the Borders to empty into the North Sea.

To the north, Scotland's contours narrow and flatten into the Central Lowlands, or Central Scotland. This is a low-lying region of green pastures, but it also boasts Scotland's largest cities, Glasgow and Edinburgh; and it's here that most of Scotland's population and industry are concentrated. Sedate and elegant on the east coast, Edinburgh, Scotland's capital, dominates the Firth of Forth, looking across the water to the Forth's northern bank, the Kingdom of Fife, where the heart of Scotland's golfing tradition beats at St Andrews. On the other side of the country, Edinburgh's antipode, workaday Glasgow, sits on the banks of the river Clyde. Above Glasgow, the west coast is a land of rugged shores and islands, spectacular scenery and temperamental weather.

Best known of Scotland's regions are the Highlands, the largest and least populous part of the country. Here are the Grampians, Scotland's highest mountains, including the highest mountain in Britain, Ben Nevis. Here are the country's wildest lochs and forests; here the ferry ports to the best-loved islands: Skye, Harris and Lewis, Orkney and Shetland. First-time visitors to the High-

lands are often surprised at their bleakness: this is a barren, tundra-like landscape, punctuated dramatically with the high silhouettes of bens and the gray and purple shadows of the roiling clouds.

Beyond these three areas, Scotland can be subdivided in a number of ways. The most recent official repartitioning, in 1996, yielded 14 administrative districts, from the Highlands to the Borders.

Climate, Crops, and Commerce

Scotland has many assets, but no one claims that its climate is one of them. Still, the cool, wet summers are tempered by mild winters (temperatures in July average around 57°F / 14°C; in January, 39°F / 4°C). This is significant for farmers as well as visitors: it's too cold and wet to grow wheat. The main grains are oats and barley (reflected in Scotland's cuisine); potatoes

Above: Ben Nevis (1344 m) is Scotland's highest mountain. Right: Seals can be spotted at the west or north coast.

and other forage plants are also grown. Only about 20% of the land is cultivated; far more terrain – around 50% – is used for rough grazing.

But it's not only Scotland's land that's cultivated. Fishing has played a major role, although it's fallen off in recent years as the schools of fish grow smaller. Shipbuilding was another mainstay; the great shipbuilding yards on the Clyde continued to produce vessels through World War II, though their heyday, too, is past.

The country's natural resources include coal, iron ore, and the more recently discovered North Sea oil, a new source of revenue in the northeast. In spite of this and other new industries, from plastics and electronics to consumer goods, unemployment in Scotland remains higher than the British average.

Wildlife

The land may look wild, but in fact man has done much to shape it. Most of

the country was originally wooded, but over the centuries and millennia, the trees were cleared away, first to make room for agriculture, later to feed the furnaces of the Industrial Revolution. Only in a few acres of woodland park (around Avie-more, for example, Glen Affric, or Loch Rannoch) can you still see original Scots pine and get a sense of what Scotland must once have looked like.

Yet the indigenous fauna are still present in a wealth and variety virtually without equal in Europe. Pheasant are a common sight, their iridescent plumage standing out in the landscape; from the road, motorists can also spot red deer and wild goats, grouse and quail. But for all the peregrine falcons and owls inland, it's along the coasts that birdwatchers come into their own. Crowded on the sheer cliffs of Scotland's northern coasts like residents of a Hong Kong apartment block, fulmars and shags, guillemots and kittiwakes live cheek by jowl. The north also boasts a considerable population of puffins, nicknamed "God's clowns" due to their droll appearance. And plenty of marine life is visible from the shore: the tails of whales, for instance, in the North Sea and Atlantic. Dolphins swim the waters of the Moray Firth, and seals sun themselves on the beaches of the north and west coasts.

Scottish Hallmarks

Since at least the 13th century, Scotland's emblem has been the St. Andrew's Flag, a diagonal white cross on a blue ground, symbol of the patron saint of Scotland. Another national symbol is the thistle. The story goes that, when Viking invaders were preparing a sneak attack on the Scots, a barefoot Viking stepped on a thistle; his cry of pain alerted the Scots, and saved the day.

Scotland even has its own church: Presbyterianism has been the national religion since the 16th century, when reformers took harsh action against the artistic treasures of medieval, catholic Scotland, leaving many of them in ruins.

THE HISTORY OF SCOTLAND

Earth's forces are palpable in the north. Millions of years ago, earthquakes and shifting plates folded the country that was to become Scotland like a piece of paper, creased along the seam of a chain of lochs later prosaically dubbed the Caledonian Canal, or along the dotted line of islands running through present-day Loch Lomond. Glaciers moved down from the north and carved deep crevasses into the land. And yet these northern reaches were a pleasant place to live.

At least, they were 5,000 years ago. Stone Age man lived well in the north of Scotland. The average height was 5'7": hardly the stature of a suffering or malnourished people. The diet was varied: people fished the seas, climbed the high sea cliffs to nab nesting birds and their

Above: The Stones of Aberlemno, relics of Pictish culture. Right: Iona was the birthplace of Christianity in Scotland.

eggs, hunted the forests for deer, gathered berries and wild onions, sorrel and dandelions, and even grew wheat – for the climate was a few degrees warmer. People lived in stone dwellings with beds, hearths, shelving, protected by snug turf roofs: a glimpse of communal life is preserved at Skara Brae on Orkney. But most of the extant testimony from this period has to do with death, not life. Burial cairns with stout walls rose from the earth in gentle mounds that were used for generations, the bones cleared out from time to time and replaced with new ones. Standing stones defined perfect circles, like Orkney's Ring of Brodgar, of which the enigmatic serenity has defied later generations anxious to divine a purpose in its order.

Time passed, and new peoples sought out the land. When Roman legionaries arrived in 82 A.D. at the northernmost extremity of their new territory of Caledonia, they found themselves resisted by local tribesmen who painted their faces blue before doing battle. This war-paint earned them the derisive nickname of "Picts" (from *picti*, or painted), not unlike the term "Yankees" or "Krauts"; but call them what they would, the Romans had trouble subduing them. Despite a variety of fortifications along various demarcations of this northern border, from Hadrian's Wall (in present-day England) to the Antonine Wall (which ran from the Clyde to the Forth, along the "waist" of Scotland), the Romans couldn't hold the line; furthermore, it was expensive to maintain garrisons in this inhospitable land. They finally withdrew in the third century A.D.

Four Peoples, One Country

The *Picts* were only one of four peoples who controlled the land over the next centuries. Certainly they were the most powerful. Evidence of the breadth of their kingdom is present in sculpted symbol stones of remarkable intricacy and beauty, found especially in the northeast of Scotland, the heart of their kingdoms. Other evidence is lacking. Conquered by the invading *Scots*, a Gaelic people who had been filtering over from Ireland since around the fourth and fifth centuries A.D., the Picts were so thoroughly eradicated (or integrated) that even their language was lost; no records remain of their histories or genealogies. To the south, the *Britons*, erstwhile allies of the departed Romans, had their own problems in the form of invading *Angles* from England: numerous skirmishes yielded to the tenuous alliance that produced the kingdom of Northumbria, which encompasses most of the present-day Borders as well as the English region still known as Northumberland.

A fifth group made its presence felt, as well: the *Norsemen*, or Vikings, kept control over the islands – present-day Shetland, Orkney, and the Outer Hebrides – and were always up for a raid on a local abbey or village along the coast.

For abbeys there were, ever since the early Irish missionaries landed on these shores: Ninian, in 397, was followed by the even more influential Columba, in 563. Scotland's west and southwest coast is sprinkled with relics of early Christianity, from Ninian's Whithorn to the island of Iona to Dunadd Fort, the capital where Columba crowned Aidan king in 574. Ultimately, it was Christianity that gave the interloping Scots the upper hand in local disputes: they could always count on help from outside – from Rome and its allies – if the going got tough. In light of persisting Norse attacks, it was in any case in everyone's best interest to get along and stand together. Thus the Scots' king Kenneth MacAlpine, who had a claim to the Pictish throne as well, ascended the latter in 843, uniting the two peoples in a single kingdom variously known as Alba, the Pictish Kingdom, or, later on, Scotland. In the early 11th century, Kenneth's descendent Malcolm II was able to gain control of the southern reaches, and brought Britons and Angles into the kingdom, as well. Sign of power of these early Scottish kings was the Stone of Destiny, which was later moved to Scone. Only a man crowned over this stone, it was believed, could be the rightful king of Scotland.

The House of Canmore

Scotland's early history is obscured both by time and by fiction: Malcolm's grandson and appointed heir, Duncan, was murdered in 1040 by another claimant to the throne named Macbeth. Actually, Shakespeare's drama more or less follows historic fact, except that Duncan was a young man when he was killed, and the real Macbeth ruled for 17 years, apparently well enough, before Malcolm III, Duncan's son, killed him in turn. One can judge Shakespeare's eye for aesthetic effect in the fact that Macbeth's wife has remained "Lady Macbeth" for posterity: her real name was Gruoch.

Apart from this interlude, however, Malcolm's line remained upon the Scottish throne for more than two centuries. Now that the peoples of Scotland were more or less solidly united, relations with neighboring England became the focal point of foreign policy, although the Norse continued to be a strong presence. In fact, Malcolm III's first wife was the daughter of a Norse noble, Ingebiorg; his second, an intelligent and devout woman now known as St. Margaret (see pp. 49, 213), was a decisive force in establishing an English-speaking church in Scotland. Margaret lost her husband and a son in fighting against the English at Alnwick, the retaliation to a number of Scottish invasions that Malcolm had led into the south – which did nothing to improve diplomatic relations. England, of course, wanted Scotland for its own; Scotland wanted Northumbria; and this state of af-

Right: Highland history explained in an exhibit in the monastery of Fort Augustus.

fairs was to persist for several hundred years.

The Norse problem was resolved in 1263, when Haakon of Norway's last invasion attempt ended in decisive defeat at a battle by Largs, on the southwest coast. In 1266, the Treaty of Perth granted Scotland all of Norway's former possessions – most of the Western Isles – except for Orkney and Shetland; the treaty marked the beginning of a Scottish-Norse friendship. Alexander III's daughter Margaret married Haakon's grandson Eric II, a union which produced another Margaret, known as the Maid of Norway.

The Maid was to come to the fore all too soon. Alexander III's reign saw the culmination of the development of a stable feudal government, both administratively and judicially. A linchpin of the feudal system were the local administrative hubs of the Royal Burghs, with artisan services and markets. However, the "Golden Age" of Alexander's reign, which lasted more than 35 years, came to an abrupt end one dark night in 1286 when Alexander, riding home to his new wife, fell off his horse and broke his neck. As all of his children had already died, his only direct heir was the Maid of Norway, Margaret, who was all of three years old at the time. The consequence was a bitter, and lengthy, battle for the Scottish crown.

The Wars of Succession

It started slowly; while regents stood in for the little girl, the watchful English king Edward I quickly arranged a marriage between Margaret and the Prince of Wales, which seemed advantageous to all parties concerned. Alas, Margaret died four years later on her way to Scotland; and it was then that all hell broke loose. No fewer than 13 candidates for the crown presented themselves, their claims based on various relationships more or less distant (one of them was Eric of Nor-

way, little Margaret's father). The two leading contenders were John Balliol and Robert Bruce, cousins who were both descended from Alexander III's great-uncle David. Trying to avert civil war, the Scottish aristocracy called Edward of England in to arbitrate the situation – which Edward took as a tacit admission of his own power in the country's affairs. The "winner" was John Balliol, the senior of the two claimants, who became effectively a puppet of the English; Scotland's autonomy was compromised.

The Scottish people weren't prepared to take this lying down. First, the nobles banded together and concluded the first official treaty of the "Auld Alliance" with France, England's enemy. Balliol, seeing unrest, shrugged off English authority, whereupon Edward marched north to subdue the upstart – who promptly abdicated, in 1296 – and take Scotland for himself. (Edward also took the Stone of Scone, making himself the "rightful" king of Scotland; the Stone was to reside under the royal throne of London's Westminster Abbey for the next seven centuries.)

At this, the common people took matters into their own hands, under the leadership of men like "Braveheart" William Wallace, an "outlaw" from southwest Scotland who had been leading minor attacks on the English for some time. Wallace and his people's army managed to defeat English troops at Stirling Bridge; but Edward's superior forces returned in 1298 and put down the movement at Falkirk. Wallace's end at the hands of the English is now a matter of Hollywood record; but long before the movie, he was a figure of legend, and a rallying-cry of national pride. One of the first works of Scottish literature was the 15th-century epic poem *Wallace*.

One person who reacted to Wallace's example was Robert Bruce, another claimant to the throne. Bruce had problems enough disentangling himself from disputes with other would-be kings; after he killed one rival, John Comyn, in 1306, crowning himself king became impera-

tive, if only for the legal protection the job afforded, and he did so at Scone a few weeks later (for a more detailed account of this period, see p. 95).

Despite his crown, it was an uphill struggle at the beginning. He had plenty of enemies – the powerful Comyn family, for a start. Scots didn't trust him because he'd once served Edward; Edward swore not to rest until he brought him down. Bruce spent much of his first year in office fleeing hostile armies, from the Highlands over to the west coast.

But his luck turned. Edward I of England died in 1307, and his son, Edward II, proved a less indomitable foe. Bruce began to win. Moving out from the south-west of Scotland, he started driving away the English. The French recognized his authority; the Scottish aristocracy followed suit. In 1314, Edward II brought a mighty army north; and Bruce and the

Above: An equestrian statue of Robert Bruce commemorates the Battle of Bannockburn.

Scots defeated him at the Battle of Bannockburn. From here on in, Scottish fortunes rose. The Pope, who had refused to recognize the country's independence, was gradually brought round, aided by the 1320 Declaration of Arbroath, the Scottish aristocracy's formal refusal to submit to English rule. In 1328, the Treaty of Northampton was England's official acknowledgement of Scotland's independence.

It's a pattern in the history of many countries that strong kings are succeeded by weak ones. At first, David II couldn't help being weak: he was five years old when his father Robert died in 1329. This was a signal for Balliol's heirs to move in, backed up by the English; in self-defence, the Scots fell back on the "Auld Alliance" and sent their little King to France for safekeeping.

When he had grown up sufficiently, David returned with dreams of leading his country to glory; but he was not the warrior his father had been: the English captured him and held him prisoner for more than ten years. England's king, Edward III, was David's brother-in-law, and while holding the childless David captive, he managed to persuade the Scottish king that passing the throne of Scotland to England upon his death might not be such a bad thing. However, Edward turned his attentions to France, where he was involved in what's now known as the Hundred Years' War, and let David go – in exchange for the payment of a "king's ransom." This fell to the people of Scotland, who, loyal in spite of their king's fickleness, struggled to keep up payments until Edward's death in 1377. By then, David had already been dead six years.

Enter the Stuarts

Robert II, the successor, was an aging nephew of the late king's. His main claim to fame was reintroducing grounds for squabble over the succession, since he had numerous children by two different marriages, one of which may or may not have been legal. It was ultimately decided legal enough that Robert II's ineffective oldest son succeeded his ineffective father as Robert III. His other children, all variously connected to important noble families, contributed to unrest in the country; infamous among them is Alexander, remembered as "the Wolf of Badenoch," who terrorized the north and burnt gorgeous Elgin Cathedral in one of his raids. These inauspicious beginnings marked the start of the Stuart line – spelled "Stewart" until its famous daughter Mary, Queen of Scots "Frenchified" it in the 16th century.

Maintaining royal authority in Scotland was no easy matter in any case: powerful noble families, like the Donalds and the Douglases, held sway over broad areas of the country and recognized little authority but their own. The situation was made no easier by the accession to the throne of a number of minors. When Ro-

bert III died, the throne went to his 11-year-old nephew, the first of many Jameses. This one was, unfortunately, in English captivity, having been scooped up on his way to safety and France. King Henry V kept the captive James safely in tow, taking him along to the battles in France; this gave the English king an excuse to execute any Scotsmen he captured fighting in the French army, since they were fighting "against their king." After Henry V died, James I, by now adult, was able to buy himself free in 1424 (ransom having by now become an established part of Scottish royal tradition), and returned home ready to show his people who was boss. In delineating the extent of his power, he necessarily (and sometimes ruthlessly) moved against strong noble families, including some of his own relations, and this awakened enmity. In 1437, an uncle and a cousin murdered James in his bedroom (in fact, in the sanctity of his privy) at the Blackfriars' house in Perth (see p. 213).

Minor followed upon minor. Six-year-old James II was known as "James of the Fiery Face" due to a large red birthmark across his visage. As he grew up, he showed signs of developing a strong political presence: but fire – gunfire – was to be the death of him. One of his own guns exploded in his face while he was curiously examining it as it fired against the English. His son was all of eight.

This son, James III, had his own problems with the aristocracy; although his reign saw territorial expansion. He grew up to marry the daughter of Christian I of Norway, Margaret; unable to afford the dowry, her father pledged the islands of Orkney and Shetland as a deposit. They were never reclaimed, and Scotland annexed them soon after. James also managed to acquire the region of Ross from the Lord of the Isles, John, leader of the powerful Clan Donald, which held sway in the north. But this king was no more able than his grandfather to withstand the powerful nobles, led by James's own brother, and later enlisting the support of his son. On June 11, 1488, in an armed battle known as Sauchieburn, James III was thrown from his horse, wounded, taken to a nearby house for medical attention, and there murdered by someone pretending to be a cleric.

War with England, Again

James IV was a Renaissance man, interested in arts and sciences, among them the art and science of good government. He spoke several languages, including a little Gaelic. This helped him make more progress than any king before him bringing the unruly islanders and Highlanders into the Scottish fold, in fact as well as in name. However, when his policy of kindness seemed to have only temporary results, he set up the Campbells and the Gordons as hereditary sheriffs. They were to remain instruments of royal law and order for centuries to come.

In terms of Scotland's foreign policy, James's reign also seemed promising: he improved relations with England by marrying an English princess, Margaret. Unfortunately, England and France were still at odds, and when the new king Henry VIII joined the Pope in a Holy League against France, James found himself bound by two mutually exclusive treaties, the Anglo-Scottish peace of 1502/1509 and the oft-renewed Auld Alliance. He was forced to keep faith to the older of the two, and marched against England in 1513, a campaign doomed to resounding disaster at the battle of Flodden Field, where the English utterly defeated the Scots, and King James IV was killed. Heir to the throne was, in the best tradition of the Stuarts, an infant: James V. Not only was he in line to the throne of

Right: John Knox gives an impassioned sermon against the corruption of the Catholic church (St. Giles's, Edinburgh).

Scotland: he was also the nephew of England's Henry VIII.

When he grew up, this James, like his predecessors, tried to bring the powerful Highland and Border lords under control; and, like his predecessors, found that this policy backfired in that it alienated some powerful allies. Despite his English roots, James was a loyal French ally. His two wives were both French, and he thus remained Catholic at a time when the Protestant Reformation was starting to make itself felt both in Scotland and in England, where his uncle, Henry VIII, had converted to Protestantism so he could divorce Catherine of Aragon. James's alliance with France, and especially his second marriage to the French Mary of Guise, whom Henry had had his eye on himself, finally provoked the uncle to move into Scotland. The pivotal battle in this conflict was at Solway Moss: another terrible defeat for the numerically superior Scots. James, already ailing, went off like a wild animal to die in his own lair at Falkland, convinced that the dynasty was at an end. He left behind him a daughter six days old: Mary, Queen of Scots.

A Rough Wooing

Young as the heiress was, there immediately began a dispute about whom she should marry. England wanted her for the crown prince Edward, son of Henry VIII; when the Scots hesitated, the English began attacking the towns of the Borders in a move locals dubbed "the rough wooing." This "wooing" continued even after Henry's death under the Earl of Hertford, regent for nine-year-old Edward VI; it led to the burning of some of the great Border cathedrals. Not that Hertford's men were the first to destroy these; Henry VIII's men had incinerated a few before Solway Moss; and for that matter, Edward II had been at them as early as 1322.

The French came to the rescue of their Scottish allies and their French regent,

Mary of Guise – on the condition that the child Mary marry the French Dauphin. Mary was accordingly brought to France and raised with the King's court, where she grew into a striking six-foot-tall red-head with a penchant for fine clothes and jewelry. Her mother continued to hold the fort in Scotland in her absence.

The Rise of the Reformation

All was far from quiet on the Scottish front. A new religion was making popular headway: followers of Martin Luther and John Calvin spoke out against the excesses of the Catholic church. One of these Protestants was Scotsman John Knox. In England, Knox did well under Henry's Protestant son, Edward VI, but he prudently left the country after that young man died of tuberculosis and the throne went to his Catholic half-sister, called "Bloody Mary" for her atrocious persecution of Protestants. Knox returned to Scotland for good in 1559, by which time the Protestant Elizabeth I had suc-

ceeded her half-sister on the English throne and was confusing her subjects by persecuting Catholics as ardently as Mary had gone after the Protestants.

By now, Scotland's Protestants, the Presbyterians, were a force to be reckoned with. In 1557, a group of them had signed the first Covenant, pledging to resist the Congregation of Satan; a distant forerunner of the 17th-century document that was to serve as a rallying-call for a generation of Protestants, this one was potent enough to spark public attacks on Catholic processions in Edinburgh two years in a row. This volatile Protestant faction found the rule of Catholic Mary of Guise increasingly galling. Some people also worried that Scotland might be absorbed by France, as their Queen, Mary, married the French Dauphin (and future François II) in 1558; upon their marriage, she indeed signed a treaty granting him, if she were to die childless, both the right to her realm and her claim to the English throne.

The common people didn't know about this treaty; nonetheless, John

Knox, preaching in Perth in 1559, found his words falling on fertile ground. Incited to action, his supporters marched on Edinburgh and voted to depose Mary of Guise in 1559. French troops came to Mary's aid; the Scots, therefore, successfully appealed to England's Elizabeth I, and the result was an Anglo-French treaty that removed French troops from English soil. The Protestants, left free rein, officially abolished the Catholic Mass in 1560. That same year, France's François II died, leaving Mary, Queen of Scots, a 20-year-old widow, Francophone and Catholic, ready to return to her people.

Mary, Queen of Scots

Relations with England were all the more tricky as many people thought Mary had a better claim to the English

Above: Mary, Queen of Scots alienated many of her subjects by remaining true to her Catholic faith. Left: Her birthplace (1542): Linlithgow Palace.

throne than Elizabeth. Since the Catholic church didn't recognize Henry VIII's divorce from Catherine of Aragon to marry Anne Boleyn, Catholics saw Henry and Anne's daughter, Elizabeth I, as illegitimate, whereas Mary was a direct, legitimate descendant of Henry VII. Upon her return, trying to appease a number of different factions, Mary agreed to recognize Elizabeth as long as Elizabeth recognized Mary's right to the English throne in the event of Elizabeth's death.

If Mary's rule was to succeed, religious tolerance was in order. She took steps to win over her Protestant subjects by publishing an edict forbidding her followers to take action against the religion that was established in the country when she got there; and she even met with John Knox to discuss religious matters. While she didn't preach her own religion, however, she remained very much a Catholic, asserting her right to have Mass said in her own palace – a thorn in the sides of many Protestant Scots.

A second thorn was her cousin Darnley, an attractive, if soft, young man who was second in line to the English throne after Mary. Mary was by now old enough to silence political discussions about whom she should marry by deciding the issue for herself: she fell in love with Darnley, and they were married within a matter of months. Unfortunately, after a few months more it was clear that Darnley was a washout. Foolish and hungry for power, he had made enemies among the Protestant nobility in Scotland, as well as with Elizabeth I, who had opposed the marriage in the first place.

The real quarrel between Darnley and Mary focused on the issue of the "Crown Matrimonial": as Mary's husband, Darnley wanted an equal share in her power. Mary, already disillusioned with him, had no intention of giving it to him; and she found support (in more than merely an advisory sense) from her secretary, the Italian David Rizzio or Riccio, who,

some Protestants feared, was actually a secret agent of the Pope. On March 9, 1566, Darnley and his henchmen broke into Mary's apartments at Holyrood, dragged Rizzio from the supper table and murdered him outside the door. In fact, Darnley was making an open bid for power, with knowledge of his cousin Elizabeth I; but Mary, in an advanced state of pregnancy, managed to rekindle the old flame long enough to win him back to her side. Peace restored, she gave birth in June, announcing to Darnley and everyone else around that "God has given you and me a son, begotten by none but you."

But, glad as she was of a legitimate heir, she didn't want his father; her new favorite was the Earl of Bothwell. It is a matter of record that she discussed, and rejected, divorce, since she wanted there to be no question about her son's right of succession. She wasn't, however, the only one who wanted Darnley gone; most of the Scottish nobles were on her side at least in this, particularly Bothwell. Darnley, meanwhile, had fallen quite ill (some

say with smallpox), and Mary went so far in a show of affection as to move him from Glasgow to Edinburgh, not, however, taking him into the castle so as to avoid infecting their infant son. One February night, she visited him with some attendants, including Bothwell, on the way to a party; in the wee hours of that morning, the house in which Darnley was staying, which had gunpowder stored in its cellar, blew up. But it wasn't the explosion that caused Darnley's end: his body was found in the garden the next morning, bearing clear marks of strangulation.

It's still unclear how far Mary was involved in the murder; but there's little question that Bothwell was a driving force in it. Popular opinion rose against both of them. It might have subsided against Mary had Bothwell not flown with her, rapidly divorced his wife, and married Mary – by force, according to the story Mary told when she was trying to clear her name – three months later. With this marriage, Mary effectively pardoned

the conspirators of her husband's murder, and it was a bit too much to flaunt in people's faces. While crowds in Edinburgh chanted "Burn the whore," the nobility moved against Mary and Bothwell. Bothwell took off for Norway, and Mary, holding her ground, was imprisoned and, on June 24, forced to abdicate. She managed to escape from her captivity and rally an army of supporters, but her return lasted no more than ten days. Defeated near Glasgow in May, 1568, she fled by way of Galloway – where she spent her last night on Scottish soil at Dundrennan Abbey – to England, and appealed to her cousin Elizabeth for help.

Elizabeth "helped" by detaining her dangerous cousin – in a more or less friendly manner, at first, but with increasing restrictions as Mary kept on involving herself in various plots to take over one or the other of her rightful thrones;

Above: Queen Elizabeth I of England at the height of her power (portrait by Robert Peake, 1580).

she was all the more dangerous to Elizabeth because of the support she had in her claims from her Catholic subjects. In Scotland, rule was left in the hands of a string of regents, all loyal to England, until the very young James VI took over, ascending the throne in 1578. James, who had barely known his mother, played a close hand and tried to keep his ties firm in all directions: to the Catholics as well as to the Protestant Elizabeth, who awarded him a pension for several years before she finally beheaded his mother, Mary, in 1587.

Stuarts on the English Throne

James VI lacked his mother's physical attractiveness; he made up for it with his intelligence. He is one of the few kings to go down in history as a man of letters, and not only for the "King James Bible," produced during his reign and still the most beautiful translation in English: he also wrote himself. He was not physically brave, finding swordplay and violence distasteful. But he was ambitious; and he had his eye on the English throne.

One thing he had in common with Mary was religious tolerance; himself a staunch Protestant (and firm ally of Elizabeth I), he was reasonably amenable to Catholics both within and outside his realm – even though his "Negative Confession" of 1581 was an explicit and strongly-worded condemnation of Catholicism. Keeping friendly with all the nobles, regardless of their religious persuasion, seemed a wise move considering the number of problems that rebellious nobles had given his Stuart forbears. It was fortunate that he was tolerant, because his queen, Anne of Denmark, converted to Catholicism at one point in their marriage – although she later converted back. Anne was a good queen in that she bore James seven children, no mean feat, given that he was homosexual.

In 1603, Elizabeth I died childless, and there was no question about who was next in line. James VI of Scotland became James I of England. His Scottish loyalties were firm enough to keep him from uniting his two kingdoms; they remained separate countries ruled by the same king. But although James emphasized his Scottish allegiance in his parting address in Edinburgh before riding south, he was – as is only human – attracted most by his new toy, this bigger, wealthier, more powerful kingdom. Leaving a group of competent ministers to govern for him in Scotland, James didn't return to his native land until 1617.

One reason for staying away was that James quickly grew to enjoy the higher standard of living in his new country. So much did he adapt to its ways that reorganizing the Scottish church along more Anglican lines became one of the big projects of his administration. He instituted bishops into the structure of the free churches, effectively giving himself a way to influence church administration;

people might have been ready to put up with this, but he went on to introduce new elements into the ceremony itself, and one reason he came back to Scotland in 1617 was to help institute his new, more English-style service. Despite initial resistance, he managed to push through these reforms, which Parliament approved as the "Five Articles of Perth" in 1621. But not everyone was content: to many Scots, the new developments smacked of the "Popery" they had worked so hard and so long to shake off.

Although the king was absent, the reign of James VI/I was long, peaceful, and generally marked with advances for Scotland. With Scotland and England under the same crown, the Borders ceased to be so bitterly contested. Clan feuds continued in the Highlands, but a measure of order was instituted there, as well: the head of the Macgregor clan was captured by means of a trick and executed, and the clan and very name of Macgregor subsequently proscribed, setting an example for other unruly clans. (A century later, "Rob Roy" Macgregor often avoided using his last name; see p. 209.) Yet the discontent James's religious reforms had sown were to bear fruit under his son and successor, Charles I, who came to the throne after his father's death in 1625.

A younger son, less attractive and popular than his older brother Henry, Charles had not been groomed for kingship; but Henry died in 1612. Charles seems to have been marked by a kind of emotional short man's complex, an urge to overcompensate to prove to the world that he could be a good king, after all. His views of monarchy were correspondingly extreme; he believed in absolute monarchy, and saw Parliament as a possibly unnecessary evil, taking whatever steps he could without them.

In Scotland, his hardheadedness went over particularly badly. Since his family had left Scotland when he was

The Struggle of the Covenant...

Ultimately, opposition to Charles in Scotland organized itself into a proper administration, the "Tables," which, the King being absent, easily moved into a position of power. This body's most significant act was to draw up a National Covenant in 1638. Repeating the "Negative Confession" of Charles's father, this document bound its signatories to support the king in the defense of true religion – a statement against Popery and Anglicanism, but not necessarily against the King himself. Charles, however, was unyielding; although thousands of people signed the document throughout the country, he refused their demand that he withdraw the bishops from the Privy Council and the Anglican liturgy from Scotland's churches, and countered with the news that the "Supplicants" of these requests could be punished as traitors. The "traitors" met this with yet more demands; they were fully prepared to set up their own government, a process which was *de facto* occurring in any case. Open conflict was inevitable.

In the first armed meeting, the Scots had the upper hand, finally forcing Charles into the concessions he had thereto avoided. The Scots were happy to negotiate; they didn't really want to fight against their King. Charles promised to recognize a free Parliament and Assembly for Scotland, and to withdraw his troops if the Scots would dissolve the Tables.

All that dissolved, however, was the peace treaty. Intoxicated with its success, the Scottish Parliament was rapidly moving to free itself from royal constraints and become an independent body. The strong Scots Army marched down and occupied the north of England, specifically the coal grounds around Newcastle. A peace treaty negotiated at Ripon showed them the clear victors.

very young, Charles had little sense of identity with his "native" country; he wasn't even officially crowned there until 1633. Subsequently, his main attentions went to changing the Scottish church – often without the benefit of approval by either Parliament or the General Assembly. Political changes included introducing bishops into the privy council and making the King the head of the church; but it was his revamping the whole liturgy, imposing Anglicanism upon Scotland's Presbyterianism, that roused the people's wrath, already provoked by James I's efforts in this direction. Riots broke out in Edinburgh's St. Giles's Church (the "Jenny Geddes riots"; see p. 54), sign of an upheaval that was soon to sweep through Scotland, England and Ireland.

Above: James VI of Scotland became James I of England in 1603. Right: Charles I's clerical reforms incited the Covenanters to open resistance.

Charles went so far as to make a special trip to Scotland in 1641 to pacify the people.

...and Civil War

Scotland wasn't the only part of his realm giving Charles trouble; the Catholic rising in Ulster was the real spark that lit the blaze of England's civil war. Part of the issue was the question of who had control of the English army, the King or Parliament; the latter had little love for Charles, since he was constantly trying to rule without it. The two camps finally began an open war in 1642: Charles and the royalists on one side, the Parliamentarians, led by the Puritan aristocrat Oliver Cromwell, on the other. Both King and Parliament made open appeals to the Scots, who deliberated about which side to back: for Scotland, the decisive question was which of the two camps was better prepared to support their own Presbyterianism.

After some seesawing, the decision fell to Parliament. The "Solemn League and Covenant" was worked out in 1643; its provisions included getting rid of Popery, upholding both reformed religion and the King's authority, and preserving peace between England and Scotland. Approved and ratified by the Scots, the Covenant was subsequently passed in both Houses of Parliament. In 1644 General Leslie led a large company of Scots to the aid of their new allies, the battered Parliamentarians, who were besieging Charles's army at York. Victories for the Parliamentarians followed.

Scots power was strong, even despite the brilliant military tactics of James Graham, Marquis of Montrose, who led a piecemeal army of Highlanders and Irishmen through the north, fighting against the Covenanters in the name of the King. Montrose was as avowed a monarchist as the King himself; in the tradition of James VI, he also wrote poetry (see p.

53-4). He fought well but ruthlessly; in fact, the brutality of his men created some sentiment against the Royalists. Yet the fact that he was able to raise a popular army at all was a sign of how far public sentiment was divided.

For the alliance with Parliament was unsteady at best. What, after all, was "the best reformed religion," as laid forth in the Covenant – Anglicanism or Presbyterianism? The English Parliamentarians weren't crazy about Presbyterianism. As for the Scots, they were all for their own religion, but not happy to be fighting against the King: they remained Royalists at heart. Furthermore, the Scots felt they were being used by the English, who clearly cared more about gaining political power than about the letter of the Covenant. Charles seemed prepared to restore Presbyterianism if restored himself. Accordingly, negotiations began with Charles – to the outrage of Cromwell and Parliament. Suddenly, the sides had switched: Scotland was marching with the king.

29

Cromwell and the Protectorate

But this didn't last long either. Cromwell came to terms with Scotland, basically as a way to forestall Scotland's interfering in his movements against the King, and in 1649, had Charles I beheaded in London. The two countries' reactions spoke volumes: Cromwell proclaimed the Commonwealth, and Scotland declared the accession of King Charles II. Seeing where his support lay, Charles II promptly declared his allegiance to the Covenant and moved with his Scots subjects against Cromwell.

The Scotsmen made a strong start, and Cromwell had a hard time of it; but the tide turned at Dunbar, when a Scottish tactical error allowed him to mow down the ranks of Covenanters. The final battle took place a year later, in 1651: Charles fled, and the age of Cromwell's Protec-

Above: Cromwell had Charles I beheaded in 1649. Right: William III forced the Highland Clans to take an oath of fealty to the Crown.

torate – effectively a dictatorship of both England and Scotland – began.

This period saw the first real attempts at Scottish-English union, much to the resentment of many Scots subjects. Still, it wasn't such a terrible time for the country. England governed well – perhaps better than many Stuart predecessors – and the economy prospered. The "yoke" of English rule made itself felt in high taxes; but Scottish resentment stemmed as much from wounded national pride as from any real suffering.

Restoration of the Monarchy

Cromwell died in 1658; his son Richard proved incapable of holding together the unstable construct of government the father had created by force of will, and the Protectorate quickly crumbled. In 1660, King Charles II returned to England and was welcomed with hysterical joy by his subjects – especially in Scotland.

Unfortunately, Stuart blood wasn't the only thing Charles II had inherited from

James VI and Charles I: he was also a firm believer in absolute monarchy. Swerving from it, after all, had led his countries into their present difficulties. Accordingly, he reverted to tradition. Scotland's Parliament passed legislation awarding him tremendous power; and the bishops began inching their way back up the governmental totem pole. Another act repealed all legislation passed since 1633. The effect of this was to make the "reform religion" that Charles had pledged to uphold not Presbyterianism, but the Anglicanism espoused by James VI and Charles I – the religious attitude that had set off the conflict in the first place. Taking the Covenant, furthermore, was declared a treasonable act. No longer the majority party in Scotland, the Covenanters had become a desperate group of outlaws; the period that followed is remembered as the "killing time," since so many Covenanters were slaughtered for their beliefs. Things didn't improve when Charles II died in 1685 – without, incidentally, ever having visited Scotland during his reign. His brother and heir, James VII, was openly Catholic.

Persecuting Protestants seemed to be all the rage in Europe: while Covenanters died in Scotland, Louis XIV was cracking down on the Huguenots in France. Hence Scotland's Protestants looked on with concern as James appointed Catholics to high office. After so many years of being united against Popery, however disparate they were in the letter of their religious law, Scotland's Anglicans and Presbyterians both found open Catholicism a bit more than they could stomach. James issued Letters of Indulgence in 1687, assuring freedom of members of both religions to worship God in the manner they saw fit – although this indulgence didn't extend to the "traitorous" Covenanters.

Indulgence or no, James's subjects weren't willing to put up with his autocratic manner combined with his reli-

gion. It was English aristocrats who invited William of Orange, who was both James's nephew and husband of his daughter Mary, to come over and referee their problems in 1688. This led to the "Glorious Revolution" – "glorious" because no blood was shed. James departed for France, and William promised to administer England and Scotland until a solution was found for the future. That solution proved to be William's coronation as King William III in 1689.

Union of the Two Countries

More tolerant than James in religious matters, William was still an authoritarian ruler, concerned with restoring control in a country which had clearly been running wild. In Scotland, he encountered some scattered opposition from Covenanters and from supporters of James and the Stuart line, thenceforth known as the "Jacobites." The loyal royalist John Graham of Claverhouse, Viscount Dundee, remembered as "Bon-

nie Dundee," mustered an army against William's forces in 1689, only to be defeated (and killed) in a much-sung battle at Killiecrankie. Another ignominious event of William's reign, elevated to scandal in modern eyes, proceeded from the king's attempt to subdue the rowdy, scattered Highland clans by demanding that they take an oath of allegiance to the crown. A few days late taking his oath, Alastair MacIain and his Clan MacDonald were made an example of, massacred by the Duke of Argyll and his Campbell troops at Glencoe (see p. 136-7).

But these were isolated events in a generally steady reign. In fact, the greatest domestic problem with William's rule was the question of what to do when it was over. The Scots had been as ready as the English to cast off James and accept William; but they were not necessarily ready to allow the English Parliament to decide all further questions of succession. Heir of the childless William was Anne, sister of his wife, Mary, and daughter of James II; but after her death, if she remained childless, Parliament wanted the succession to pass to the House of Hanover, into which her nearest Protestant relative had married, and the Scots tended still to support James II's son, James Edward Stuart (styled the "Old Pretender" by his opponents), who became heir upon James's death in France in 1701. All that kept support from being unanimous was that the Old Pretender was Catholic. To William, it seemed that the best cure for all this dissension was to unite the countries of England and Scotland as quickly as possible.

William died in 1702, and Anne duly ascended the throne, prepared to continue William's policies and work together with a Parliament that was coming more and more to take over the business of government. Relations with France had been steadily worsening, and war was declared two months after her accession; given this, she could hardly ally herself

Right: The Jacobites beat the English at the Battle of Killiecrankie (gorge) in 1689.

with Scotland's Jacobites, since France supported their claimant to the throne (furthermore, such an alliance would have meant recognizing the Pretender's right to rule at the expense of her own). The only option for stabilizing English-Scottish relations, therefore, was a rapid push toward complete union; in 1706, a group of commissioners from both countries, appointed by the queen, negotiated this in a matter of months. Both sides had reasons for haste: the English didn't want to deal with a Scottish threat, since they were already at war with France; and the Scots wanted greater freedom of trade – the English had been steadily moving to restrict them as a way to drive them into the union fold – as well as to avoid the risk of civil war or, Heaven forfend, a Catholic king should the Jacobite faction carry the day. In 1707, Scotland's Parliament ratified the Act of Union, and the Kingdom of Great Britain was born.

United with England under a common name, a common flag, and a common Parliament, Scotland kept some measure of autonomy, notably its own legal system and law courts (which continue to this day). In addition, Scotland received a large cash payment to balance out the burden it was shouldering in the form of England's National Debt, which was much higher than Scotland's. Loyal Scots citizens, watching with dismay as their country, as they saw it, was swallowed up by its age-old rival, felt that Scotland had been sold for economic gain. There was mob violence in the cities; petitions were circulated; protests organized: but the Act of Union had been ratified, and there was no going back.

England didn't do much to mollify the Scottish population in its actions after union; in fact, it fanned the flames of popular fears by acting with an eye to its own advantage now that the Scottish "problem" had been "solved" forever. In Scotland, Presbyterians feared the advance of Anglicanism, which seemed in

line to become a state religion (even the Toleration Act of 1712 included a proviso requiring men of the cloth to take an oath that stuck in Presbyterians' throats). Economically, Parliament's legislation seemed consistently to penalize Scotland and favor England, trying to impose taxes and tariffs on Scottish products such as whisky, linen, and timber.

The Jacobite Risings

Scottish dissatisfaction was so pronounced that it became inevitable that the Jacobites, the supporters of the deposed Stuart line, would make a concrete bid for the throne and for a renewal of Scotland's independence. In fact, they made three such bids, two of real significance. None was successful; none actually had a broad enough base of popular support to carry the day, especially given the Catholicism of the Old Pretender and his son. But coming as they did in the wake of Union, at a point when Scotland's independence was not long past and still seemed within reach, they have remained romanticized in the national consciousness as Scotland's last shining hour before the country's final, definite absorption into the new entity of Great Britain.

The first abortive attempt, in 1708, was an effort of the French, who sent a fleet (with the Old Pretender) toward the Firth of Forth; bad weather prevented a landing, and the ships turned back. But the rising of 1715 got off to a much better start. Queen Anne had died in 1714, and the Scots, already sick of Union, were not thrilled about the Hanoverian king that had forced on them by England's Parliament, George I.

A nobleman who had served in Anne's government and been snubbed by George's, the 11th Earl of Mar (whose sobriquet was "Bobbing John"), decided that Union was an unworkable construct, went north, and quickly mustered a huge army, partly by force of his good cause

lowing years to bring the Highlands under control. Leader of this effort was General Wade, who in the years after 1725 disarmed the Highlanders and created a wide-reaching network of military roads, studded with bridges and forts, throughout the north of Scotland. This period saw the formation of the Highland Black Watch regiment, one of Britain's most distinguished military bodies. The British Government seemed to have tamed the Highlands once and for all. And the Jacobite threat seemed weakened: the Old Pretender had been expelled from France after the Peace of Utrecht – larger considerations of state having taking precedence over his ineffectual machinations – and he had moved on to Rome, since the Pope was the only potentate left who still recognized him as King. Still, his son, Charles Edward, grew up believing that one day he would assume his "rightful" throne.

and partly, in the Highlands, by coercion. Starting with a huge advantage over the smaller royalist forces, he took over much of the north in September. But he was unable to carry through to decisive victory. In the pro-English south of the country, the sparks of rebellion fell on damp ground, there to fizzle and die. No French aid was forthcoming: Louis XIV of France died in September, and the regent who succeeded him wanted peace with England. Even the Chevalier, as the Old Pretender was also known, didn't show up until December, by which time Mar had lost much of his momentum. The army gradually disbanded, and Mar and the Chevalier ingloriously left the country by sea, leaving their followers to the mercies of a (surprisingly lenient) English government.

King George and his administrators were sufficiently respectful of this attempt to take concrete action in the fol-

"The Forty-Five"

Lo and behold, France got back into the picture. Seeking revenge on the British for an earlier military incident, Louis XV, in 1744, planned an attack which was to include Charles Edward Stuart, the Old Pretender's son. Bad weather prevented this French action, but "Bonnie Prince Charlie," summoned from Rome and raring to go, decided to go ahead under his own steam. Equipped with little in the way of money or experience, the 23-year-old sailed to Scotland and landed at Moidart on July 25, 1745, prepared to reclaim his kingdom for his father.

What followed was one of the more romantic episodes in a romantic history: a kind of living fairy tale about a boy prince returning in glory to his hereditary homeland. It may never have had a ghost of a real chance; but it made great copy. Landing in the Highlands, which the English, believing "tamed" by General Wade's work, had somewhat neglected,

Above: "Bonnie Prince Charlie" led the clans in the last battle against English rule. Right: The battlefield of Culloden Moor.

he raised his standard at Glenfinnian and waited while members of the clans marched in to give aid to "their" prince (see p. 139). Supported by this army, complete with kilts and bagpipes, he marched through the country and "took" first Perth, then Edinburgh.

But Charlie's army was small and predominantly Highland in composition; and the British government, albeit disorganized, had begun to take steps against him within days of his landing. Given his precarious position, Charlie's only recourse was to keep moving. Accordingly, he took the army and started to march south toward London itself. But although he took Carlisle, his men grew tired as they continued, and there were no reinforcements; moreover, the towns he had taken in Scotland had fallen back into government hands. Therefore, when he reached Derby he reluctantly turned his troops around and marched back.

By this time, the English had marshalled their resources, and there were two considerable armies moving against the upstart prince. Once again on Scottish soil, Charlie fought a couple of successful actions (at Falkirk and Stirling Castle), and then began to retreat in earnest, pursued by a massive force under the Duke of Cumberland. When the Highlands were in sight, a practical option might have been for the army to melt away into their native hills (a tried and true tactic of Highland warfare); instead, they turned to stand and fight at Culloden Moor on April 16, 1746. It was the last major battle on British soil; and it was a rout. The weary Highlanders were no match for the British. More than a thousand died, and no mercy was shown to prisoners; not for nothing did Cumberland earn his sobriquet of "Butcher." Seeing himself beaten, Charlie fled.

His "flight through the heather" to the west coast is as much a part of the Charlie myth as his last stand. For five months, he traveled incognito, sometimes disguised as a woman, sheltered by loyal supporters from the prowling British troops – a notable example of Highland

35

ecuted or transported to America, estates expropriated, and wearing a kilt or playing the bagpipes were banned, punishable by strictly enforced law. Not until 1782 was the ban on kilts lifted, and some estates were returned to their owners in 1784; by that time, Highland strength and independence had receded into the legend, and landlords were already beginning to clear out their tenants to make room for sheep, emptying the region forever. The Highlands would never be quite the same again.

This is one reason why "the Forty-Five" and Bonnie Prince Charlie have remained vivid for Scots today. On April 16, 1996, the 250th anniversary of the Battle of Culloden, thousands converged on the battlefield for commemorations, including a minute of respectful silence – "for all the world," said a visitor, "as if it had happened 50 years ago, not 250."

loyalty, since there was a price of £30,000 on his head. He finally came to Skye under the protection of Flora MacDonald (see p. 160-1), whose relationship to him has been much romanticized. Taking his leave of her with the optimistic statement that "for all that has happened, I hope, Madam, we shall meet in St. James [in London] yet," he returned to the mainland and was picked up by a French ship which brought him back to the Continent and a dissolute life spent between various European capitals, with plenty of alcohol and not much to show for himself, until his death in 1788.

British retribution was severe; there was to be no risk of such a thing happening again. This time, it wasn't just a question of "taming" the Highlanders: Cumberland and his forces saw to it that their backs were broken. Prisoners were ex-

Above: Kilts and bagpipes were strictly forbidden for many years. Right: The Highland Clearances got rid of people to make room for sheep.

Clearances and Commerce

While romantic battles played themselves out in parts of the country, Scotland was busily developing into a hive of prosperity. The whole 18th century saw the flourishing of overseas trade with the Americas; Glasgow, especially, became a thriving tobacco center (and suffered especially hard when the American Revolutionary War of 1776 cut into its turnover by some 40%). The linen industry already had a firm foothold early in the century; mining was another source of revenue. Some of Scotland's industries, like fishing, long suffered under competition from other countries: but war with France, combined with the establishment of three British Fisheries stations in Scotland in 1786, proved an aid to its development; it continued to play a major role in the economy throughout the 19th century.

Fishing, and many other industries, received plenty of new manpower (and cheap labor) with a huge wave of displaced Highlanders. Agricultural im-

provement was all the rage among wealthy landowners in the late 18th century; but "improvement," and "profit," wasn't the same thing as commitment to one's dependent tenant farmers – whose traditional feudalistic services had become less important, in the new industrial age, than simple hard cash. "Improvement" and "profit" were juxtaposed most ironically – not to say tragically – in Sutherland: while the Duke, largest landholder in the Highlands, spent money on improving roads and harbors, his men forcibly evicted his tenants from their villages, moving them to the coast – where, it was alleged, they could make a better living as fishermen – and, just in case they had any thoughts of returning, burning their villages behind them. Other landlords acted in the same manner. The "Highland Clearances" are generally dated from around 1780 to 1860; in addition to brute force, famine and the difficulty of living off the infertile Northern land drove thousands of Highlanders to the coasts, into urban slums or onto crowded ships sailing for America. Those who settled in the cities provided a ready workforce for the new factories of the Industrial Revolution.

From Unrest to Complacency

The start of the 19th century saw considerable political unrest. From 1774 to 1805, Scotland had been more or less governed – "ruled" might be a better term – by Henry Dundas, Viscount of Melville, who began as an M.P. and Lord Advocate of Scotland, and went on to hold various offices in the British Cabinet. Dundas's primary concern was to establish a broad power base, by whatever means necessary, to enable him to govern as he wished, and achieve what he determined was best for Scotland – "Dundas Despotism" was one label for his *modus operandi*. The Radicals, incited against such absolute rule and encouraged by the examples of the American and especially the French revolutions, were burning Dundas in effigy by the 1790s; however,

it wasn't just Dundas – who was impeached for corruption in 1805 – but the whole system that was at fault. Scotland's electoral districts were hopelessly antiquated; elected officials didn't begin to represent the needs and opinions of the actual population. Labor riots, strikes, and other demands for reform of the outdated, corrupt system peaked in the Scottish Insurrection or "Radical War" of 1820. Finally, the opposition built up enough of a head of steam that the Scottish Bill for Parliamentary Reform was enacted in 1832, redrawing the country's electoral districts and extending the voting franchise to a larger segment of the population.

There was upheaval in the church as well. One issue that divided the General Assembly was that of patronage: the right, that is, of landowners to appoint clergymen, set forth in the Patronage Act of 1712.

Above: The textile industry saw its first great flowering in the 18th century. Right: Samuel Johnson, eminent 18th-century Scotland tourist.

Many held that this compromised the church's independence. In 1843, Dr. Thomas Chalmers led more than 400 clergymen, out of a total 1,200, to leave their manses and establish the Free Church of Scotland. It was an act both surprising and successful; within a few years, the Free Kirk, with hundreds of its own churches and schools, was a force to be reckoned with, viewing itself as the true church of Scotland. Not until 1874 was the Patronage Act finally repealed; and it wasn't until 1929 that the Free Church rejoined the Auld Kirk to form the United Established Church of Scotland (although a splinter group of Free Churchmen, known as the "Wee Frees," kept the old flame of independence alive).

Meanwhile, Scotland was coming into vogue both in England and abroad. In the spirit of the Romantic Age that was just breaking, people started to take new interest in this wild territory at the edge of Europe. Effectively the first tour guide to Scotland, *Pennant's Tour in Scotland*

1769, appeared in 1771; soon after, Samuel Johnson had set off with Boswell on his own exploration. This trickle of pioneer travelers swelled into a flood after the books of Sir Walter Scott began appearing in the early 19th century. In addition to its scenic beauties, Scotland offered curative airs and waters – spa towns began to develop – while excursion steamers bore great crowds up the west coast on day trips out of Glasgow. (Admittedly, the steamers' popularity wasn't entirely due to the scenery; since an 1853 Act of Parliament had prohibited drinking on Sundays to everyone except travelers, the steamships were the only place you could get alcohol.)

But the true seal on Scotland's popularity came with George IV's epic visit in 1822: the first Hanoverian monarch to set foot in Scotland, he set loose a Scotland fad (complete with a tartan craze) that persisted – indeed, that grew apace – throughout the long reign of Queen Victoria. Victoria herself became one of Scotland's biggest fans – to the extent of taking Presbyterian communion and even of espousing Jacobite views (now that the Jacobites had receded far enough into history to cease to be a threat to the reigning British monarch).

The Twentieth Century

As the Act of Union faded farther and farther into the background, the history of Scotland became increasingly part and parcel of the history of Great Britain as a whole. British or Scottish, it was an urbanized, prosperous, middle-class society that suddenly found itself confronted with the outbreak of World War I. Scots turned out in force to enlist, particularly from areas such as Dundee or the Outer Hebrides, where unemployment was high. And Scottish losses were disproportionately huge. It's claimed that more than 20 percent of Britishers killed in the war were Scots.

The war inflated industry hugely: the shipbuilding yards of the Clyde and the jute mills of Dundee were kept producing at a rate that postwar demand was wholly incapable of supporting. Moreover, working men and women all over Europe were becoming newly aware of their rights, and of how far these had been violated throughout the development of the industrial modern age. Labor unrest in Glasgow gave rise to the term "Red Clydeside." In 1919, the military was called in to put down a strike for a 40-hour work week; tanks arrived to steamroll the seeds of revolution, and the police turned on the crowd with their nightsticks at a rally in George Square on a day remembered in Glasgow as "Bloody Friday."

Between the wars, Scotland had a hard time of it. Prohibition in the United States had a disastrous effect on an important industry, the export of Scottish whisky; and the Great Depression struck Clydeside shipping hard. Politically, the region tended to go Labour; but its difficult situation led many people to rethink the Act

of Union once again. The National Party of Scotland was formed in 1928; in 1932, it merged with the Scottish Party to form the Scottish National Party. Ever since, the SNP has done its best to get Scotland to vote itself free of what some people still see as the "English yoke."

World War II recreated a demand for shipbuilding; it also devastated Clydeside in 1941 when German bombers flew in to put a temporary stop to production by destroying the area. As in World War I, Scotland provided many thousands of soldiers; it also played a significant role in Britain's naval activities. Orkney still has many relics of the years it spent as a naval base.

The Fires of Nationalism

Despite the Labour government that came in after the war, Scotland gradually

Above: Scotland provided the British Army with many men in the two World Wars. Right: Since the 1970s, the North Sea oil fields have stimulated economic growth.

slipped into a downturn once again. The nationalization of many industries, such as coal, meant that headquarters tended to be based in the south: Scotland provided labor, but no longer leaders of industry. As grumblings against England in the 1700s fueled the Jacobites' cause, so did popular frustration in the 1950s stoke the fires of the Scottish National Party's drive for Home Rule.

A major event at the end of the 1960s helped swing the economy around: the discovery of oil in the North Sea. This brought prosperity to a formerly depressed region – and a new reason for national pride. Riding on the crest of this enthusiasm, the SNP, with 11 M.P.s, almost managed to push through a Home Rule bill which would have given Scotland its own elected assembly. The British government, of course, didn't want to lose the income from the new oil fields, and made it a condition for the passing of the bill that more than 40% of Scotland's voters approve it in a referendum. The bill failed; and Margaret Thatcher's rise

to power effectively silenced debate on the issue for years.

But the SNP hasn't given up hope. While some hold that Scotland, after two and a half centuries of union, is inextricably intertwined with England's economy, others still believe that Scotland's best interests can only be represented if Scotland has independent government (actor Sean Connery is one prominent SNP advocate). Since 1989, a cross-party Scottish Constitutional Convention has met regularly, coming up with various proposals for a more or less independent Scottish administration.

Scotland's Self-Image Today

In 1996, when John Major's unpopularity signalled the imminence of new elections, and thus a chance for Scotland to speak its mind once again, a Gallup poll of Scotland's population showed that 69% of the people supported some form of Scottish parliament, either fully independent or within the context of the pres-

ent government. While this seems a strong show of support, it's nonetheless down from the 81% who felt this way in 1993; in fact, it's the lowest show of nationalism in the last 10 years, and the figure shrunk to 54% when the condition was introduced that a separate parliament could mean higher taxes. Still, Scottish identity continues to thrive: 49% of those asked saw themselves as "Scottish first and British second," and 18% even called themselves "Scottish only."

And John Major tried to appeal to this spirit. Unexpectedly, after seven centuries, the Stone of Scone was returned to its rightful homeland in 1996. Some Scots saw this as an insult, implying that Scottish nationalism was based on sentiment and superstitious tradition; Major, they felt, was making an empty gesture of concession to the Scots while denying them any of their concrete political wishes. Others saw it as an event that Scotland had been fighting for since 1296, and a sign that Scotland was preparing to resume its rightful independence.

41

EDINBURGH
The Athens of the North

CASTLE
OLD TOWN
NEW TOWN
LOTHIANS

"Between the beauty of the weather and the scenery, and the kindness of good people, I am typsy with pleasure." The writer was George Eliot, on a visit to Edinburgh in 1852. Now as then, Edinburgh weather remains variable; but the people are still warm and visitors still typsy with pleasure.

George Eliot called Edinburgh "Auld Reekie," after a poem by local son Robert Fergusson. The nickname, deriving from the sootiness of the city, might have been a term of abuse but was in fact used affectionately – and not just by Eliot – for a couple of centuries. Today the smoke is largely gone, and Edinburgh's other name, the Athens of the North, is far more appropriate for the intellectual, artistic, and financial center of Scotland, with the elegant coolness of its stone architecture.

Edinburgh received its town charter from King Robert the Bruce as long ago as 1329. The capital of Scotland for more than five hundred years (ever since King James IV decided to hold his parliament here in the late 1480s), the city tumbles down from a central rock on which its

Preceding pages: Dancing in the streets during the Edinburgh Festival. Marshalling the military: the Royal Tattoo. Left: Summer lovers on Princes Street (New Town).

formidable castle rises – not unlike the Acropolis of its unofficial namesake.

A trout-filled little river, the **Water of Leith**, rills through gorges from Edinburgh to the sea, while the **Pentland Hills**, which shelter the city (and rise to almost 2,000 feet/600 m), are the haunt of grouse – and, during the season, the haunt of those anxious to shoot them. On the way from the Pentlands to the sea, the Water of Leith powered the mills of the villages of Dalry, Dean, Stockbridge, Silvermills and Canonmills, which in the 19th century became incorporated in the city. Other delightful corners of the city which were once separate villages include Corstorphine (with its 551-foot/168-m high hill and Edinburgh's **Zoological Gardens**, home to the world's largest collection of penguins) and **Duddingston**, with a loch, bird sanctuary and the oldest licensed premises in Scotland, *The Sheep's Head*.

From Edinburgh you can look down to the sea, represented by the **Firth of Forth**, with its two superb bridges, road and rail, masterpieces of engineering and also beautiful, the first built in 1964, the second in 1890. Because of this close proximity to the sea, in the past the Lord Provosts of Edinburgh had the status of Admirals of the Fleet, with the right, until the 20th century, to issue passports.

CASTLE

As Wordsworth described the city, stately Edinburgh is throned on crags. One thousand years old, **Edinburgh Castle** dominates the rock, 443 feet (135 m) above sea level and visible from virtually everywhere in the city.

This was a perfect site for a fortress, endowed with springs of water. On one side, the sheer cliffs seem veritably impregnable. Edwin, King of Northumbria, (from whose name "Edinburgh" is said to derive) rebuilt am earlier fortress here in the 7th century. The castle became a royal home in the 11th and 12th centuries, and even a royal prison in 1482 when disaffected nobles incarcerated King James III there. Despite the castle's seeming invincibility, it's been taken three times: Henry II of England took it, as did the forces of Edward I (though the King himself had died in Cumberland on

Above: A mighty fortress: Edinburgh Castle seems invincible.

the march north). Next, in 1650 Oliver Cromwell besieged the castle; the garrison surrendered only when he threatened to use explosives to blow up the entire rock. Later in the same century, the castle was again besieged, this time by William of Orange in order to expel the supporters of his exiled father-in-law James VII/II.

The castle's memories include the moment when Mary Queen of Scots gave birth here, in a little room, to the son who would become James VI of Scotland and James I of England. A window looks out from this room over the **Grassmarket**, and tradition has it that the Catholic Mary secretly lowered her son out of this window in a basket, to have him baptized in her own faith.

Above this room are housed the **Honours of Scotland**, ancient insignia which were used at the coronation of Scottish kings since the time of Robert Bruce. These regalia include the scepter and crown of Scotland, and the sword of state which Pope Julius II gave King James IV in 1507. On the scabbard are enamelled the Pope's coat-of-arms. Repeatedly the English tried to take the regalia to London and were repeatedly foiled.

In the 17th century, they were hidden in Dunottar Castle, Angus (see p. 194), but Oliver Cromwell learned of their whereabouts and took that castle, as well. In the meantime, however, the wife of a local minister spirited the treasures away and hid them under the floor of Kinneff Church, and there they stayed until the restoration of the monarchy.

Edinburgh Castle is blessed by the oldest building in the city, Romanesque **St. Margaret's Chapel**. Margaret, born in Hungary in the mid-11th century, was a queen as well as a saint. She came to England with her mother and young brother Edgar; after the death of Harold at Hastings, Edgar was king-elect. After the Norman Conquest, Margaret fled for safety to Scotland; there, her beauty, piety and learning conquered the heart of King Malcolm III Canmore, King of Scotland since the death of Macbeth in 1057. Margaret founded this chapel in 1076. It houses no more than twenty-six worshippers.

St. Margaret died in 1093, after learning that her husband and son had been slain at the battle of Alnwick. Her chapel survived the capture of Edinburgh Castle in 1313 by Robert the Bruce, who ordered the destruction of every building save this. At its door is a massive cannon known as **Mons Meg**, which was forged in the mid-15th century and could fire its five hundredweight cannonballs some one and a half miles (and was used to besiege, for instance, Threave Castle; see p. 98). Unfortunately, in 1680 Mons Meg fired a royal salute for Charles II and burst in the process.

The magnificent **Scottish National War Memorial**, controversial when it was first erected in 1927 to the designs of Sir Robert Lorimer, stands behind the chapel, depicting in stained glass and bronze those who served in World War I (and commemorating the 100,000 Scots who died). Lorimer insisted on also paying tribute to carrier pigeons, mules, and the mice and canaries who detected gas in the trenches of Flanders fields.

Still garrisoned, the castle witnesses a secular ceremony each weekday when the one-o'clock gun is fired on what is known as Half-Moon Battery, a habit the citizens of Edinburgh copied from Paris in 1861. Some visitors have been known to dive for cover when they heard the sound of the explosion, only to be baffled at seeing the citizens of Edinburgh continuing blithely about their business, oblivious to what is to them a daily event.

Beyond this is the spacious **Esplanade**, where the bagpipe parades of the Military Tattoos take place each August. Beyond the Esplanade on the right stands **Cannonball House**, built in 1630, with a cannonball lodged in its wall (according to a romantic tradition, fired by the Jacobites when they rebelled in 1745). Opposite is a spot of grisly reputation, the **Witches' Well**, so called because some three hundred women, alleged to be witches, were here burned at the stake between the 15th and the 18th centuries.

Close by, **Ramsay Lane** is named after Allan Ramsay, who came to Edinburgh in 1701, apprenticed to a wigmaker. His talents as a poet gained him favor, and in 1718 he opened a bookshop, publishing *The Tea Table Miscellany*, volumes which set new Scottish verse to old Scottish music. Ramsay's most celebrated book, *The Gentle Shepherd*, appeared in 1725, and his best-known poem is the enchanting love-song, "Peggy":

My Peggy is a young thing,
Just enter'd in her teens,
Fair as the day, and sweet as May,
Fair as the day, and always gay;
My Peggy is a young thing,
And I'm not very auld,
Yet well I like to meet her at
The wawking of the fauld.

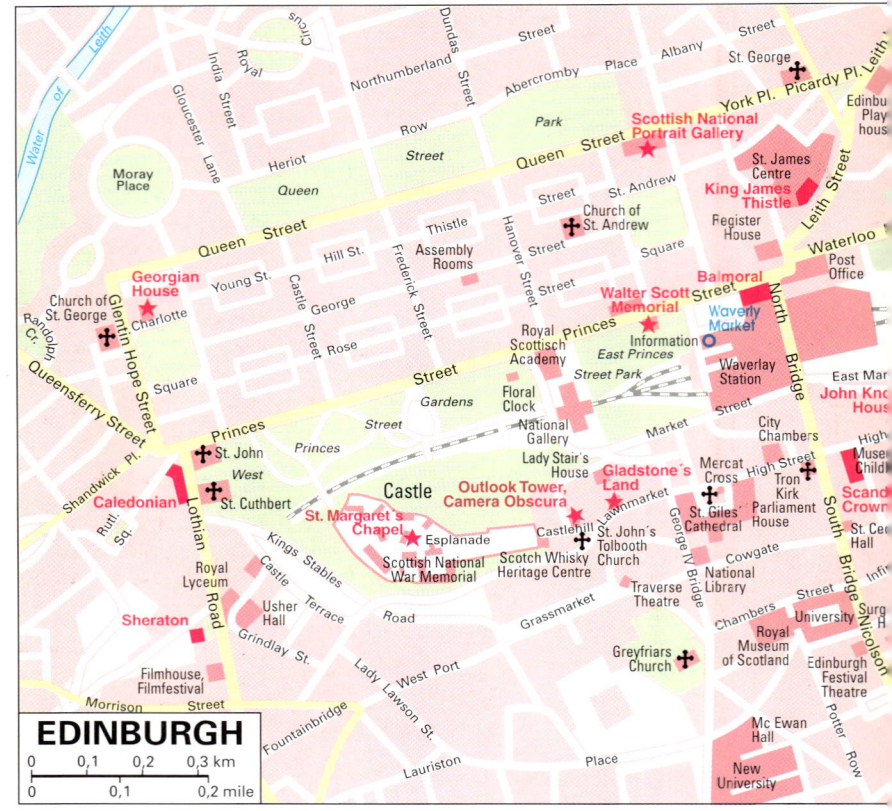

EDINBURGH

0	0,1	0,2	0,3 km
0		0,1	0,2 mile

Ramsay's son, also called Allan, became one of Scotland's finest 18th-century artists, and portrait painter to George III. Many of his brilliant portraits hang in the Scottish National Portrait Gallery on Queen Street. The Ramsays' home still stands here and is known as Goose Pie on account of its curious octagonal shape.

On the corner of Ramsay Lane rises the city's **Outlook Tower** with a fascinating 1850s **Camera Obscura**, an early kind of cinema; its revolving mirrors and lenses project new views of modern Edinburgh. Another kind of history, this time liquid, can be savored opposite, in the **Scotch Whisky Heritage Center**. Walk on to reach the early 19th-century church of **St. John's Tolbooth**.

OLD TOWN

And then you reach the **Old Town**. Edinburgh's Old Town was built on the eastern side of the rock, where the slope is gentler. Its glory is the "Royal Mile," so called because it extends between two royal houses, Edinburgh Castle at one end and the Palace of Holyroodhouse at the other. As you stroll along the royal mile, its name changes enchantingly (or confusingly): Castle Hill, Lawn Market, High Street, Canongate.

Walking from the rock down Castle Hill and along the Lawn Market, the first part of the Royal Mile, you arrive at **Gladstone's Land**, a beautifully restored six-storey, 17th-century building with an

floors between, so that as Robert Louis Stevenson put it, "the population slept 15 to 15 deep in a vertical direction." Today, the house is refurbished, complete with market booths with 17th-century wares, and open to visitors.

Close by Gladstone's Land is another house with an external staircase, this one called Riddle's Close and once the home of a magistrate (or Baillie) named Macmorran. In 1595, Macmorran was called in to resolve a strike by high school students who were protesting because they had been refused a holiday. One schoolboy shot him dead.

Another neighbor was Deacon William Brodie, a man of double character. By day he posed as a respectable citizen; by night he was a burglar – eventually apprehended and hanged in 1788. Robert Louis Stevenson and W. E. Henley celebrated his life in their play *Deacon Brodie*, and Brodie also played a part in inspiring Stevenson's *Dr. Jekyll and Mr. Hyde*. Today, citizens of Edinburgh celebrate in nearby *Deacon Brodie's Tavern*.

Lady Stair's House (built by Sir William Gray in 1622 but named after Lady Elizabeth Stair, a noted 18th-century hostess) is also close by, with a staircase tower and elegant balcony. It's now a museum with mementos of Scotland's most celebrated writers: Robert Burns, Sir Walter Scott and Robert Louis Stevenson.

Just before the Royal Mile reaches the High Kirk of St. Giles, look for the heart fashioned in the cobbles of the street. Here once stood the Old Tolbooth, Edinburgh's prison, the scene of a 1736 riot which Walter Scott recreated in his novel *The Heart of Midlothian*. In that year a crowd had gathered to protest at the execution of a popular smuggler named Wilson. An officer of the city guard, Captain John Porteous, ordered the troops to fire on the crowd; six people were killed, and twenty wounded. Although Porteous was initially condemned to death as a murderer, he was pardoned

outside staircase, intricate gables and splendid painted ceilings. Finished in 1620, when the Old Town was so crowded that the only way for a house to expand was upward, Gladstone's Land derives the first part of its name from the Edinburgh burgess and textile merchant Thomas Gledstanes, who owned it and sold his wares from the ground floor.

"Land" in Scots means tenement, and each unit of Gladstone's Land is called a house. Such tenements were common in the Old Town in the 17th and 18th centuries. Every inhabitant shared the common staircase: the poor lived in the attics, or at street level; the richer lived on the main floor; the rest lived according to their wealth on the variously amenable

by George II's wife Caroline. Incensed at this, on September 7 a lynch-mob broke into the Tolbooth, dragged Porteous to the Grassmarket and hanged him from a dyer's pole.

You reach the Grassmarket today by crossing George IV Bridge and walking down Candlemakers Row. Today peaceful, until the 19th century the Grassmarket remained the scene of Edinburgh's public hangings. Porteous was not the only one to be executed here: a cross in the pavement recalls 100 Covenanters who were put to death for insisting on worshipping as Presbyterians. On the way, at the corner of George IV Bridge and Candlemakers Row, you pass the little statue of a pet dog, **Greyfriars Bobby**. The master of this Skye Terrier died in 1858 and was buried in the nearby churchyard of Greyfriars Kirk. For the next fourteen years Bobby watched over his grave, fed by friendly citizens.

Above: People-watching on the Royal Mile.
Right: A pint is still the standard liquid measurement in an Edinburgh pub.

Greyfriars Kirk, dedicated on Christmas Day, 1620, rises on the site of a 15th-century Franciscan friary. Here, on February 28, 1638, was adopted the National Covenant, whereby many patriotic Scots pledged themselves to defend their King (Charles I) but rejected his insistence that they abandon their Presbyterian beliefs and support Anglicanism. Some of them gashed their veins and signed in blood. Many others were weeping as they signed. Inside the church the Covenant is proudly displayed.

Grassmarket abuts onto **Cowgate**, a refuge in the 19th century of Irish escaping from the Great Famine, who lived in cramped conditions along the street. Among them was James Connolly, who worked as a printer on the *Edinburgh Evening News*, was a soldier with the Royal Scots and was executed in 1916 for his part in the Dublin Easter rebellion. Cowgate also boasts **St. Patrick's Roman Catholic Church**, which used to serve its Irish Catholic residents, and the elegant **St. Cecilia's Hall**, a concert hall

built in 1762 in imitation of the Opera House of Parma. Parallel to Cowgate is Chambers Street, where the **Royal Museum of Scotland** displays exhibits of history and technology from ancient Egypt to the space age.

Old Town's Past

This whole part of Edinburgh drips with history. The name of **George IV Bridge**, for example, recalls King George IV's visit to Edinburgh in 1822. The King wore pink tights and an exceedingly short kilt, which prompted citizens to declare that they were well satisfied by seeing as much of their king as possible.

Naturally, every Stuart King played his part in the history of the city. So did Mary Stuart and her redoubtable foe John Knox. The Protestant Knox was enraged when Mary allowed a Roman Catholic mass to be celebrated in the Palace of Holyrood. Knox vehemently condemned Mary in a sermon preached in St. Giles, and he remained her implacable enemy

until his death in 1572. But Mary's downfall came before then. She didn't only hold masses in Holyrood, but also masques, and she was attending one in 1567 when the house in which her dissolute husband Darnley was sleeping (at Kirk o'Field, a little way outside the southern walls of Edinburgh) was blown up; his corpse was later discovered in the garden (see p. 26-27). Three months later Mary married the Earl of Bothwell, who was thought to have arranged Darnley's murder. Scottish lords, enraged, went up in arms, forcing Mary's abdication.

Then there was the hapless James Graham, Marquis of Montrose. This 17th-century Scottish general (and poet) vacillated enormously throughout the turmoil of the Civil War, losing most of his army in 1650 in an ill-judged attempt to avenge the execution of King Charles I. Captured in the same year, he was hanged on Edinburgh's High Street on May 21. Eleven years later his earthly remains were collected together and buried in the **High Kirk of St. Giles**, halfway along the Royal Mile, where they lie under an impressive monument of 1888.

A better memorial is his verse, for example, "I'll Never Love Thee More," which, alluding to his prowess as a soldier as well as a lover, concludes:

But if thou will prove faithful then,
And constant of thy word,
I'll make thee glorious by my pen
And famous by my sword;
I'll serve thee in such noble ways
As never heard before;
I'll crown and deck thee all with bays,
And love thee more and more.

After inspecting his monument, you can turn your attention to the church itself. Much restored in the 19th century, it remains an impressive Gothic building, retaining four octagonal pillars from its predecessor, which was founded in 1120. Its 15th-century crown tower is a remarkable construction: eight flying buttresses, a sculpted turret and an open spire. Here (legend has it) in 1637, when Dean Lindsay, following the wishes of Charles I, was trying to introduce Anglicanism and the English Prayer Book into Presbyterian Scotland (see p. 28), a vegetable-seller named Jenny Geddes flung her stool at the bishop, crying out, "Thou false thief, dost thou say mass at my lug?" An inscription on the floor of the nave marks the spot where she made her outburst.

St. Giles is the site of the annual meeting of the General Assembly of the Church of Scotland; every May, it fills with soberly-clad Presbyterian ministers. But this High Kirk, founded in 1120 and restored and embellished many times since, also contains older traditions. Here, you'll find the **Chapel of the Thistle**, the spiritual home of the Scottish Knights of the Thistle (Scotland's equivalent of the English Order of the Gar-

Right: The Chapel of the Thistle: heraldic gem of St. Giles's Cathedral.

ter). Designed by Sir Robert Lorimer of National War Memorial fame in 1911, it has carved oaken stalls, heraldic windows and a lovely vaulted ceiling.

The finest window in the High Kirk, however, was designed by the Pre-Raphaelite artist Burne-Jones. And admirers of Edinburgh-born Robert Louis Stevenson can see the tablet inscribed with lines from his tomb on Mount Vacca, Samoa:

Under the wide and starry sky
Dig the grave and let me lie.

Allegedly buried in **Parliament Square** is John Knox, next door to the Church of St. Giles where he was minister from 1561 until his death. In the same square is an equestrian statue of King Charles II. Here, too, stands **Parliament House**, where the Scottish Parliament met from 1639 until Scotland and England were united in 1707. (It later housed Scotland's most important courts, for which Sir Walter Scott was for twenty-five years clerk.) Parliament House is worth a visit simply to glimpse its superb 17th-century hammer-beam roof.

Opposite St. Giles rise the **City Chambers**, built as a Royal Exchange in 1761 by John and Robert Adam. And next to the High Kirk is **Mercat Cross**, which once stood at the center of the street. This is the heart of Old Town, once a market but also yet another place of execution.

Here, in 1513, the citizens heard that King James IV, along with two bishops, thirteen earls and 10,000 Scottish soldiers, had attacked England and perished at the hands of the troops of the Earl of Surrey at Flodden Field. Mercat Cross saw the deaths of one of Mary Queen of Scots' retainers, Kircaldy of the Grange, who was keeper of the castle, as well as that of Montrose. From the platform of its tower, members of the Court of Lord Lyon still read royal proclamations.

Walk on to what ought to be a more peaceful spot, **Tron Kirk**, which was

built in 1637. Its curious name derives from the tron (or weighing beam) which once stood outside the church and weighed all goods coming into Edinburgh. Its peaceful aspect is belied by the fact that traders who falsified their weights were pinned to the tron by their ears. Look inside the church to admire its hammer-beam roof.

John Knox's House, where he lived from 1561 until his death 11 years later, stands on the left further along the Royal Mile, which here stretches into Canongate (so called because the canons of Holyrood Abbey used to enter the city by this route). A noble building, it dates from 1490. Ironically, in view of Knox's hatred of Mary Queen of Scots, the house had also been inhabited by her goldsmith, James Mossman. Knox is said to have harangued the people from the steps of his house as well as from the pulpit of St. Giles. Today, the house is a museum dedicated to him and to Mossman.

It's worth remembering that there was more to the past than the names and dates

presented in history books; and two museums along the Royal Mile serve as reminders, illustrating everyday aspects of days gone by. Across the street from Knox's house is the **Museum of Childhood**, whose displays cover not only antique toys and games, but various aspects of raising, clothing, and tending children in the past. In 16th-century **Canongate Tolbooth**, once home to the district's courts and jail, you can visit **The People's Story**, a museum about the daily lives of normal working Edinburgh men and women from the 18th century until today.

Canongate Church is an example of Edinburgh taking up the Tuscan classical mode late after its 17th-century arrival in Britain. James Smith designed it in the late 1680s. Above its diminutive Doric portico an inscription reads, "In 1688 King James VII ordained that the mortification of Thomas Moodie granted in 1649 to build a church should be applied to the erection of this structure." In its graveyard lie the political economist

Adam Smith, the 18th-century poet Robert Fergusson and Robert Burns's friend "Clarinda." When Burns arrived in Edinburgh, Fergusson's grave was unmarked, and though impoverished, Burns paid for a memorial stone. As for "Clarinda," her real name was Agnes Maclehose, and though she was married with two children, Burns fell deeply in love with her. (Her husband was conveniently abroad.) She inspired his lines:

Had we never lov'd sae kindly,
Had we never lov'd sae blindly,
Never met – or never parted,
We had ne'er been broken-hearted.

As celebrated in history as Canongate Church is **Moray House**, which rises on the left of Canongate, dates from 1628, housed King Charles I, and was the headquarters of Oliver Cromwell, who had him executed. On May 1, 1650, the Duke and Duchess of Argyll, along with their wedding guests, stood on this balcony and watched the wretched Montrose carried past in a cart, on the way to his own execution. More than a hundred years older is **Huntly House**, further along Canongate and off to the left, which – though much reconstructed – dates from 1517. Today it serves as Edinburgh's local history museum. There are also fine 17th-century buildings gracing this part of Canongate. One is **Acheson House**; another is **White Horse Close**, which retains a 17th-century inn that was the starting point for coaches to and from London. Here, in 1773, Dr. Samuel Johnson relished his first visit to Edinburgh as guest of James Boswell, in preparation for their tour of the Hebrides. On their return, Johnson stayed at Boswell's home in James's Court (since burned).

Johnson enjoyed his stay, but one of his running jokes with Boswell was his

Right: The Palace of Holyrood House nestles at the foot of "Arthur's Seat."

antipathy to the Scots. One day, Boswell records, Johnson met a Mr. Ogilvie, who began to praise the rich land around Edinburgh, observing also that Scotland had a great many noble wild prospects. Johnson replied, "Sir, let me tell you, the noblest prospect which a Scotchman ever sees, is the high road that leads him to England." "All these sallies," Boswell fondly noted, "were said sportively, quite in jest, and with a smile, which showed that he meant only wit." Others disagreed with Boswell's estimate of Johnson; Mrs. Boswell, in particular, disliked the way the two men caroused together, observing, "I have often seen a bear led by a man, but never till now have I seen a man led by a bear."

Ironically, for a time the skeptical 18th-century Scottish philosopher and historian David Hume also lived in James Court, in the same house as the devout Anglican Dr. Johnson.

Holyrood Palace

Finally you reach **Holyrood Palace**. Just before it is an open space where until 1880 debtors could find refuge, immune from arrest. The letter S, set at intervals in the road, marks the boundary of this place of sanctuary. As for the palace, its name, which signifies Holy Cross, indicates its origins as a medieval abbey. Beside the palace and the ruined abbey, you can still see the graceful remains of the abbey church with its exquisite Gothic tracery. King David I is said to have dedicated the abbey to the cross on which Jesus died, because he was miraculously saved from death in a hunting accident: an enraged stag, chasing him through the forest, turned into a cross when the despairing king grasped its antlers. Another tradition holds that the abbey was named for a fragment of the True Cross St. Margaret brought from the Holy Land.

For more than five hundred years this palace has continued to be embellished

by the rulers, first of Scotland, and later, of the United Kingdom. Many times burned to the ground, it was most recently (partly) destroyed by the troops of Oliver Cromwell. King Charles II ordered his surveyor in Scotland, Sir William Bruce, to rebuild it (retaining some of the older palace), and Charles's own French taste influenced the palace you see today. William Bruce deserves high praise for designing his own east tower to match the early 16th-century west tower that had survived.

Then and now, Holyrood Palace has served as a royal home, used by King James VII/II when he was still Duke of York. When his campaign of 1745 seemed to be going well, Bonnie Prince Charlie gave a ball here. As Prince of Wales, Edward VII often stayed in the palace. Today, it welcomes the general public at times when no Lord High Commissioner or member of the British royal family is in residence (the Queen generally comes every summer). Visitors can see the audience chamber of Mary Queen

of Scots and the room where David Rizzio was murdered. In the past, a continually renewed bloodstain marked the treacherous spot, but this has been replaced by a more prosaic brass plaque. Here are supposed portraits of early Scottish kings, all fakes, painted by James de Witt in 1684, as well as genuine Flemish and French tapestries and elegant 18th-century furniture.

Holyrood Park is a treat. Covering 648 acres (260 ha), it is dominated by **Arthur's Seat**, a hill 822 feet (251 m) high. The citizens of Edinburgh are adept at finding bizarre names for natural features, and they call the curious basalt rock to the west "Samson's Ribs."

NEW TOWN

The romantic Gothic spikiness of Edinburgh's Old Town contrasts startlingly with Edinburgh's **New Town**. Reach it by way of Abbey Hill, turning into Regent Road and arriving first at Calton Hill. Here is a tangible clue to the

origins of Edinburgh's sobriquet "the Athens of the North": as a memorial to the Scots who died in the Napoleonic Wars, the architect William Hill began building a **National Monument** modelled on the Parthenon. He never finished it, since the available cash ran out.

Another clue is the **Royal High School** at the foot of Calton Hill, modelled by Thomas Hamilton in 1829 on the Temple of Theseus in Athens.

Beside Edinburgh's unfinished Parthenon is **Nelson's Monument**, a 102-foot (31 m) column, with a time ball that descends daily at 1 p.m. to tell the time to the sailors in the Firth of Forth. Calton Hill overlooks **Princes Street**. On the way there you pass James and Robert Adam's lovely, classical **Register House** (built from 1772 to 1792), and you are in Edinburgh's New Town. This is Georgian orderliness and regularity at its most

Above: The setting sun gilds the facades of New Town. Right: Two more bright New Town facades.

beguiling. Laid out in the Georgian style in the late 18th and early 19th centuries, the district's northeastern perimeter is marked by Drummond Place, and it ends to the southwest at exquisite Charlotte Square.

Starting from Scratch

Building an entire new city district is no small task. The city needed to drain a loch (where today Princes Street Gardens are laid out) before building its New Town, but the energy of the fabled Lord Provost George Drummond was equal to this. To the east of the loch was marshy land, which Drummond and the Town Council decided should be spanned by the North Bridge. Built in 1772, it is 70 feet (21 m) high and has a span of 1,130 feet (346 m). Two million cartloads of soil were transported to create a mound – called, in fact, *The* Mound – linking Princes Street with the Old Town. And Edinburgh's New Town sprang up at astonishing speed – driven, perhaps, by

the urgency of the city's need to expand from the narrow, cramped streets of its Old Town.

In 1770, the Edinburgh Corporation had commissioned the architect James Craig to build gracious St. Andrew Square and Charlotte Square, connecting them with George Street. Other superb architects added their genius to the area. **Charlotte Square** is not so much the work of James Craig as of Robert Adam, who was responsible for the houses on the north side: these three-storey houses, with pillars and pediments, are a consummate masterly example of 18th-century town architecture. One of these, the **Georgian House** at No. 7, is open to visitors interested in examining a corresponding period interior. Apogee of the square is the green-domed **Church of St. George**.

All of this Georgian elegance is perhaps a fitting frame to the business of Charlotte Square: these sedate buildings mark the center of Edinburgh's financial center. Edinburgh is in fact Britain's leading financial capital after London: here abound banks, insurance companies, and other related offices.

Close by, parallel to George Street, runs Queen Street, whose finest 18th-century building is the **Augustan Library** of the **Scottish Royal College of Physicians**. Here, too, the **National Museum of Antiquities of Scotland** and the **National Portrait Gallery** occupy opposite wings of the same building. The former is devoted to artifacts of Scotland's history, from prehistoric days through the Romans and Vikings to the 18th century; the latter attaches concrete images to many names familiar from history and travel books.

The Popular Mile

Princes Street also runs parallel to the Royal Mile, with one side lined with shops and the other open to views of the towering Castle. Promenading up and down this street at sunset, residents and visitors can window-shop, peruse the

castle, and examine each other as they pass along a main artery of Edinburgh. Shoppers walk the aisles of the venerable department store **Jenner's**, built in the 1890s, or turn off into the modern, sculpture-adorned terraces of the mall called **Waverly Market**. Anyone who wants to stop for a drink can detour up to parallel, pedestrian **Rose Street**, lined with atmospheric pubs.

In East Princes Street Gardens the 1846 **Walter Scott Memorial**, where the author's statue sits alongside a statue of his dog Maida under a Gothic canopy, is the largest monument in the world dedicated to a writer. It was designed by George Meikle Kemp, who, alas, drowned in the Edinburgh canal before the monument was finished. Niches carry sixty-four representations of characters from Scott's writings. For a fine view of the city, visitors can climb the 287 steps to its pinnacle. Another monument in

Above: The treasures of Scotland's National Gallery.

Princes Street Gardens commemorates the poet Allan Ramsay the Elder.

Since Scott was born in Edinburgh and lived most of his life here, plaques in his memory litter the city like confetti. One on 8 Chambers Street notes that he was born not there but "near this spot." Over the door of 39 Castle Street, where he and his wife Charlotte Carpenter lived for 28 years, is a statuette of him seated.

All along this thoroughfare you have a stupendous view of the Old Town, rising above. Princes Street also boasts the **Royal Scottish Academy** with, nearby, the **National Gallery of Scotland** (both a little to the north); the buildings rise like two Greek temples, the first dating from 1823-36, the second from 1845-58, both designed by William Playfair. Scotland's National Gallery houses no fewer than four works by Titian, as well as a magical "Finding of Moses" by Tiepolo and paintings by Rembrandt, Velasquez, El Greco, Goya, Degas, Monet and Gauguin. They hang alongside works by such Scottish masters as Allan Ramsay (among the finest are his portraits of his two wives and of David Hume, resplendent in a red jacket embroidered in gold) and Henry Raeburn (who was knighted by George IV, and whose most engaging portrait in the gallery depicts the Reverend Robert Walker nonchalantly skating on frozen Duddingston Loch).

Nearby is Edinburgh's celebrated **floral clock**, the oldest in the world. Planted in 1903, 26 feet (8 m) in circumference, the clock, bedecked with 24,000 plants, is driven by electricity and accurately tells the time.

The New Town is filled with other notable monuments, such as the quaint elliptical church of **St. Andrew** which stands on George Street. (Its architect had visited Rome and been impressed by the similarly elliptical church of Sant'Andrea al Quirinale by Bernini on the Via del Quirinale.) And some way further down George Street are Edinburgh's late 18th-century **Assembly Rooms** and **Music Hall**.

At the east end of George Street, **St. Andrew Square** was laid out to match Charlotte Square at the west end. It centers around a column designed to match the Trajan column in Rome and bearing the statue of Henry Dundas, 1st Viscount Melville, who was one of Pitt's ablest supporters and died in 1811.

James Craig's scheme was such a success that in the 1820s the city fathers decided to extend it, and the New Town expanded. **Heriot Row** (a few paces across Queen Street Gardens) is where this new development begins. No. 17 Heriot Row bears a plaque declaring that here Robert Louis Stevenson lived from the age of five. Born in Edinburgh in 1850, Stevenson became famous with the publication of *Treasure Island* in 1883. Romantics hold that the ornamental lake with its tiny island in Queen Street Gardens was the inspiration for this book. Sterner scholars rightly remember that here Stevenson wrote *A Child's Garden of Verses*.

Back to Gothic

In the 1870s, amidst the classical decorum of New Town, Sir George Gilbert Scott created a magnificent return to Scottish Gothic. **St. Mary's Cathedral**, Edinburgh, which he designed for the Scottish Episcopalian Church, was consecrated in 1879, a year after his death. Scott insisted that the cathedral's architecture pay due regard to the finest medieval Gothic churches of Scotland, so that the clerestory hints at Coldingham Priory, the triforium in the nave suggests Dunblane and the west door incorporates elements taken from Elgin, Jedburgh and Holyrood Abbey itself. But the massive central tower and spire, nearly 330 feet (100 m) high and weighing 6,000 tons, dominating classical Melville Street, in the southwest of town, displays everything that Scott had learned as a restorer of English cathedrals, too. Four huge buttresses rising from the corners of the transepts and the main building support an octagon pointing back to the one Scott had partly renewed at Ely, before turning into pillars guarding the soaring octagonal spire. Farther west on Belford Road, the **National Gallery of Modern Art** has an outstanding collection of 20th-century masterpieces, from Picasso to Hockney, as well as paintings by Scottish artists.

North of New Town is **Leith**, the city's port, and once one of the prominent ports of Europe. However, the area saw a decline as shipping and industry moved north to the oil harbors of Grampian or south to busier English harbors. Today, it's undergoing a kind of renaissance as the site of in restaurants and pubs, and developers are converting old shipping facilities to suit new residential and commercial uses.

Estival Festival

One of Edinburgh's main attractions is seasonal. Fortunately so; for an influx of

more than 200,000 people into the city on a regular basis would tax Edinburgh's resources to the utmost. As it is, the three-week **Edinburgh Festival** season in August means constantly overcrowded restaurants and accommodations booked out many months in advance. It also means one of the best assemblages of the performing arts to be found anywhere in the world.

Begun shortly after World War II in an effort to revive the cultural scene after wartime desolation, the festival has blossomed into a popular triumph. To seek a direction or defining principle would be futile: it's a true city festival in that it offers everything. There are world-class theater, concert, opera and dance performances; there are also low-budget, avant-garde performance events, many associated with the Festival Fringe, technically a separate festival, which involves many hundreds of companies in smaller

Above: Impromptu street spectacles are a byproduct of the Edinburgh Festival.

venues, from church basements to the great outdoors.

Booking tickets to one of the larger events – such as opera – may be difficult, but with the variety of fringe events around, you're certain to get into something. And the city's streets pulse with new life during the festival, filled with visitors and informal street performers.

The Edinburgh Festival has put the city on the international cultural map. It's also managed to break down some of the barriers between "popular" and "high" culture – no mean feat in the often-elitist climate of the European arts scene.

AROUND EDINBURGH: LOTHIANS

East Lothian, Midlothian and West Lothian surround the ancient capital of Scotland and are blessed with splendid countryside, fine country houses, lovely towns and a rich history.

Scenically, East Lothian has verdant countryside, woodlands, the **Garletan**

AROUND EDINBURGH

Hills and the powerful massive rise of Traprain Law. Heather covers the **Lammermuir Hills** in the southern uplands, which are sprinkled with lochs. East Lothian also boasts 40 miles (65 km) of sandy coastline; its two most celebrated sand beaches are those of North Berwick.

At the eastern end of East Lothian the major town is **Dunbar**, sheltered by the Lammermuirs, and supposed to be the driest and sunniest place in all Scotland. Today a flourishing holiday resort, Dunbar is a fishing port which became a royal burgh as early as 1369. As one would expect in this part of Scotland, Mary Queen of Scots stayed here, as did her Prime Minister James Stuart, Earl of Moray. When she was imprisoned, he became regent of Scotland. Turning against Mary, embracing the Protestant religion, he nonetheless managed to pacify the rival factions in the realm. Unfortunately, he came to a brutal end in 1570, when he was shot dead in West Lothian at Linlithgow.

Save for some bare remnants on a rocky eminence over the harbor, the castle in which these stirring events mostly took place is no more, but present-day Dunbar is not without noble buildings. Its old **Town House**, with a quaint hexagonal tower, was built in 1620. Its parish church, rebuilt in 1821, has a square, 108-foot (33 m) high tower. Inside, the impressive tomb of George Hume, who was 1st Earl of Dunbar and Lord High Treasurer of Scotland, dates from 1610. In 1828, Dunbar was the birthplace of John Muir, inventor of America's national parks; his humble home at **128 High Street** is now his museum. Another memorial to this pioneering conservationist is the **John Muir Country Park**, some 8.5 miles (14 km) of cliffs and dunes, woods and salt marsh. Beside the harbor are some uncomfortable-looking modern fishermen's houses designed in the 20th century by Sir Basil Spence.

Due west of Dunbar, **East Linton** lies on the River Tyne, which here flows

63

through a gorge and is spanned by a 16th-century bridge. The river powers a 16th-century water mill, **Preston Mill**, still in operation. The parish church also dates in part from the 17th century, when its square tower was built, and its chancel is four centuries earlier. This picturesque village was the birthplace in 1761 of engineer John Rennie, who built three Thames bridges. Part of his house, the mansion of **Phantassie**, still stands; and its beehive doocot (or dovecote) is a notable example of its kind.

Oliver Cromwell's troops turned **Hailes Castle**, a couple of miles southwest of East Linton, into an exquisite ruin. Sheltered by the 724-foot (221 m) hill of **Traprain Law**, the castle has a 13th-century watergate and dungeons. In 1567 Bothwell and Mary Queen of Scots took refuge here after the murder of Mary's husband.

Above: Pastoral scene in the Lammermuir Hills. Right: Sea birds roost around the lighthouse on Bass Rock.

Nearby **Haddington** is rife with lovingly restored buildings, so that it veritably breathes the air of the past.

Almost due north on a rocky headland, moated, rose-colored, and ruined, **Tantallon Castle** has guarded the coastline for more than 600 years. Built for the Earls of Douglas, it was virtually impregnable, owing to its ditches, ramparts and the 100-foot (30 m) cliffs which rise sheer from the sea. Its 14th-century gatehouse, its curtain wall and its round towers remain impressive, despite the degradations wrought by General Monck in 1651, at the behest of Oliver Cromwell. Even Cromwell's artillery needed twelve days of almost continuous fire in 1651 to force its defenders to surrender. Offshore, **Bass Rock** rises 350 feet (107 m) out of the sea, topped by a lighthouse.

A tour of the coast from here reaches first **North Berwick**, another royal burgh and 20th-century holiday resort some 3 miles (5 km) to the west. It lies picturesquely on the south side of the Firth of Forth. Its most evocative building is the ruined Cistercian abbey. Nearby is **North Berwick Law**, a conical hill, once a volcano, which is topped by a watchtower built in 1803 to guard the land from a possible Napoleonic invasion.

Dirleton, some 3 miles (5 km) southwest of North Berwick, is exquisite. Like many a town in East Lothian, it surrounds a green whose borders are lined by 17th- and 18th-century houses and by the **castle**. The stones of this once-massive castle, which rises sheer from a rock, date in part from the 13th century, and though the troops of Cromwell ravaged it, a three-storey Renaissance wing still stands. Look out for its 16th-century doocot/dovecote (one of many in the Lothians) and admire its 17th-century bowling green, which is shaded by yew trees. Another green fronts Dirleton's early 17th-century parish kirk.

The Heart of Midlothian

Midlothian, the central section of the Firth of Forth coast, is equally entrancing. Its hills are steep enough to encompass ski slopes. and so as to enable skiers to indulge themselves all year round, Midlothian has created artificial ski slopes as well. Less energetic sports in this region include clay pigeon shooting and angling, particularly in the limpid, cool North and South Esks, as well as in the reservoirs of Rosebery, Gladhouse and Glencourse. Craftsmen and -women flourish here; of particular note are those who create Edinburgh crystal at Penicuik.

The mists of history wreathe Midlothian. At **Dalkeith** Queen Victoria, a fanatical devotee of Scotland, spent her first night in the country in 1842, staying in the palace which Sir John Vanbrugh designed around 1700 for Anne, Duchess of Buccleuch and Monmouth. Victoria worshipped in its ancient parish **church of St. Nicholas**. Another aristocratic survival is **Arniston House**, designed by William Adam for the Dundas family at the beginning of the 18th century.

To the southeast, the village of **Borthwick** retains the 15th-century barrel-vaulted aisle of a church that was mostly destroyed in a conflagration of 1775. Happily, 15th-century **Borthwick Castle** remains virtually intact, with its huge rectangular tower and its great hall, although it isn't open to the public.

East of Edinburgh, **Inveresk** is another delightfully picturesque Midlothian village. In Roman times a camp and a settlement were established here. Today, its houses date back to the 17th and 18th centuries, while its parish church of **St. Michael** dates from 1805. 17th-century **Inveresk Lodge** opens to the public its delightful terraced garden, pungent with the delicate scent of its shrub rose border and the climbing roses.

Do not neglect **Penicuik**, a mere half-hour's drive from Edinburgh. In the past this town flourished from its paper mills, driven by the River Esk, beside which stands ruined **Brunstone Castle**.

Scarcely 2 miles (3 km) northwest of Penicuik, on the eastern slope of Carnethy, is **Rullion Green**. A monument here indicates the battlefield where on November 28, 1666, nine hundred Covenanters were defeated by a royalist army commanded by Sir Tam Dalyell.

One of Midlothian's most remarkable survivals is close by at **Roslin**, a mining village on the North Esk 7 miles (11 km) south of Edinburgh. Here, in 1446, the 3rd Earl of Orkney founded a chapel. Only its choir, Lady Chapel and part of the transept were completed, but in this tiny space is a wealth of carving; the earl brought craftsmen from Europe to carry out the work. Outstanding is the *Prentice Pillar*, with exquisite entwined ribbons climbing to its peak. It is said that it was created by an apprentice while the master mason was abroad; so jealous was the master when he saw the pupil's work that

Above: Door to the north: the Forth Rail Bridge was one of the great enginering feats of the 1890s.

66

he killed the apprentice. The Bishop of St. Andrews long postponed consecrating the chapel because it had seen the spilling of innocent blood. On the chapel wall are sculpted heads of the mason, the apprentice, and his weeping mother. Roslin also boasts a powerfully buttressed **castle**, with dungeons, which rises impressively on a cliff above the river. Sir William Sinclair founded it in the early 14th century, and its keep was built for his grandson. Partly destroyed in 1544, the castle was well restored in the 1580s.

Southeast, still beside the North Esk, nestles **Hawthornden**. Here, poet William Drummond restored **Hawthornden House** in 1638. His *Invocation* well describes some of Midlothian's skyscapes:

Phoebus, arise!
And paint the sable skies
With azure, white, and red.

Another magnificent Midlothian castle is **Crichton**, above the River Tyne, in part modelled in the late 16th century on the Palace of Ferrara at the behest of the Earl of Bothwell.

Balerno is a typically charming Midlothian village, this one today a suburb of Edinburgh but prized for its site along the Water of Leith and shaded by the **Pentland Hills**. A second suburban village along the Leith Water is **Currie**, with its 18th-century church.

West Lothian

Following the ever-narrowing Firth of Forth, you enter **West Lothian** and an industrial belt that includes Livingston and Bathgate. **Livingston** is one of Scotland's newest towns, designed in the 1960s to accommodate working men and women from Edinburgh's growing population. The industrial town of **Bathgate** has a long history. Here, in 1711, Sir James Simpson first used chloroform as an anaesthetic; and in the mid-19th century Dr. James Young was the first to manufacture paraffin. As for engineering, **Queensferry** boasts both the **Forth Railway Bridge** (2,765 yards/2,537 m long and 351 feet/107 m above the waters) and the suspension bridge (with a central span of 3,330 feet/1,018 m).

But industrial monuments are not the major tourist attractions of West Lothian: even Queensferry boasts St. Mary's Church, with a 16th-century tower and barrel vaulting. And there are more picturesque things to be seen even on the periphery of Edinburgh as you leave it driving west. **Dalmeny**, 7 miles (11 km) northwest, has a tree-shaded village green. Its church, built in the mid-12th century, is dedicated to St. Cuthbert and rich in Romanesque carvings. Do not miss the carved south door. **Barnbougie Castle**, close by, looks out at the Firth of Forth. And **Dalmeny House** is a mansion built by William Wilkins in the Tudor Gothic style in 1815. It contains superb 18th-century portraits and 18th-century French furniture and tapestries.

South of Queensferry, **Kirkliston** has a 12th-century parish church with a saddleback roof and an astounding carved Romanesque porch. A couple of miles southwest of the village is **Newliston House**, built by Robert Adam in the early 1790s. And west of Queensferry is **Abercorn**, where the first Scottish bishopric was founded in the 7th century. Inside its parish church is preserved part of an ancient crozier which may have belonged to its first bishop. Nearby **Hopetoun House**, built by William Bruce and later enlarged by William and Robert Adam, with splendid paintings, is set in a park grazed by red deer and St. Kilda sheep.

Visit the **House of the Binns**, some 15 miles (24 km) west of Edinburgh. This was the 17th-century home of the Dalyell family. Its moulded plaster ceilings date from the 1730s, and its museum houses the Bible and sword of General Thomas Dalyell. Some of Scotland's turbulent past is encapsulated here, for, as we have noted, General Dalyell not only defeated the Covenanters in 1666 at the battle of Rullion Green in the Pentlands but also raised the Royal Scots Greys at the Binns in 1681. Tam Dalyell was a devout royalist, and after the execution of King Charles I he never shaved his beard.

At **Linlithgow**, visit the ruined palace, once one of Scotland's most magnificent, and the birthplace not only of Mary Queen of Scots but also of King James V. King James I built the main body of the palace, which stands on a mound overlooking Linlithgow Loch, sanctuary to rare birds. The last king to sleep here was Charles I; a century later, the Duke of Cumberland's men, on their way home from defeating Bonnie Prince Charlie at Culloden, accidentally set fire to it. A few houses on Linlithgow's High Street date back to the 17th and 18th centuries. The 15th-century parish church of **St. Michael** is magnificent; the flamboyant tracery of its **St. Catherine's Aisle**, breathtaking.

EDINBURGH

Telephone area code: (0131)

Accomodation

For information about all kinds of Edinburgh accommodation, call 5579655. The Tourist Information Desk at Edinburgh Airport also has an accommodation booking service, tel. 3332167.

LUXURY: **The Balmoral**, 1 Princes St., tel. 5562414, fax 5573747, lavish, castle-like, with two restaurants and leisure center. **The Caledonian**, Princes Street, tel. 4599988, fax 2256632, acknowledged Edinburgh leader. **The Sheraton Grand Hotel**, 1 Festival Square, tel. 2299131, fax 2296254. **Stakis Grosvenor Hotel**, Grosvenor St., tel. 2266001, fax 2202387. **Royal British Hotel**, 20 Princes St., tel. 5564901, fax 5576510, right on the main drag.

MODERATE: **Malmaison Hotel**, 1 Tower Place, Leith, tel. 5566868, fax 5556999, refurbished contemporary hideaway. **Bank Hotel**, 1 South Bridge, Edinburgh, tel. 5569043, fax 5581362, central, with in-house bar, yet more affordable than many around. **Brunswick Hotel**, 7 Brunswick St., tel. 5561238, fax 5571404. Two-star hotel in Georgian listed town house. **Grosvenor Gardens Hotel**, 1 Grosvenor Gardens, tel. 3133415, fax 3468732, not far from airport, cozy. **Kildonan Lodge Hotel**, 27 Craigmillar Park, tel. 6672793, fax 6679777, family-run, Victorian house. **The Lodge Hotel**, 6 Hampton Terrace, West Coates, tel. 3373682, fax 3131700. W of city, spruced-up family hotel of very high standard.

BUDGET: **Clan Campbell Hotel**, 11 Brunswick St., tel. 5576910. Listed Georgian building. **St. Bernard's Guest House**, 22 St. Bernard's Crescent, tel. 3322339. Georgian house not far from center. **Cairn Lodge**, 2 Downie Terrace, Costorphine, tel. 5392117, fax 5398117, Victorian villa, near zoo, family-run. **Belford Hostel**, 6-8 Douglas Gardens, tel. 2256209, fax 5398695, in old church. **High Street Hostel**, 8 Blackfriars Street, tel. 5573984, fax 5562981, central, v. popular (waiting list in season). **Mrs. Rosemary Bruce-Jones**, 35 Orchard Road South, tel. 3328209. Homey en-suite B&B.

Restaurants

EXPENSIVE: **The Atrium**, in the Traverse Theater, Cambridge Street, tel. 2288882, eat upmarket Scottish food from tables made of old railway sleepers. **The Witchery**, 352 Castlehill, 2255613, elegant Scottish fare, Old Town ambience. **The Doric**, 5 Market Street, 2251084, upscale bistro. **L'Auberge**, 56 St. Mary's St., tel 5565888, fine French cuisine. **Oyster Bar** at the **Cafe Royal**, 17 West Register St, tel. 5564124, lavish Victorian interior, lavish prices. **Martin's Restaurant**, 70 Rose Street, tel. 2253106, prides itself on its selection of Scottish and Irish cheeses.

MODERATE: **Iggs**, 15 Jeffrey Street, 5578184, tapas top Scottish menu near the Royal Mile. **The Shore**, 3-4 The Shore, Leith, tel. 5335080, seafood with water views. **The Vintner's Room**, 87 Giles St., Leith, tel. 55467679, old wine storage faciility, now a candlelit restaurant, French/Scottish cooking, and proud of its game dishes as well as its seafood. **Dubh Prais**, 123B High St., tel. 5575732, small cellar restaurant serving very good Scottish cooking. **Pierre Victoire**, 10 Victoria St., tel 2251721, with other branches including 38 Grassmarket, tel. 2262442, renowned institution serving affordable French bistro cooking; very cheap lunches. **Pierre Lapin**, 32 West Nicholson St., tel. 6684332, is an affiliate restaurant with vegetarian meals.

BUDGET: **La Cuisine D'Odile**, 12 Randolph Crescent, tel. 2255366, in the basement of the Institut Français of Scotland, lunch only, no alcohol. **Lancers Brasserie**, 5 Hamilton Place, tel. 3323444, Indian food with Raj-era flavor. **Indian Cavalry Club**, 3 Atholl Place, tel. 2283282, remarkably exotic Indian restaurant. **Blue Moon Cafe**, 36 Broughton St., tel. 5562788, popular hangout, notably with gay crowd.

Pubs

The Drum and Monkey, 80 Queen St., tel. 5588111, good grub. **Maggie Dickson's**, 92 Grassmarket, tel. 2256601, new "theme" pub. **Bennet's**, 8 Leven St., tel. 2295143, Victorian style, with good food. **The Basement**, 109 Broughton St., popular hangout. **The Cumberland Bar**, Cumberland St., real ale, not too loud. **The Bow Bar**, 80 West Bow, huge selection of ales.

Tea Rooms

Cafe Florentin, 8 St. Giles St., tel. 2256267, French pastries, light meals nr High Street. **Queen Street Cafe**, Nat'l Portrait Gallery. *trés* Edinburgh coffee shop. **Laigh Kitchen**, 117A Hanover St., tel. 2251552, long-standing tradition, flagstone floors.

Museums and Sights

Camera Obscura, Castlehill, tel. 2263709, Apr-Oct 9:30 am-6 pm, Nov-Mar til 5 pm. **Edinburgh Castle**, tel. 6688800, daily Apr-Sep 9:30 am-5:15 pm, Oct-Mar til 4:15 pm. **Georgian House**, 7 Charlotte Sq., tel. 2252160, Apr-Oct Mon-Sat 10 am-5 pm, Sun 2-5 pm. **Gladstone's Land**, 447B Lawnmarket, tel. 2265856, Apr-Oct Mon-Sat 10 am-5 pm, Sun 2-5 pm. **Greyfriars Kirk**, tel. 2251900, Easter-Sep, Mon-Fri 10 am-4 pm, Sat 10 am-2 pm. **High Kirk of St. Giles**, tel. 2259442, daily 9 am-5 pm. **Huntly House Museum**, 142 Canongate, tel. 5294143, Jun-Sep Mon-Sat 10 am-6 pm, Oct-May til 5 pm. **Lady Stair's House**, Lawnmarket, tel. 2242424, Jun-Sep Mon-Sat 10 am-6 pm, Sun & Oct-May til 5 pm. **Museum of Childhood**, 42 High St, tel. 5294142, Oct-May Mon-Sat 10 am-5 pm, Jun-

Sept to 6 pm. **National Gallery of Scotland**, the Mound, tel. 5568921, Mon-Sat 10 am-5 pm, Sun 2-5 pm. **Palace of Holyroodhouse**, Canongate, tel. 5561096, exc. state visits, Apr-Oct Mon-Sat 9:30 am-5:15 pm, Sun 10:30 am-4:30 pm, Nov-Mar daily 9:30 am-3:45 pm. **The People's Story**, 163 Canongate (Tolbooth), tel. 5294057, Oct-May Mon-Sat 10 am-5 pm, Jun-Sept to 6 pm. **Royal Botanic Garden**, Inverleith Row. tel. 5527171, May-Aug 10 am-8 pm, Apr & Sept til 6 pm, otherwise 10 am-4 pm. **Royal Museum of Scotland**, Chambers St., tel. 2257534, Mon-Sat 10 am-5 pm, Sun 12-5 pm. **Scottish National Portrait Gallery**, 1 Queen St., tel. 5568921, Mon-Sat 10 am-5 pm, Sun 2-5 pm. **Scotch Whisky Heritage Centre**, 354 Castlehill, tel. 2200441, Jun-Sep 9 am-6:30 pm, Oct-May 10 am-5 pm. **Edinburgh Zoo**, Corstorphine Rd, tel. 3349171, Apr-Sep 9 am-6 pm, Oct-Mar til 4:30 pm.

Theater and Music
Edinburgh Festival Theatre, 13-29 Nicolson St., tel. 5296000, gorgeous old-style theater, varied program. **Usher Hall**, Lothian Rd., tel. 2288616, city's leading concert hall. **Traverse Theatre**, Cambridge St., tel. 2281404, cutting-edge productions.

Festivals
Edinburgh International Festival, 21 Market St., tel. 2264001, fax 2251173. Music, theater, dance; held every August. **Edinburgh Festival Fringe**, 180 High St., tel. 2265257, fax 2204205. **Edinburgh's Hogmanay**, tel. 5573990, festival at New Year's.

Sports
GOLF: An Edinburgh Golf Pass entitles you to 2 or 4 days of golfing at 12 Edinburgh courses at reduced rates. Call 5581072 or the Tourist Board, below.

Tourist Information
Scottish Tourist Board, 23 Ravelston Terrace, tel. 3322433. **Edinburgh & Lothians Tourist Board**, 3 Princes St., tel. 5571700. **National Trust for Scotland**, 3 Charlotte Square, tel. 2265922

LOTHIANS
West Lothian
Accommodations / Restaurants
UPHALL: *EXPENSIVE:* **Houstoun House Hotel**, tel. (01506) 853831, fax 854220. 16th-century tower house surrounded by gardens. **LINLITHGOW:** *MODERATE:* **The Earl o' Moray Inn**, Bonsyde, tel. (01506) 842229, fax 846233, Georgian manor, palace views. **The Four Marys**, 67 High St., tel. (01506) 842171, pub with malt whiskies & good food. **Champany Inn**, junction of A904 and A803 (2 mi/3 km NE of town), tel. (01506) 834532, prides itself on steaks.

Museums & Sights
Dalmeny House, South Queensferry, tel. (0131) 3312451, Jul-Aug Mon, Tue 12-5:30 pm, Sun 1-5:30

pm. **Hopetoun House**, South Queensferry, tel. (0131) 3312451, mid-Apr-Sept 10 am-5:30 pm.

Midlothian
Accommodations / Restaurants
DALKEITH: *MODERATE:* **County Hotel**, 152 High St., tel. (0131) 6633495, family-run, central. **NORTH MIDDLETON: Middleton Country Inn** (S of Gorebridge), tel. (01875) 821978. **PENICUIK:** *MODERATE:* **Navaar House Hotel**, Bog Road, tel. (0131) 4473087, main hotel in town. *BUDGET:* **Peggyslea Farm**, Nine Mile Burn, tel. (01968) 660930, pleasant B&B. **ROSLIN:** *MODERATE:* **Old Original Roslin Hotel**, 4 Main St., tel. (0131) 4402384, 19th-century inn.

Museums & Sights
Dalkeith Park, tel. (0131) 6653277, open Apr-Oct daily 10 am-6 pm, landscaped in the 18th century. **Edinburgh Crystal Visitor Center**, Eastfield, Penicuik, tel. (01968) 675128, Mon-Fri 9 am-5 pm, Sun 11 am-5 pm, factory tours in season (no children under 8). **Scottish Mining Museum,** Newtongrange, 10 mi/16 km S of Edinburgh on A7, tel. (0131) 6637519, Mar-Oct 10 am-4 pm.

East Lothian
Accommodation / Restaurants
DUNBAR: *MODERATE:* **Courtyard Hotel & Restaurant**, Woodbuch Brae, tel. (01368) 852287, on the water; good food. *BUDGET:* **St. Beys Guest House**, 2 Bayswell Rd., tel. (01368) 863571, Victorian; home cooking. **DIRLETON:** *EXPENSIVE:* **Open Arms Hotel**, tel. (01620) 850241, by village green, Scottish food. **GIFFORD:** *MODERATE:* **Goblin Ha' Hotel**, Main St., tel. (01620) 810244, 18th-c. inn. **GULLANE:** *EXPENSIVE:* **Greywalls Hotel**, Muirfield, tel. (01620) 842144; designed by Sir Edward Luytens; Gertrude Jekyll laid out gardens. *MODERATE:* **La Potiniere**, Main St., tel (01620) 843214, exc. French cooking & wines. **NORTH BERWICK:** *MODERATE:* **Point Garry Hotel**, 20 West Bay Rd., tel. (01620) 892380. Victorian house, sea view.

Museums & Sights
John Muir House, 126-128 High St, Dunbar, tel. (01368) 863353, June-Sept, by appt. **Lennoxlove**, Haddington, tel. (01620) 823720, home of Duke of Hamilton; death mask of Mary Queen of Scots. May-Sept, Wed, Sat, Sun 2-5 pm. **Phantassie Doocot & Preston Mill**, 6 mi/10 km W of Dunbar, tel. (01620) 860426, Apr-Sept, Mon-Sat 11 am-1 pm and 2-5 pm, Sun 2-4 pm, Oct Sat & Sun only. **Prestongrange Industrial Heritage Museum**, Morison's Haven, tel. (0131) 6532904, Apr-Sept.

Tourist Information
Tourist Information Centre, 143 High St., Dunbar, tel. (01368) 863353. **Tourist Information Centre**, The Cross, Linlithgow, (01506) 844600.

THE BORDERS
Religion and Politics

PEEBLES
MELROSE
DRYBURGH
JEDBURGH
KELSO

Medieval monasteries were built beside rivers, and villages grew up around the monasteries. Thus in the Borders of Scotland the remains of these monasteries and the limpid rivers aren't only there to please the eye of modern visitors; they were in fact vital in the creation of the region's historic towns. These towns – Peebles, Selkirk, Melrose, Jedburgh, Kelso, and Berwick upon-Tweed – all grew up around monasteries along clear, fish-filled streams. And because this was truly border country, fought over again and again by rival dynasties, this is also a region of mighty fortresses and castles, some of them, too, in ruins.

Of these rivers none is more redolent of history and literature than the salmon-filled **Tweed**, which flows for 97 miles (156 km) through hilly country, from the southern uplands of Scotland to Berwick-upon-Tweed and the sea. The cloth produced on its banks is famous, though it derives its name not from the river Tweed but from a corruption of "twill," the term for a textile fabric in which weft-threads pass first over one warp-thread and then under two more, creating vivid (or, de-

Preceding pages: A symphony of greens in the Scottish Borders. Left: Wool country: fabric samples from local manufacturers.

pending on the colors, subtle) diagonal lines. However, "tweed" it has become and tweed it remains (see "From Tweed to Tartan," p. 227). Some Border towns, such as dour Hawick with its sturdy 19th-century buildings, derive their prosperity chiefly from tweed (though Hawick also boasts a profitable sheep auction, and its inhabitants ride to hunt).

A living commemoration of this rich past are the Border Ridings: now annual summer pageants held in many towns, these colorful festivities recall (and reenact) the days when mounted patrols toured the borders of a county to guard against bands of marauding outlaws.

PEEBLES

Washed by the Tweed, the county town of **Peebles**, south of Edinburgh, is as beguiling a spot as any to start a visit to the Borders. Peebles has been a royal burgh since King David II granted it a charter in 1367. Still earlier, in 1261, King Alexander III founded **Cross Kirk** where pious villagers had discovered an ancient cross. Around it, beside the wide River Tweed, grew a monastery; though this was dissolved at the Reformation, Cross Kirk continued as Peebles' parish church until 1784, and then was allowed to fall into its present ruined state. You can still admire its 15th-century tower and explore the monastery's remains.

Even earlier, close by Cross Kirk, the **Church of St. Andrew** was founded in 1195. The marauding English set it on fire when they were busy sacking much of this region's religious heritage, and its present tower dates only from 1883.

Scottish learning has flourished in Peebles. Here were born the brothers William and Robert Chambers (in 1800 and 1802). Publishers, they created *Chambers Encyclopedia*, compiled dictionaries and wrote histories of their native land; they also published the poems of Robert Burns. William became Lord Provost of Edinburgh, and from his own pocket paid for the restoration of the High Kirk of St. Giles. In Peebles, a plaque on a little house on the street Biggiesknowe marks their birthplace. And William left to the town **Chambers Institute**, now its civic center and museum.

Another plaque on High Street records that the famous explorer Mungo Park settled here as a surgeon after his marriage in 1799. He had already traversed the River Niger and published his *Travels in the Interior of Africa*. But Park was restless, and in 1805 he set off again for Africa, where natives attacked his company; during the conflict, he was drowned.

Neidpath Castle, the Douglas family seat, rises west of the town above the Tweed, its oldest walls 11 feet (3 m) thick; its newer parts date from the early 15th century. When William Wordsworth visited in 1803, he was incensed, for to raise money its spendthrift absentee landowner, the 4th Duke of Queensberry, had cut down the trees on his estate, impoverishing those who worked the land on his behalf. Wordsworth wrote a poem excoriating him as "Degenerate Douglas! Oh, the unworthy Lord!"

Travel 8 miles (13 km) southwest to discover ancient trees, the magnificent specimens in **Dawyck Botanic Gardens**, many of them more than a hundred years

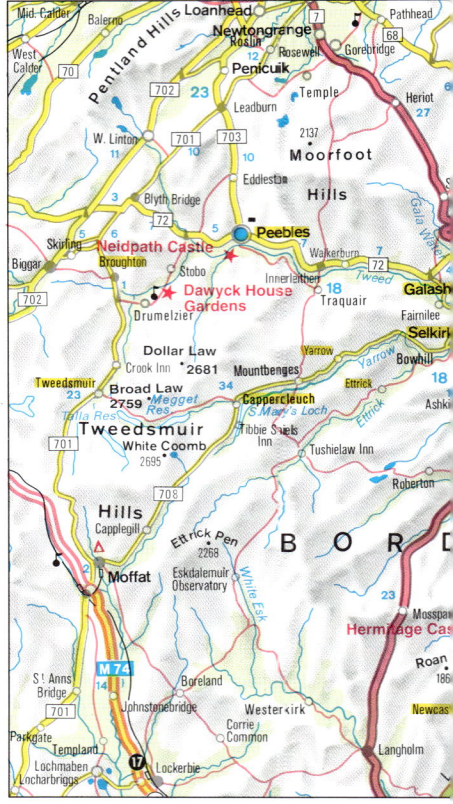

old. Further on lies the village of **Broughton**, set on Biggar Water near the valley of the River Tweed. A ruined church here abuts on the cell of an early settler: Liolan, a 7th-century Pictish hermit. The village nurtured John Buchan, whose grandparents had a home here; Buchan often holidayed here with his sister. The **John Buchan Center** at Broughton celebrates his life. Already famous for his *The 39 Steps* (see p. 232), Buchan was also a distinguished politician and diplomat, and when he became governor-general of Canada was also made a peer. He took as his title Lord **Tweedsmuir**, from the name of a lovely village south of Broughton near the source of the River Tweed. On a mound

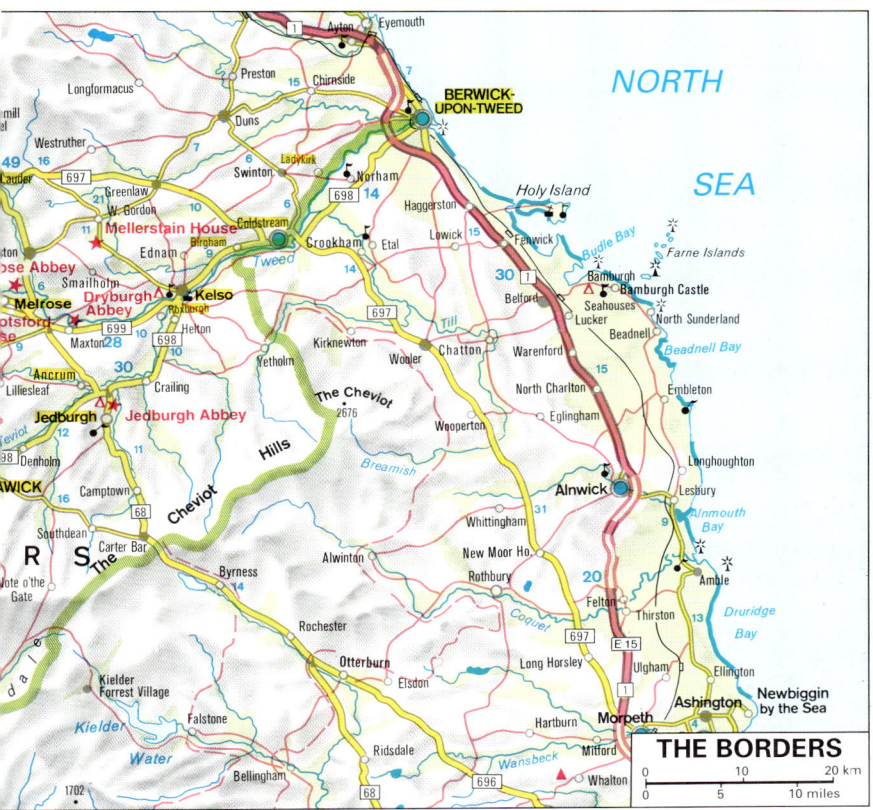

THE BORDERS

0   10   20 km
0   5   10 miles

close by lovely Victorian **Tweedsmuir Church** you can trace the stones of an ancient fortress. And just outside the village, **Oliver House** stands on the site of what was once Oliver Castle, built in the reign of David I and one of a chain of towers which line the River Tweed. About 1.5 miles (2.5 km) from town stands 17th-century **Crook Inn**, a haunt of Buchan, Sir Walter Scott and Robert Burns, now catering to local anglers.

South of Tweedsmuir is the river's source. Near here are the two highest spots in the Borders, 2,750-foot (841 m) **Broad Law** and 2,650-foot (810 m) **Dollar Law**. This is impressively craggy country. Driving southeast from Tweedsmuir you come first to **Talla Reservoir**, home to brown trout; the reservoir was created in 1905, but there was a lake here before that. Continuing on, you next reach **Megget Reservoir**; and finally, at **Capercleuch**, **St. Mary's Loch**, one of the few lochs in the Borders. Sheltered by steep hills, the loch derives its name from the ancient church of St. Mary on its northwestern shore. A little to the north rises one of the Borders' most formidable defensive towers, **Drythorpe Tower**, birthplace in 1550 of Mary Scott, one of Sir Walter's ancestors. Further south, toward Moffat, the waterfall **Grey Mare's Tail** cascades from the hills.

On the isthmus between St. Mary's Loch and tiny Loch of the Lowes is the former **Tibbie Shiel's Fishing Inn**.

Named after Tibbie Richardson Shiel, who ran it from her husband's death in 1824 until she died herself, aged 96, in 1878, it was introduced to his Edinburgh cronies by William Chambers, who relished her "wholesome and agreeable country fare." Walter Scott became a regular, as did James Hogg, the remarkable poet and novelist known as "the Ettrick Shepherd."

Born in 1770, a shepherd in youth, educated only in fits and starts, Hogg nonetheless managed to have some of his works printed in Edinburgh when he was there selling his employer's sheep. He was lucky enough to meet and impress Walter Scott, who saw to the publication of his later works. *The Confessions of a Justified Sinner* is Hogg's masterpiece.

In his *Life of Scott*, J. G. Lockhart recalls the first time Hogg took dinner with Scott. The rustic genius had little notion of fashionable manners, and when he entered Scott's drawing room he saw that Mrs. Scott, then in a delicate state of health, was reclining on a sofa. "The Shepherd, after being presented, and making his best bow, forthwith took possession of another sofa placed opposite to hers, and stretched himself thereupon at all his length; for, as he said afterwards, 'I thought I could never do wrong to copy the lady of the house.'" Lockhart adds that as Hogg was wearing clothes suitable for attending a cattle market, and his hands bore traces of a recent sheep-shearing, Mrs. Scott did not take kindly to his novel use of her chintz. However, the Shepherd didn't notice. He "dined heartily, drank freely, and, by jest, anecdote and song, offered plentiful merriment to the more civilized part of the company."

"A wren's nest round and theekit wi' moss" is how Hogg once described Tibbie Shiel's inn, and he longed for a memorial in "a quiet spot fornent Tib-

bie's dwelling." His wish was granted: today a monument 20 feet (6 m) high commemorates him and his dog Hector. He is buried in the local cemetery, close by the grave of Tibbie Shiel.

Northeast of Tibbie's Inn you reach **Yarrow**, which lies in the vale of Yarrow Water. Turn south for **Ettrick**, Hogg's birthplace, passing through Ettrick forest. This part of the Borders owes its sheep to King James V, who in 1529 gave the forest some 10,000 of them; their descendants still graze here. If you continue down the B709 you'll come upon a more unusual import: the pagodas of a **Tibetan Monastery**, going strong since 1967.

Hawick, set in a cleft of the Border Hills, is the most extensive town in this area. Here, in 1711, a far-sighted citizen introduced stocking-frames, which were successfully exploited throughout Scotland. The town benefited from its site at the confluence of the River Teviot and Stirling Burn, for water is essential to the cloth trade; today Hawick is famous for its cardigans and sweaters.

Hermitage Castle, some 12 miles (20 km) south of Hawick, received an unexpected visit from Mary Queen of Scots in 1566. The Queen was anxious for the health of the Earl of Bothwell, who had been wounded in an unexpected fight. This is one of the best-preserved of the old Border keeps. Protected to the south by the Hermitage Water and the marshlands around the tower, it stands near a small medieval hermitage (whence its name). Parts of it date back to the first castle of 1296. In more warlike eras, Hermitage Castle menaced enemies with a powerful tower, which occupies the site of an earlier one built by the English in an oblong central courtyard. The other parts of Hermitage Castle, built by the Scots (with a substantial 19th-century restoration), include small square towers added at the corners of the main tower.

After Bothwell's death, the castle came into the hands of the Scotts of Buccleuch,

Right: This little piggy... The lighter side of an agricultural show.

who in 1793 created a piquant example of 18th-century town planning. At **Newcastleton**, 3 miles (5 km) south of Hermitage Castle, the 3rd Duke of Buccleuch set up a village devoted to handloom weaving. Sitting in the flat Liddlesdale valley, the town has a central square and a High Street with squares at either end.

Selkirk, a royal burgh overlooking Ettrick Water, has seen both turbulence and peace. Turbulent were the days when the English razed the town after their victory at Flodden. Only one of the 80 soldiers Selkirk sent to Flodden returned – but he was bearing a captured English standard. His statue stands in the market square. Other statues in Selkirk depict Walter Scott and Mungo Park, while a plaque over a shop doorway states that Montrose stayed here before his defeat in battle in 1645. 17th-century **Halliwell's House** is now a museum of local history. Also worth a visit is **Bowhill House**: built in 1812, it contains the art collection of the Buccleuch and Queensberry family, in-

cluding works by Reynolds, Gainsborough, and some attributed to Leonardo.

Galashiels spreads itself across Gala Water, a tributary of the Tweed which flows for 21 miles (34 km) from its source in the nearby Moorfoot Hills. Sir Robert Lorimer left his mark on Galashiels by designing its huge **clock tower** (behind the World War I memorial). The town has been a center of Scottish woollens since the early 16th century, some 70 years earlier than its **Mercat Cross**, which dates from 1695. As for the town crest, with its motto "Sour Plums," it depicts a fox attempting to reach the boughs of a plum tree and relates to an incident in 1337 when the defenders of Galashiels came upon unsuspecting English soldiers picking wild plums and slaughtered them.

Lauder, north of Galashiels, deserves to attract visitors if only because of **Thirlestaine Castle**. It rises from a 12th-century foundation and inside are some of Scotland's finest 17th-century plaster ceilings as well as handsome furnishings and paintings. Once the family seat of the

Earls of Lauderdale, Thirlestaine Castle also houses an exhibition detailing Borders agriculture.

MELROSE

Melrose, southeast of Galashiels, is magical. Monks from Iona (among them St. Aidan and the shepherd-saint Cuthbert, patron of Northumbria) founded a monastery here in the mid-7th century, but the evocative ruin we now see dates mostly from the 15th century. Undoubtedly one of Scotland's most spectacular ruins, Melrose was refounded in the mid-12th century by Cistercian monks whom King David I had invited from Rivaulx. But in the next century the troops of Edward I repeatedly savaged it, viciously slaughtering some of its monks. And in 1385 an offensive led by Richard II burned the abbey to the ground.

Above: Magical Melrose, one of Scotland's loveliest Border abbeys. Right: Friendliness is part of the Scottish national character.

Here the heart of Robert the Bruce was buried (or maybe not: another tradition has it taken to Spain and flung at the Moors by the dying Sir James Douglas, who cried, "Go first, brave heart"). Yet it cannot be said that the Scots themselves cherished the monastery. The Douglas family, who took possession of Melrose Abbey in 1568, used many of its stones to build their house at the end of the cloisters. Fortunately in 1822 Sir Walter Scott, funded by the Duke of Buccleuch, put the buildings in order. At the east end of its church the walls still reach the height of the roof; shells of both transepts and chapels of the south aisle also survive. Note the gargoyles, particularly one of a pig playing the bagpipes.

Abbotsford House, near Melrose and set on the right bank of the Tweed, was the home of Sir Walter Scott from 1812 until he died in 1832. When he bought it, this was a mere farm (known as Cartley Hole). Scott transformed it into a palatial (if stylistically eclectic) baronial home, and planted the surrounding woodlands.

It remains as he left it, housing some 20,000 rare books as well as a collection of historical relics of the Border Wars, Bonnie Prince Charlie, Napoleon Bonaparte and Robert Burns. Scott wrote all his Waverley novels here. (See p. 232.)

DRYBURGH

Southeast of Melrose, in woodlands, is **Dryburgh Abbey**. Since the first syllable of Dryburgh means "oak" in Celtic, many conjecture that Druids, who venerated that tree, worshipped here. Hugh de Morville founded the abbey in the mid-12th century for Northumbrian monks. Although much of the abbey church was destroyed under Henry VIII and only the transepts remain, Dryburgh's medieval cloisters are the best-preserved of any in Scotland, save for those at Iona and Inchcolm. You can still see the steps leading to the canons' sleeping quarters, as well as the barrel-vaulted chapter house. Resting in the well-preserved 13th-century north transept are the mortal remains of Sir Walter Scott.

Nearby, a panorama of the valley of the Tweed and of the three peaks of the Eildon Hills is now called **Scott's View**. Scott once observed that he could stand here and point out 43 spots famous in war and verse. And at his funeral, his horses, pulling his hearse, stopped here briefly, remembering that they had always done so in the past.

JEDBURGH

Further southeast, across **Dere Street**, a Roman road built nearly two thousand years ago, is **Jedburgh**, where Augustinian canons who had sailed from St. Quentin's Abbey at Beauvais in France founded a priory in 1138 at the request of King David I. This county town is a mere 10 miles (16 km) from the English border, and nestles in the valley of the Jed Water, a tributary of the River Teviot.

Inevitably, given its position as a gateway to Scotland, Jedburgh was much ravaged by the English. In 1174 the Treaty of Falaise even ceded it to them as security for the ransom of King William the Lyon (grandson of David I), who had been captured near Alnwick Castle and taken across the Channel to Normandy. King Edward I stayed here in 1296, partly to secure the election of an abbot favorable to the English.

In 1409, the Scots decided that a castle so frequently occupied by the English ought to be demolished. Its site is now occupied by a building still known as the Castle but in fact built in 1832 as the county jail. The abbey itself was battered with shot and shell in 1523 by the troops of the Earl of Surrey. In 1544, an English army set fire to some of its buildings.

Yet Jedburgh remained a favored royal seat. Malcolm IV died in its castle in 1195. In the abbey in 1295, King Alexander III was married to the daughter of the Count de Dreux, but the ceremony was apparently clouded when a ghost ap-

peared and told the king that he would soon die tragically. A year later he was dead, killed instantly when his horse fell one dark night. A monument at Pettycur, southwest of Kinghorn, marks the spot.

Mary Queen of Scots arrived here in October 1566 to preside over the circuit court. She stayed in Queen Street at what is now called **Queen Mary's House** (where you can see some of her personal effects, including her watch). From here, she galloped to Hermitage Castle (see p. 76) and the wounded Bothwell. Her 40-mile journey there and back (65 km) almost cost her her life, for she became seriously fevered and didn't recover until a month later – along with Bothwell, who also regained his strength.

Bonnie Prince Charlie also lodged at Jedburgh, at no. 11 Castlegate, during his doomed rising against England. This was also a haunt of Walter Scott, whose first

Above: New meets old at a roadside snack bar. Right: Battered by the English: the roofless nave of Jedbergh Abbey.

appearance as an advocate in a criminal trial was here, in 1793: he successfully defended a poacher and a sheepstealer.

Centerpiece of town is the superb ruined **abbey**. Much of its church rises proudly, if damaged; its nave is roofless, but otherwise almost intact. Its west end, in the Transitional Gothic style, is magnificent. Three gables surmount a skillfully sculpted Romanesque doorway; above it rise blank arcades and a round-headed window, supporting a gable with a delicious, half-Gothic rose window. Inside, the shafts are slender and clustered. The north transept is rebuilt, while the south one is an evocative ruin; the ruined chancel arcade retains cylindrical piers and corbels. South of the nave you can trace out the lie of other monastic buildings: two undercrofts; what might have been the monastery kitchen; the base of the pier from which sprang the vault of the square chapter house, where the monks met each day to discuss daily concerns.

Northeast of Jedburgh, **Ancrum** looks back into prehistory, with a couple of

Iron Age forts nearby. Here, at the battle of Lilliards Edge in 1545, Scots soldiers routed an English force – one of the last Scottish victories in the Border Wars. Further on, **Penielheugh Hill** supports a 150-foot high (46 m) memorial set up in 1815 by the Marquis of Lothian to celebrate Britain's victory at Waterloo.

Roxburgh, on the south bank of the Tweed, and protected by the fortress of Marchmount, once controlled a major border crossing. After its capture by the English, King James II of Scotland besieged Marchmount in 1460. On August 3, a cannon exploded and killed the king. Mary, his widow, urged on the Scottish troops, and they succeeded in routing the English and demolishing the fortress.

KELSO

Sir Walter Scott judged **Kelso**, on the rivers Tweed and Teviot, to be the most romantic and probably the most beautiful village in Scotland. In 1754, a bridge over the Tweed enhanced the prosperity of this market town, and in 1800 the brilliant civil engineer John Rennie began constructing a new five-arched bridge across the river, which served as the model for Rennie's 1811 London Bridge.

But people don't come to Kelso for 19th-century civil engineering. Once upon a time, Kelso possessed the largest and richest of the Borders' medieval abbeys. **Kelso Abbey** was founded in 1128 by King David I, who brought in French Benedictine monks he had originally settled at Selkirk. David believed his foundation would be protected by the nearby royal burgh of Roxburgh, but it was demolished by the English in 1545. Ignominy had already been conferred on Kelso earlier in the century when King James V insisted that one of his illegitimate sons be made abbot. Yet though a ruin, Kelso Abbey's church remains remarkable in Scotland for its two sets of transepts, with a tower over each crossing.

Northwest of Kelso, visible from Rennie's bridge and set amidst extensive, landscaped grounds, stands imposing **Floors Castle**, built by Sir John Vanbrugh in 1718 on behalf of the 1st Duke of Roxburgh and remodelled by William Playfair between 1839 and 1849. Another magical building no more than 6 miles (10 km) northwest of Kelso is **Mellerstain House**. Here, William Adam and his son Robert designed one of Scotland's greatest Georgian houses, a masterpiece of early 18th-century harmony, for the Baillie family. Inside, Georgian delicacy rules over the moulded ceilings (especially in the library), the mantelpieces, light fittings and doorways. The furniture is by the likes of Chippendale, Sheraton and Hepplewhite; the paintings, by Veronese, Gainsborough, Constable, and van Dyck. Outside, terraced gardens, laid out in the Italian style in 1909, slope towards an ornamental lake.

Birgham lies on the west bank of the Tweed, at the west end of its reach which defines the border between Scotland and

England. In a battle on the other side of the river, Lothian was won for Scotland in 1018, and the village was subsequently the venue of numerous meetings between the diplomats of the rival countries. Their greatest success seemed to be the Treaty of Birgham, negotiated in 1290, which arranged the marriage of the infant Queen Margaret of Scotland to England's Prince Edward, who would come to the throne as Edward II. Alas, within three months Margaret died, and the new alliance dissolved into acrimony and war.

Further on towards Berwick-upon-Tweed, **Coldstream** sits at the spot where an ancient ford crossed the River Leet, still in use until 1766 when John Smeaton built a five-arched bridge. Although the headquarters of the Coldstream Guards was established here in 1659, that celebrated regiment had earlier collaborated with General Monck in his pacification of Scotland on behalf of

Oliver Cromwell and was equally loyal to him in his successful bid to restore the monarchy in 1660. The guards' name derives from the fact that they set out for this perilous task from Coldstream.

Ladykirk, not quite halfway between Coldstream and Berwick-upon-Tweed, is where in 1599 King James IV, later to die at Flodden, almost drowned in the Tweed. As an offering of thanks for his life, he endowed a church here, which still stands; its belfry was added in 1743.

Finally, you reach **Berwick-upon-Tweed** and the North Sea. Today, Berwick-upon-Tweed is in England, but it changed hands between England and Scotland no fewer than thirteen times between 1147 (when William the Lyon ceded it) and 1482 (when the future Richard III finally took it for England). The town wall, and the layout of its cobbled streets, are remarkable medieval survivals. If you drive north along the coast, you pass the ruins of 13th-century **Coldingham Priory** before reaching the sheer cliffs of **St. Abb's Head**, a home for sea birds.

Above: Sun breaks through the clouds over a Border farm.

THE BORDERS
Accommodation
PEEBLES: *MODERATE:* **Park Hotel**, Interleithen Road, tel. (01721) 720451, view of the Cademuir Hills. **Venlaw Castle Hotel**, Edinburgh Rd., tel. (01721) 720384, baronial manor outside town.
MELROSE: *MODERATE:* **Burts Hotel**, Market Square, tel. (01896) 822285, with especially good restaurant. **King's Arms Hotel**, High St., tel. (01896) 822143, ancient coaching inn. *BUDGET:* **Dunfermline House Guest House**, Buccleuch St., tel. (01896) 822148, close by Melrose Abbey.
ETTRICK VALLEY: *MODERATE:* **Tushielaw Inn**, tel. (01750) 62205, beside Ettrick Water. 18th-century coaching inn, home cooking.
SELKIRK: *EXPENSIVE:* **Philipburn House Hotel**, tel. (01750) 20747, 18th-century house, marvelously low-key atmosphere. *MODERATE:* **Ettrickshaws Hotel**, Ettrick Bridge, tel. (011750) 52229, Victorian country house in river valley.
GALASHIELS: *MODERATE:* **The Abbotsford Arms**, Stirling St., tel. (01896) 752517, unpretentious and delightful. **Kingsknowes Hotel**, Selkirk Road, tel. (01896) 758375 and **Woodlands House Hotel**, Windyknowe Road, tel. (01896) 754722, two powerful Victorian mansions.
HAWICK: *MODERATE:* **Elm House Hotel**, 17 North Bridge St., tel. (01450) 372866, family-run.
ST. MARY'S LOCH: *BUDGET:* **Tibbie Shiels Inn**, tel. (01750) 4231.
DRYBURGH: *EXPENSIVE:* **Dryburgh Abbey Hotel**, St. Boswells, tel. (01835) 823945, in the abbey grounds.
JEDBURGH: *MODERATE:* **Kenmore Bank Guest House**, Oxnam Road, tel. (01835) 862369. **Glenfriars Hotel**, The Friars, tel. (01835) 862000. Victorian house with some 4-poster beds. *BUDGET:* **The Willow Court**, The Friars, tel. (01835) 863702, low price for high quality; views over town.
KELSO: *EXPENSIVE:* **Sunlaws House Hotel**, Heiton, tel. (01573) 450331. Pleasant country house hotel, award-winning restaurant. *MODERATE:* **Cross Keys Hotel**, The Square, tel. (01573) 223303, coaching inn, one of Scotland's oldest. **Ednam House Hotel**, Bridge Street, tel. (01573) 226319, 1761 Georgian mansion overlooking Tweed; extensive gardens. *BUDGET:* **Bellevue House**, Bowmont St., tel. (01573) 224588. 19th-century home of angler-poet Thomas Tod Stoddart.

Restaurants
PEEBLES: Kailzie Garden Restaurant, 2.5 mi/4 km from Peebles on the B7062, tel. (01721) 722807.
WALKERBURN: Tweed Valley Hotel, tel. (01896) 870636. Try the oak-paneled restaurant for game and home-made puddings.

MELROSE: Marmion's, Buccleuch St., tel. (01896) 822245. Pleasantly busy, low-key bistro.
GALASHIELS: Clovenfords Inn, Clovenfords, tel. (01896) 850203, famed for Aberdeen Angus beef and local salmon.
EYEMOUTH: The Old Bakehouse, tel. (01890) 750265. **Dunlaverock House**, tel. (01890) 771450, overlooks Coldingham Bay.
BERWICK-UPON-TWEED: Canty's Brig, Paxton, tel. (01289) 386255.

Museums and Sights
Neidpath Castle, Peebles, tel. (01721) 721333, Easter-Sept, Mon-Sat 11 am-5 pm, Sun 1-5 pm, also Tues in Oct. **Dawyck Botanic Garden**, 8 mi/13 km S of Peebles, tel. (01721) 760254, Mar 15-Oct 22, 10 am-6 pm. **Traquair House**, 8 mi/13 km fr Peebles, tel. (01896) 830323, dating from 12th c., with relics of Mary Queen of Scots. May-Sept daily 1:30-5:30 pm, Jul-Aug from 10:30 am. **Borders Wool Center**, North Wheatlands Mill, off the A72 NW of Galashiels, tel. (01896) 4293, Mar-Oct Mon-Fri 9 am-5 pm, Sat til 4 pm. **Dryburgh Abbey**, tel. (01835) 822381, Apr-Sept Mon-Sat 9:30 am-6:30 pm, Sun 2-6:30 pm, Oct-Mar til 4:30 pm. **Jedburgh Abbey**, tel. (01835) 863925, same hours as Dryburgh, above. **Mary Queen of Scots House**, Queen St., Jedburgh, tel. (01835) 863331, mid-Mar-mid-Nov Mon-Sat 10 am-4:45 pm, Sun til 2:30 pm. **Manderston**, near Duns, tel. (01361) 883450, open mid-May-Sept 2-5:30, Adam-style house in 56-acre formal gardens. **John Buchan Center**, Broughton, tel. (01899) 21050, Easter-Sept daily 2-5 pm. **Thirlestaine Castle**, Lauder, tel. (01578) 722430, Jul-Aug Mon-Fri & Sun 2-5 pm, May, Jun, Sep Mon, Wed, Thu 12-5 pm. **Melrose Abbey**, tel. (01896) 822562, hours as Dryburgh, above. **Abbotsford**, Sir Walter Scott's home nr Melrose, tel. (01896) 752043, late Mar-Oct 10 am-5 pm, Sun 2-5 pm. **Melrose Motor Museum**, Annay Rd., tel. (01896) 822624, Easter-Oct, 10:30 am-5:30 pm. **Kelso Abbey**, Bridge St., tel. (0131) 2443101, daily, year-round. **Mellerstain House**, 7 mi/11 km NW of Kelso, tel. (01573) 410381, May-Sept, Sun-Fri 12:30-4:30 pm. **Coldstream Museum**, 12 Market Squ., Coldstream, tel. (01890) 882630, Easter-late Oct, Mon-Sat 10 am-5 pm, Sun 2-5 pm. **Paxton House**, 5 mi/8 km W of Berwick, tel. (01289) 386291; Adam interiors, Chippendale furniture, Regency picture gallery. Easter-Oct, 12-4:15 pm.

Tourist Information
Scottish Borders Tourist Board, 70 High St., Selkirk, tel. (01750) 205054, fax 21886. **Jedburgh Tourist Information Center**, Murray's Green, tel. (01835) 863435. **Hawick Tourist Information Center**, Drumlanrig's Tower, Tower Knowe, tel. (01450) 372547.

THE SOUTHWEST
Dumfries, Galloway, and Ayrshire

DUMFRIES
THE SOUTH COAST
AYRSHIRE'S WEST COAST

Tucked into a corner of the country, off the main North-South routes from England to Glasgow and Edinburgh, the southwest of Scotland – Dumfries, Galloway, and Ayrshire – is less frequented by tourists than the more spectacular Central or Highland regions. This area has always stayed apart from the Scottish mainstream: Galloway means "land of the stranger Gaels," and the southwest of Scotland remained a Pictish stronghold long after most of the rest of the country had united in the 9th century.

Yet it has much to offer. Dubbed the "Scottish Riviera," the south coast of Galloway alternates small beaches with jagged rocks tearing white foam gashes into the blue water. Like the original Riviera, its villages house not only fishermen, but also communities of artists, drawn by the region's charm. Inland, the landscape moves from green meadows dotted with black-and-white "Belties," Galloway belted cattle, to deserted moorland, purple with heather. And the wilderness comes into its own in the woodlands of Galloway Forest Park.

On the west coast, Ayr sets the tone for the whole coastline: a resort town in the

spirit of England's Brighton, with a broad seaside promenade, fun fairs, and mini-golf. Other west coast towns are also geared to vacationers, belying the fact that this region was also touched by the spread of industry outwards from Glasgow in the 19th century.

Separate as it is, Scotland's southwest was the cradle of much of Scottish history. It saw the dawnings of Christianity in Scotland when St. Ninian landed in Isle of Whithorn in 397 A.D., before any other missionary; it saw Robert Bruce's battles against the English in the 14th century; it saw the "Killing Time" in the 17th century, when under the Restoration monarchy hundreds of Covenanters were murdered for their religious beliefs.

And to the general public, Ayrshire, Dumfries and Galloway are perhaps best known as the stomping-grounds of Scotland's very favorite native son.

Burns Country

To non-Scots, the poet Robert Burns is known for "Auld Lang Syne," sung in English-speaking countries around the world to usher in the New Year. To Scots, Burns is an embodiment of national consciousness, and chief bard in a language (not, locals aver, a dialect) that has faded over the years, but never died.

Preceding pages: Born free: Caerlaverock Nature Reserve. Left: Love among the ruins: Sweetheart Abbey'.

Few poets, living or dead, enjoy such rampant popularity. Celebrated during his lifetime, the poet attained cult status immediately upon his death in 1796: Burns Clubs sprang up throughout the country (the first one, in Greenock, began in 1801), and by 1885, they had formed an International Federation. "Burns Suppers" still take place in many parts of Scotland, especially in the southwest. The meal has evolved into an elaborate ritual, served with much Scotch whisky and reciting of poetry, often held on "Burns Night," January 25, Burn's birthday. In some areas, women costume themselves as the witches in "Tam O'-Shanter," one of Burns's finest pieces (and the one of which he was proudest).

Yet Burns's life was not in itself particularly remarkable. He was born in 1759 in the village of **Alloway**, near Ayr (the **Birth House** is now a museum), son of William Burnes (the "e" was discarded after his father's death). While the family was not well-off, Burnes senior placed great importance on his children's education, and by the age of 14, the young Burns had, as he later put it, "first committed the sin of RHYME." He grew into a dashing young man plagued by financial worries and alert to the pleasures of female company. After a stint in **Irvine** learning the trade of flax-dressing, a career which he fortunately abandoned, he returned to run the family farm after his father's death; but when he got the lovely young Jean Armour pregnant, he made the farm over to his brother to protect it against the claims of Jean's indignant father. In 1786, with the publication of the **Kilmarnock** edition of his poems, Burns was established as a poet. He spent time in Edinburgh, where he was the darling of society; but, as he needed to settle down and make a living, he rented the farm **Ellisland**, north of Dumfries, in 1788 and moved there with Jean, now (several children later) officially his wife. Ellisland proved fertile for poetry – much

DUMFRIES AND GALLOWAY

| 0 | 10 | 20 km |
| 0 | 5 | 10 miles |

of his best work dates from this time – but not for agriculture; Burns was forced to work as an exciseman, riding through the region checking up on imports and looking out for smugglers. He left the farm in 1791 and moved to Dumfries, where he died at the age of 37, partly as the result of a doctor's ill-advised prescription that he bathe daily in the icy waters of **Brow Well**, which exacerbated his long-standing heart condition.

DUMFRIES

For travelers coming up from England, the last station of Burns's life is one of the first stations in Scotland's southwest. Here, fans can look in at the **Burns House** (his last residence), or a **Burns Center** and museum. Burns was often in the audience of the **Theatre Royal**, Scotland's oldest working theater; after a

Above: Local hero: poet Robert Burns. Right: Dumfries's Old Footbridge arcs across the placid River Nith.

show, you can look in at his hangout (or "howff"), the **Globe Inn**, tucked away in an alleyway off High Street, oozing atmosphere, and not too tarted up for tourists. Preserved in an upstairs bedroom are relics of Burns's penchant for writing poetry on windowpanes (proving that diamond is harder than glass, and that Burns wore one).

Dumfries is a pleasant town, lounging comfortably along either side of the River Nith. Hard by the **old footbridge**, part of which dates from the 15th century, is Bridge House, the town's oldest dwelling (17th century), now furnished with an eclectic mix of "period" paraphernalia and open as an incidental museum. Less convenient, but perhaps more rewarding, are the **sculptures** scattered through the fields around the **Glenkiln Reservoir**, about 8 miles (13 km) west of Dumfries (turnoff Shawhead): there's something haunting about a Rodin standing alone in the middle of the countryside. There used to be six sculptures here, but Henry Moore's King and Queen had to be removed after a vandal decapitated them and threw their heads into the lake: perhaps a misguided expression of Scottish resistance to foreign rule, and certainly a wholly inappropriate one.

Southeast of Dumfries, the B725 leads to the fabulous bird-watching center of **Caerlaverock Nature Reserve** (especially notably for the barnacle geese who winter here) and **Caerlaverock Castle**, a satisfying edifice for storybook-castle fans. The estate dates back to the Norman Conquest; the site was key for control of access from England to the entire southern coast, and the first castle (a little ways behind the present ruin) probably started out as an English stronghold. Today's castle, or what's left of it, was first built in 1270, and destroyed and rebuilt many times thereafter. This distinctive triangular building is entered over a drawbridge across the surrounding moat (which today appears more pastoral than protec-

tive). Inside, a weathered but still ornate 1634 facade sports whimsical carvings of heads or plants over the doorways, which have yawned empty since the Covenanters besieged the place in the Civil War; Charles I's men finally allowed the garrison to capitulate honorably.

Continuing along this road, Burns pilgrims can pay homage to their idol at Brow Well, where he took the infamous cures that killed him. A bit further on, at **Ruthwell**, the history of poetry in Scotland comes full circle, from the death of Burns to the 8th-century **Ruthwell Cross** in the town church, which bears the runic text of Caedmon's *Dream of the Rood*, said to be the earliest known poem in the English language. The Covenanters judged this monument idolatrous and smashed it, leaving posterity to patch it together again. The man who rediscovered its pieces in 1810 also founded the country's first **savings bank**, also in Ruthwell, now a museum.

Further east, right on the English border, the **Old Toll House** in **Gretna** is the first house in Scotland for anyone coming up from the south. After the 16th century, English couples unable or unwilling to deal with the expense of an English church wedding traveled to Scotland, where a declaration of intent before two witnesses was enough to "tie the knot." **Gretna Green**'s **Old Blacksmith's Shop** was another frequent wedding venue until marriage by declaration became illegal in 1856.

North of Dumfries, one of the best Burns sites is Ellisland Farm, where he moved with Jean Armour in 1788. Ellisland is still a working farm, but one section displays Burns-iana and a film about the poet's three Ellisland years. Farther north is a far more splendid country house: **Drumlanrig Castle**, a Renaissance-style palace of 1680s vintage set in neat green parkland. Behind the imposing sandstone facade is a magnificent collection of Old Master paintings and family portraits (from Rembrandt to Reynolds), and French furniture, amassed for the First Duke of Buccleuch and Queens-

berry (apocryphally said to have spent but a single night on the premises, outraged at the building's high cost). The second Duke of Queensberry may have had simpler tastes: his ornate marble tomb is in the modest, lovely little village church of **Durisdeer**, tucked away in the woods, an unlikely place for an aristocrat's funerary chapel.

A longer-term residence of the first Duke was **Sanquhar**; which the second Duke left when he moved into Drumlanrig. Sanquhar is also associated with the Covenanters, whose first and second "Declarations of Sanquhar," affixed to the town's now-vanished market cross in 1680 and 1685, were defiant statements of allegiance to the true faith, rejecting, in the spirit of the Covenanters, the efflorescences of Catholic Popery and with it the authority of Charles II. A similar declaration was issued in Lanark; in the town of **Biggar**, the **Covenanters' House**, set up

Above: Artistic expression can turn up in the most surprising places.

in a former farmhouse, commemorates the lives of Covenanters in the region.

Religion and politics aside, this northeast section of the southwest also boasts plenty of memorials to daily life. One of Sanquhar's more prosaic claims to fame is the world's oldest working **post office** (1738). Mining is associated with **Wanlockhead**, supposedly the highest village in Scotland, and long a center for mineral activity. Disused since 1860, the Lochnell lead mine is now a museum; other mines here were worked until into the 20th century. Gold and silver are even more valuable exports: local gold has been used by royalty from James V – in his crown – to the current Queen Mother – in a brooch. Amateurs who want to pan for gold still flock here; the town hosts an annual gold-panning championship.

In Biggar, the prominent relic of the industrial age are the **coal gasworks**, in use from 1839 until the 1970s. Once a feature of most towns, gasworks only became interesting after they were closed down in favor of natural gas, whereupon Biggar's became an interesting historical monument rather than an unsightly blemish.

Further west on the banks of the Clyde is **New Lanark**, testimony to the utopian dreams of a social reformer in the early 1800s. Founded in 1784 as an industrial village for textile mill workers, New Lanark was transformed by Robert Owen, son-in-law of the original owner, who strove for better living conditions for his workers. Having improved and enlarged the run-down living quarters, he added such radical elements as a cooperative grocery store, a free school, cheap medical care and old age pensions, making New Lanark an anomaly in industrial Britain of that period and a model for such visitors as Friedrich Engels, who was impressed by the project.

Lanark has its bit of history, as well: it was in this royal burgh that "Braveheart" William Wallace, a sometime local resident, first got on the wrong side of the law. After he killed an English soldier in a squabble, he fled to the hills, but, when he learned that his wife had been murdered in retaliation, he gathered up supporters and returned to wreak havoc on the English troops stationed in town.

Less noble outlawry has an unofficial memorial in the striking **Devil's Beef Tub**, a deep natural bowl in the hills north of Moffat: cattle-rustlers used it as concealment for stolen Border livestock. **Moffat** itself is bisected by the widest main street in Scotland, supposedly for the benefit of drovers bringing through herds of cattle. Nearby, there's an endearing display of how present-day herders deal with their livestock: the **Tweedhope Sheepdog Center**, which breeds and trains the border collies still essential to a modern shepherd's work.

THE SOUTH COAST

"What," Queen Victoria asked Scotsman Thomas Carlyle, "is the loveliest road in my realm?" "That from Gatehouse of Fleet to Creetown," he said. "Ah," said the Queen, taken aback (she had been expecting a plug for her own favorite area, Deeside), "and what is the second loveliest?" "That from Creetown to Gatehouse of Fleet," replied Carlyle.

Carlyle's oft-quoted statement seldom meets with agreement today. There may well be lovelier roads in the British Isles. But there are plenty of uglier ones, too: and the gentle views of river estuaries bleeding at low tide out into the sea, seen over the rolling green hills, are nothing to sneeze at.

In view (on a clear day) of the English Lake District, not far from Ireland, the south coast has been a focal point for historic comings and goings for centuries. In fact, it was here that Christianity broke onto Scottish shores. In 397, a Welshman named Nynia or Ninian, made a Bishop in Rome, arrived to preach the Word to the Pictish heathen. Founding Scotland's first Christian church in Whithorn – this *candida casa*, white house, gave the town its name through the Northumbrian translation *hwit aern* – Ninian had tremendous success. His church and dwellings were popular places of pilgrimage well into the Middle Ages. Ninian even antedates the founding of Portpatrick, on the west coast of the peninsula called the Rhins of Galloway, so called because Saint Patrick supposedly landed here when he crossed (in a single step, some stories have it) over from Ireland.

But the first Christian monument you pass as you drive west from Dumfries is testimony to a much later era of the church. Sweet little **Sweetheart Abbey** was founded by Devorguilla, wife and mother to two John Balliols. Balliol *fils* was a rival of Robert Bruce, and initially beat him out as claimant to the Scottish throne; his father was evidently endearing enough to possess his wife's undying affection. When he died in 1248, she had his heart embalmed and carried it with her at all times as she did good deeds (including founding Oxford's Balliol College); when she died 42 years later (aged 90), she was buried with the heart before the church's high altar. Further west is a ruined 12th-century abbey, **Dundrennan**, where Mary, Queen of Scots spent her last night on Scottish soil before crossing over to England.

On so open a coast, defenses were as important as worship. The **Motte of Urr**, near Castle Douglas, is the largest motte-and-bailey construction in the country, dating back to the days of the Saxons. **Castle Douglas**, however, is neither a castle nor named for the Douglas family who were so prominent in the country's history; rather, it was a little settlement bought up by Glasgow merchant William Douglas in 1789 and laid out as an estate village. It's now one base for visitors arriving to fish, walk, sail or swim the waters of **Loch Ken**, a man-made reservoir which has developed into a popular leisure center.

But there is a real Douglas castle nearby, and a forbidding one at that: the ominous square tower of **Threave Castle**, accessible by boat. This castle was clearly built to defend and control, with walls eight feet thick and an infamous stone knob over the gateway from which evildoers – anyone, that is, the current Douglas heir didn't like – were hung (William, the 8th Earl, once boasted that it "hadn't been without a tassle for 50 years"). Ultimately, James II led troops against the castle to bring the haughty Douglases under control. The story goes that the locals so disliked the Douglases that they helped cast the mammoth cannon used in the siege, christened "Mons Meg" after the blacksmith's wife and now displayed in Edinburgh (in fact, the cannon was a gift from the Duke of Burgundy). Regardless of its provenance, it managed to blow off the hand of the

Right: Brown trout are one enticement Scotland offers recreational anglers.

Earl's wife when it was fired as she sat taking tea, although the castle was able to hold out for three months after that.

There are also more peaceful, picturesque things in the area, such as splendid **Threave Gardens**. And the picturesque elements have been amply documented by the artists' communities which grew up along the coast in the last century, notably in **Kirkcudbright** (pronounced Kirk-COO-bree). Local son E.A. Hornel, a leading member of the group of artists known as the "Glasgow Boys," settled here in 1890, and helped establish a community of artists. Hornel's house, **Broughton House**, is a museum displaying his paintings, library, and garden; while the 17th-century **Tolbooth** and the **Harbour Cottage Gallery** both display the work of local artists past and present. The tolbooth once briefly imprisoned John Paul Jones, born in nearby Arbigland, who went on to become an American naval commander in the Revolutionary War.

Besides the charming fishing harbor, an element of the town that may have provided artistic inspiration is **MacLellan's Castle**, actually a 16th-century town house: its remains loom dramatically out of the fog on rainy days, ideal subject for any would-be painter.

Gatehouse of Fleet, another lovely town, continued the artistic tradition in that Dorothy Sayers wrote here her Lord Peter Wimsay mystery *Five Red Herrings*. The book deals mainly with the artists of Kirkcudbright – or their fictional cousins, at any rate. A visitor center in an old cotton **mill** – cotton was once a mainstay of the local economy – provides an entertaining glimpse of local history.

Another of Gatehouse's literary claims to fame is that Burns supposedly wrote "Scots Wha Hae," a dramatic monologue depicting Robert Bruce inciting his troops to victory, while he was staying in town. The story goes that Burns composed the poem in his head while riding

across the moors in thunderstorm, and committed it to paper either at the Murray Arms or the (now-vanished) Bay Horse.

It's at Gatehouse that Carlyle's favorite stretch of coastal road begins. High on a rise off the road, commanding the same view of Wigtown Bay and the peninsula known as The Machars, are the dramatic standing stones of **Cairnholy**, now-roofless burial chambers. Inland, the views of the moorland are equally spectacular; the rugged heath and gorse are protected as a nature preserve known especially for its bird life. This is the kind of terrain traversed by Richard Hannay as he fled his pursuers in John Buchan's classic novel *The Thirty-Nine Steps*.

The Bruce and the English: Galloway Forest Park

More than pastoral poetry and lovely landscapes, Galloway also saw the birth of Scotland's history, the events that led to the establishment of one of the country's two longest royal dynasties. It

didn't begin very elegantly: in fact, with internecine squabbling about who had the right to inherit the crown, what Galloway actually saw was civil war in 1286. Two of the leading contenders were John Balliol, Devorguilla's son, and Robert Bruce. Balliol, the first to ascend the throne, became effectively a British puppet (see p. 19); Bruce was a leader in the revolts that subsequently swept the country. England wasn't the only enemy; there were also the other claimants to the throne, such as John Comyn, who almost killed Bruce in Selkirk Forest in 1299, and whom Bruce killed in Dumfries's Minorite House in 1306. Bruce was now open to charges of murder, sacrilege, and (from the point of view of Comyn's followers) treason; the only logical way out was to become King as soon as possible.

While his endeavors to achieve and maintain this goal took him all over Scotland, Galloway continued to be a focus of his activities. Early 1307 found him on the island of Arran, where, legend has it, watching a persevering spider struggling

southwestern base and his position as rightful Scottish king, he swept through the country on his way to the final victory at Bannockburn.

Apart from memories of Robert Bruce, **Galloway Forest Park** is a paradise for walkers and anglers. Combining natural and man-made beauties, it contains a red deer range and a wild goat park; spouting waterfalls, such as the Little Grey Mare's Tail; and the striking **monument** to **Alexander Murray**, a hilltop obelisk thrusting into the sky. It's all right not to have heard of Murray, who was a 19th-century professor of Oriental Languages at Edinburgh University; but seeing his birthplace, the ruins of a modest shepherd's house in the middle of nowhere (also in the park), make it clear that he's worthy of commemoration simply for having come so far.

Westward Ho

The history of Christianity is writ large on the peninsula known as the Machars. At its tip is the little fishing village **Isle of Whithorn** (not an isle at all), where stand the ruins of **St. Ninian's Chapel**. While the 13th-century ruins you see were built on the site of an older building, this probably wasn't an edifice of Ninian's own making, but rather a stop-off for the numerous pilgrims who traveled here to do him homage. A couple of miles out of town is **St. Ninian's Cave**, where he was said to have lived and prayed for a time; the pilgrims all trekked here, some leaving crosses etched in the rocks.

But the "house that Ninian built," the Candida Casa, is in **Whithorn**, a little ways inland. The "white house" was thus named because it was covered in white plaster, a contrast to the dark stone or wattle-and-daub huts more common at the time. It became such a popular place of pilgrimage in the centuries after the saint's death that a whole complex grew up around the site, with a monastery and

to build its web encouraged him to try, try again (a number of different places claim to be the site of this story). Certainly he needed perseverance: when his forces landed at Loch Ryan, near Stranraer, the English troops killed Bruce's two brothers.

But at **Glen Trool**, in the heart of what's today **Galloway Forest Park**, his luck began to turn. Trapped by English forces in the shadow of the **Merrick**, highest peak in southern Scotland, he managed to escape. The modern monument to him overlooking Loch Trool, called **Bruce's Stone**, is perhaps not unlike the boulders he and his men rolled down on the heads of the English. There's another Bruce's Stone in the park, by Clatteringshaws Loch; Robert supposedly leaned on this stone while directing his troops against the hapless English. Another victory took place near Ayr; having thus defended his

Above: Wild orchid: one example of Scotland's profusion of flowers. Right: Summer concert on the grounds of Culzean Castle.

ultimately a cathedral. The tiny museum has an excellent display of early Christian crosses and stones, giving a context for other relics of early Christianity, such as the **Kirkmadrine Stones** on the Rhins of Galloway, the oldest in the British Isles. There's further excavation into the past at the archaeological site dubbed the **Whithorn Dig**; begun in 1986, this excavation has uncovered evidence of Norse settlements and burial grounds as well as a forerunner of the monastery. Open to the public, the Dig provides a chance to see how archaeologists really work.

Further north, **Wigtown** is associated with Christians who lived much later: the martyrs Margaret Lachlan and Margaret Wilson, Covenanters who in 1685 were condemned to die for their religious beliefs. A **Martyr's Stake** has been erected approximately on the spot in the tidal flats where they were tied to a post and left to be drowned by the incoming ocean. Their graves are in the churchyard; a larger monument stands on a hill high over the town.

Like so many Christian buildings in the area, 12th-century **Glenluce Abbey** is a ruin, albeit a striking one. It's best known for a 13th-century denizen, the wizard Michael Scot. Buried here, so it's said, are his books on the occult, which helped him to lure the plague here so that he could imprison it, thereby saving the population. After the abbey's decline, stones from it were used in the building of the Castle of Park in 1590.

Stranraer, at the neck of the hammer-shaped peninsula of the Rhins of Galloway, is a hub for ferry traffic to Ireland; the local accent is sometimes disparagingly dubbed "Stranraer Irish." For centuries, however, most travel to and from Ireland went through Portpatrick. Botanic gardens such as **Castle Kennedy Gardens**, **Ardwell House Gardens**, or **Logan Botanic Gardens**, attest to the mild climate, courtesy of the passing Gulf Stream. The peninsula culminates in the cliffs of the **Mull of Galloway**, from where you can see to England and Ireland, weather permitting.

AYRSHIRE'S WEST COAST

Leading from Stranraer up to Glasgow, the road along the west coast connects towns that combine their traditional function as fishing villages with the newer one of resort. Panoramic views of sea and shore are punctuated by the corpulent form of an offshore island: **Ailsa Crag**, called "Paddy's Milestone" because it's halfway between Belfast and Glasgow. Now the province of nesting birds, the island was once owned by **Crossraguel Abbey**, the 13th-century ruins of which you can visit on the mainland; the abbot used the island as a place to punish intransigent brothers.

The area immediately around Crossraguel has a number of monuments to the more or less distant past, from the ruins of **Turnberry Castle** (a possible site of Robert Bruce's birth) to the elegant estate of **Culzean Castle**. The latter is far from a ruin; perhaps the greatest masterpiece of Scottish architect Robert Adam, it's one of the leading attractions in the country. Built in 1777, the Kennedy family's country seat sits in beautiful gardens at the heart of a 650-acre country park, with a view out over the ocean. An architectural highlight is the distinctive oval staircase; also notable are the plasterwork ceilings. Culzean is a familiar sight even to Scots who haven't been there: it's depicted on the Scottish five-pound note.

At the other end of the scale is the simple dwelling dubbed **Souter Johnnie's Cottage**, the home of a cobbler (souter) who was the real-life model for the character in Burns's "Tam O'-Shanter." This building signals that you're reentering Burns Country. For **Alloway**, the poet's birthplace, is another center of Burns pilgrimage. The monuments here are legion, from the Birth House to the **Brig** (bridge) **o'Doon**, over

Right: Robert Burns was born in this modest thatched cottage.

which Tam rides in the poem, and the roofless ruin of the 16th-century **Auld Kirk** (church), the setting of the witches' dance in the poem, where Burns' father is buried. There's a Burns Museum in **Mauchline**, home of Jean Armour; another in Kilmarnock; and, in **Failford**, **Highland Mary's Monument**, to a young love whose life and death Burns immortalized in his poetry. Even the room where he lived as an apprentice in Irvine is now a museum, in an area of town called the Glasgow Vennel, restored to its 18th-century flavor.

Ayr

With its broad promenade lined with beach on the one side and parks and fun fairs on the other, **Ayr** is every inch the bustling, contented resort town. It even still boasts one of Scotland's last remaining variety theaters, the Gaiety; and hosts the annual horse-racing event of the Scottish Grand National. Summer excursions are offered on the world's last sea-going paddle-wheel steamer, the **Waverley**, which calls in up and down the coast between here and Glasgow.

Ayr has seen its share of history, as well, since it became a Royal Burgh in 1205. In 1299, fighting for sovereignty (Scotland's from England, and his over Scotland), Robert Bruce destroyed its castle; later, after he became king, he rebuilt it and kept it in his own hands, and it was here that the Scottish Parliament convened to determine who should succeed him. In a later civil war, Oliver Cromwell emulated Bruce by building a citadel here, using parts of the 12th-century castle from nearby Ardrossan for the purpose. Today, Fort Street is the only reminder of this edifice.

Prestwick Airport, north of town, was once the hub for transatlantic flights through Scotland, but lost pride of place when Glasgow Airport was built. It does retain the distinction of being the only

place in Britain where Elvis Presley set foot; he made a brief landing on his way home from military service in Germany.

The name of the lovely seaside resort **Troon** may derive from *troone*, nose, describing the point of land on which it sits. On one side of town, the harbor is still protected by the grassy dike of the Ballast Bank, which the Duke of Portland built to protect it in 1840, using the ballast from local ships. On the other is the **Royal Troon Golf Course**, one of the leading courses in an area rich in good links, which hosted the British Open in 1996. Golf fans should also note the Prestwick course, where the Open Championship first started in 1860. In fact, this area has been nicknamed the "Golf Coast."

A maritime past is evident in the royal burgh of **Irvine**, in the form of the **Scottish Maritime Museum**, where you can view everything from the world's oldest clipper ship, *The Carrick*, to a Clyde puffer. A restored Victorian tenement flat shows the erstwhile living conditions of shipyard workers. Farther north are the so-called "Three Towns" of **Saltcoats**, **Stevenson**, and **Ardrossan**. In Saltcoats, the North Ayrshire Museum documents the history of local life, from tools and costumes to a history of Ayrshire sewn muslin, once a prominent cottage industry throughout the area. From Ardrossan, where there are still some remains of the 12th-century castle which Cromwell dismantled, ferries depart for the island of Arran (see "West Coast," p. 130). At **Kilwinning**, there are ruins of a 12th-century abbey as well as the **Dalgarven Mill**, working since the 17th century.

Largs is one of the prettiest Clyde resorts; it's also the terminus for Scotland's shortest ferry ride, the ten-minute crossing to **Cumbrae**. An annual Viking Festival commemorates the Norsemen whom the Scottish finally defeated here in 1263.

The last resort before Glasgow is **Gourock**, also a ferry port. **Greenock** is better known for sugar refineries and shipbuilding than as the birthplace of Captain Kidd and James Watt.

THE SOUTHWEST
Transportation

The first railway line in Scotland ran from Kilmarnock to Troon. Today, the Galloway Line runs from Glasgow along the West coast to Stranraer; there's also service from Glasgow to Dumfries. Train information: (0345) 212282. Stranraer is a ferry port for boats to and from Northern Ireland (about 90 minutes). Stena Sealink offers day trips to Northern Ireland, combined with bus tours; tel. (01776) 702262 or (01233) 647047. Ferries to Ireland are also operated by SeaCat, tel. (0345) 523523.

DUMFRIES

Telephone area code: 01387

Accommodation

EXPENSIVE: **The Station Hotel**, Lovers Walk, tel. 54316, fax 50388. 19th-century red sandstone building, refurbished with period flavor and modern flair. Restaurant. *MODERATE:* **Embassy Hotel**, Newbridge (N of Dumfries), tel. 720233, fax 721008. Country house, rooms a bit overpriced for what they offer, but large and comfortable; cozy pub.

Restaurants

The Globe Inn, 56 High Street, tel. 01387 252335. Favorite hang-out of Robert Burns.

Museums

Burns House, Burns Street, tel. 255297. Open daily 10 am-1 pm, 2-5 pm (closed Sun & Mon Oct-Mar). **Robert Burns Centre**, Mill Road, tel. (01387) 264808. Open Oct-Mar, Tue-Sat 10 am-1 pm, 2-5 pm, Apr-Sept Mon-Sat 10 am-8 pm, Sun 10 am-5 pm. **Old Bridge House**, Mill Road, tel. (01387) 256904. Oldest house in Dumfries. Open Apr-Sept Mon-Sat 10 am-1 pm, 2-5 pm, Sun 2-5 pm. **Dumfries Museum**, The Observatory, tel. 253374. Local history, with antique **Camera Obscura** (open Apr-Sept only). Open Mon-Sat 10 am-1 pm, 2-5 pm, Sun 2-5 pm, closed Sun & Mon Oct-March.

AROUND DUMFRIES
Accommodation and Restaurants

MOFFAT: *BUDGET:* **The Black Bull Hotel**, Churchgate, tel. (01683) 20206, fax 20483. Old-style restored inn with bar meals, Burns connection. **BIGGAR:** *LUXURY:* **Shieldhill Hotel**, Quothquan (off the B7106), tel. (01899) 220035, fax 221092. Luxury hotel in a mansion which has been in the family for 700 years; parts date back to 1199.

Museums

WANLOCKHEAD Lead Mining Museum (signs from A76), tel. (01659) 74387. Apr-Oct 11 am-4:30 pm. **SANQUHAR Tolbooth Museum**, High Street, tel. (01659) 50186. Local history. Open Apr-Sept, Tue-Sat 10 am-1 pm, 2-5 pm, Sun 2-5 pm. **BIGGAR: Greenhill Covenanters' House**. Easter-mid-Oct, daily 2-5 pm. **Gasworks Museum**. June-late Sept, daily 2-5 pm, Sun (Jul & Aug)

12-5 pm. Biggar museum info: (01399) 21050.
LANARK: New Lanark Visitors Centre, tel. (01555) 661345. Planned industrial village made famous by Robert Owen's pioneering social reforms in the 18th century, open to visitors daily 11 am-5 pm.

Sights and Activities

DRUMLANRIG CASTLE and Country Park, on the A76 4 mi/6.5 km N of Thornhill, tel. (08148) 330248. Stately home; extensive grounds; a falconry with flying demonstrations; artisan shops in the old stables. Castle open May-Aug, daily exc Thu 11 am-5 pm; grounds open year-round.
MOFFAT: Tweedhope Sheep Dogs, the Fishery, Hammerlands, tel. (01683) 221471. Sheepdog center (cuddly puppies) with demonstrations daily 11 am & 3 pm, Easter-Oct (weekends and winter by appointment only) of the dogs' remarkable skills.
BIGGAR: Biggar Little Theatre, tel. (01899) 220631, Victorian-era puppet theater which stages daily shows, with puppet museum. Open Mon-Sat 10 am-5 pm, summers also Sun 2-5 pm.

SOUTH COAST
Accommodation

NEW ABBEY: *MODERATE:* **Criffel Inn**, tel. (01387) 850305. Pub with good bar meals and rooms, on the main street; the equally cozy **Abbey Arms Hotel**, tel. (01387) 850489 is across the way.
COLVEND: *MODERATE:* **Clonyard House Hotel**, Colvend (near Dalbeattie), tel. (01556) 630372, fax 630422. Small Victorian country-house hotel near the coast; good restaurant.
ROCKCLIFFE: *LUXURY:* **Baron's Craig Hotel**, tel. (01556) 630225, fax 630328. Huge country house hotel, fine restaurant. Open Apr-Oct.
KIRKCUDBRIGHT: *MODERATE:* **Selkirk Arms Hotel**, High Street, tel. (01557) 330402, fax 331639. Family-run 18th-century establishment with very good restaurant. *BUDGET:* **Gordon House Hotel**, 116 High Street. DG6 4JQ, tel. (01557) 330670. Small pleasant rooms over a small pleasant pub, homey and unpretentious.
NEW GALLOWAY: *BUDGET:* **The Cross Keys Hotel**, High Street, tel. (01644) 420494. There are several small hotels in New Galloway, but this is the one to go to; its pub is *the* local hangout.
GATEHOUSE OF FLEET: *EXPENSIVE:* **Cally Palace Hotel**, tel. (01557) 814341, fax 814522. Luxury country house hotel in the 18th-century manor house of the town's former patron. *MODERATE:* **Murray Arms Hotel**, Ann Street, DG7 2HY, tel. (01557) 814207, fax 814370. Venerable town hotel, with restaurant. Burns slept here.
GALLOWAY FOREST PARK: *BUDGET:* Loch Grannoch Lodge; hostel-type accommodation for up to 20 people. Reservations: The Forestry Commission, 21 King Street, Castle Douglas, Kirk-

cudbrightshire, DG7 1AA, tel. (01556) 3626. *CAMPING:* Tent and trailer facilities. Information: Forest District offices at Castle Douglas, tel. (01556) 503626, or Newton Stewart, tel. (01671) 402420.

Restaurants
Many hotels listed above also have restaurants.
KIRKCUDBRIGHT: The Auld Alliance, 5 Castle Street, tel. (01557) 330569. The restaurant's name says it all: blend of French and Scottish influences, with an emphasis on local seafood.

Museums and Sights
NEW ABBEY: Shambellie House Museum of Costume, tel. (01387) 850375, fax 850461. Huge collection of antique clothing in 19th-century family mansion. Open daily April-October, 11 am-5 pm. **New Abbey Corn Mill**, tel. (01387) 850260. Restored 18th-century oat mill, still in working order. **Sweetheart Abbey** (tel. 01387/850397). Both open April-Sept, Mon-Sat 9:30 am-6:30 pm, Sun 2-6:30 pm; Oct-March Mon-Wed & Sat 9:30 am-4:30 pm, Thu 9:30 am-12 pm, Sun 2-4:30 pm.
CREETOWN: Creetown Gem Rock Museum, Chain Road, tel. (01671) 820357. Precious stones and gems from around the world.
KIRKCUDBRIGHT: Broughton House (Hornel Art Gallery), High Street, tel. (01557) 330437. E. A. Hornel's house with his paintings, furniture, and library. Open daily Easter-Oct. **Tolbooth Art Centre**, tel. (01557) 331556 (open daily June-Sept, Mon-Sat Mar-Oct, and Sat only Nov-Feb). **Harbour Cottage Gallery** in Castlebank, tel. (01557) 330207 (open Mar-Dec). **Museum of Stewartry** (St. Mary Street, tel. (01557) 331643), town history. Open Mar-Oct Mon-Sat, Nov-Feb Sat only.

Sports
FISHING: **Newton Stewart Angling Association**, tel. (01671) 402193; **Galloway Guns & Tackle**, 36a Arthur St., Newton Stewart, tel. (01671) 403404. **Boat charter** out of Kirkcudbright, tel. (01557) 330337, or Isle of Whithorn, tel (01671) 402102, among others. *GOLF:* Not a golfing center, Dumfries and Galloway still boast 29 golf clubs, from New Galloway, tel. (01644) 420255, to Gatehouse of Fleet, tel. (01557) 814734. *SAILING:* **Galloway Sailing Center**, Loch Ken, Castle Douglas, Kirkcudbrightshire, tel. (01644) 420626. Courses, boat rental, and launching facilities on Loch Ken. *WALKING:* For info on walks around Loch Ken: Castle Douglas Planning Department, tel. (01566) 502351. For info on Galloway Forest Park, see Camping, above. Dumfries Tourist Office has maps and brochures of other area walks.

WEST COAST / AYRSHIRE
Accommodation
ALLOWAY: *MODERATE:* **Northpark House**, tel. (01292) 442336, fax 445572. Restored 1720s farmhouse with fabulous in-house restaurant.
AYR: *LUXURY:* **Fairfield House Hotel**, 12 Fairfield Road, tel. (01292) 267461, fax 261456. Ayr's deluxe address in an old tea merchant's mansion, with gourmet restaurant. *MODERATE:* **Savoy Park Hotel**, 16 Racecourse Road, tel/fax (01292) 266112. Family-run hotel in a rambling mansion house. *BUDGET:* **The Richmond Guest House**, 38 Park Circus, tel. (01292) 260111, fax 285348. Homey family-style place in residential area.
GIRVAN: *BUDGET:* Maxwelston Farm B & B, Dailly (B741 from Girvan) tel. (01456) 811210. Nice, clean B & B on a working farm.
TROON: *MODERATE:* South Beach Hotel, South Beach Road, KA10 6EG, tel. (01292) 312033, fax 318438. Reasonable rates, near the water.
TURNBERRY: *LUXURY:* Turnberry Hotel, tel. (01655) 331000, fax 331706. One of the leading hotels in Scotland.

Restaurants and Pubs
AYR: Fouters Bistro Restaurant, 2A Academy Street, tel. (01292) 261391. Reasonably-priced, in converted bank vaults; Ayr's best for 20 years. **Stables Restaurant**, Queens Court, 41 Sandgate, tel. (01292) 283704. Scottish food in 18th-century stables. **The Hunny Pot**, 37 Beresford Terrace, tel. (01292) 263239. Coffee shop, afternoon teas.
TROON: Wheatsheaf Inn, Symington, off A77, tel. (01563) 830307. Fabulous pub food.
GIRVAN: Wildings, 56 Montgomerie St, tel. (01465) 713481. Good, fresh, straightforward food.
LARGS: Nardini, the Esplanade, tel. (01475) 674555. Legendary seaside cafe best known for ice cream, but with full Italian menu at the back.

Nightlife
In **AYR**: **Club de Mar**, 1 Arthur Street, tel. (01292) 611136; **SALTCOATS: Metropolis**, Hamilton Street, tel. (01294) 602213.

Museums and Sights
CULZEAN CASTLE, Apr-Oct 10:30 am-5 pm.
LARGS: Vikingar! Greenock Road, tel. (01475) 689777, multi-media visitors' center. Open daily, Apr-Sept 10:30 am-6 pm, Oct-Mar 10:30 am-4 pm.

Sports
GOLF: Seaside courses include the links at **Portpatrick**, tel. (01776) 810273, and the championship course at **Stranraer**, tel. (01776) 870245. Contact tourist offices for complete listings. *WALKING:* **Southern Upland Way**, Scotland's longest official footpath, leading 350 km across Southern Scotland, starts in Portpatrick and leads to the east coast. Info: Scottish Natural Heritage, tel. (01397) 704716.

Festivals
IRVINE: Marymass Fair in late August dates from 12th century, associated with Mary Queen of Scots.

GLASGOW

SACRED BEGINNINGS
GLASGOW TODAY AND
YESTERDAY
GLASGOW MUSEUMS
AROUND GLASGOW

Glasgow used to be stereotyped as a dirty, gritty, industrial city, the proletarian counterweight to stately Edinburgh on the opposite coast. And it's true that Glasgow came to prominence as a trade center. The city on the River Clyde, whose name supposedly derives from the Gaelic for "green place" (*glas cau*), was a quintessential product of the Victorian industrial age, smokestacks and all. Not that this was necessarily a bad thing: in fact, the industrial age saw Glasgow's great flowering. With growing prosperity came the Victorian dwellings and offices that still characterize the cityscape today. In the 19th century it was Glasgow, not Edinburgh (or Manchester or Birmingham) that was seen as "Britain's second city" after London, and thus one of the great metropolises of the British Empire.

In this century, "dirty" gained the upper hand over "busy": working-class Glasgow became increasingly associated with slums and crime. But the 1980s saw a real turnaround. The opening of the world-renowned Burrell Collection in 1983 proved a renewed impetus for city fathers and denizens to roll up their

Preceding pages: Glasgow – decked out in new colors for the 1990s. Left: Wild and weird installation at the Gallery of Modern Art.

sleeves and set to work cleaning up Glasgow's act. Old, blackened Victorian facades were cleaned of their dirt and restored to their original colors; downtown areas were renovated into new, elegant shopping arcades. The awarding of the title Cultural Capital of Europe in 1990 marked the dawn of a new age for Glasgow; both at home and abroad, the city's image had transformed. When people think of Glasgow now, it's for its culture – its splendid museums, the Scottish Opera, or active fringe theater scene – as much as for shipping on the river Clyde.

Just because Glasgow is rich in culture doesn't mean it's highbrow. Glaswegans are proud of their city, but they're not snobs; that's an attitude more associated with Edinburgh, the North Pole to Glasgow's South. The rivalry between the two cities is common knowledge ("Glasgow's miles better," proclaims one advertising slogan; you don't have to be a Glaswegan to figure out what it's better than); the perception remains that Edinburgh is for the intellectuals, Glasgow for the people. And the people, in general, are friendly and open. A familiar "Jimmy" remains the standard form of address for strangers ("What'll it be, Jimmy?"). Glasgow is a spirited, tough, living city with spunk. In the 1920s, author H. V. Morton described Glasgow

SACRED BEGINNINGS

Historically speaking, Glasgow was a late bloomer. While officially founded by William the Lion in 1175, it didn't become a Royal Burgh until 1611. And true prosperity waited until the city's ships came in – from America, laden with tobacco, creating "tobacco lords" who built stately homes in the 18th century.

Still, the town has been settled for a long time. It began as a religious rather than a business center; supposedly, Saint

as Scotland's anchor to reality, which calls to the rest of the country to leave its romantic memories of its past and "take a hand in the building of a new world."

Ninian (who landed in southwest Scotland in the 4th century) consecrated ground on the spot, and St. Kentigern, affectionately known to locals as Mungo, built the first church here in the 6th century. He didn't select the spot himself; rather, having found Saint Fergus dying by the roadside, he placed him on an cart and told the oxen to take him wherever God wanted. It was the bulls who stopped on the site Ninian had blessed a couple of hundred years before, where Mungo duly buried the saint and set up shop.

Today's **Glasgow Cathedral**, otherwise known as St. Mungo's, considerably postdates this first building. The modern cathedral was founded in 1136; the oldest parts you see today (the Lower

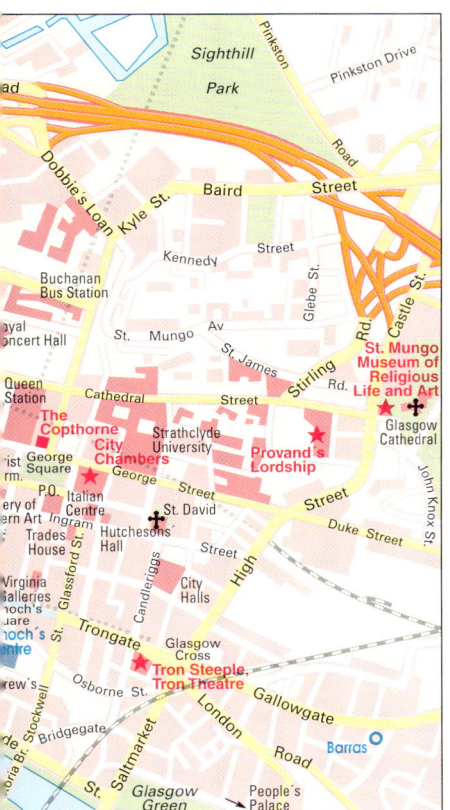

The church's lower level is the oldest part of all. Sticking out like an extra appendage about halfway along the building's length is the so-called Blachadar Aisle. This 15th-century wing is located on the traditional site of the land which Ninian blessed and where Fergus lies buried; a carving of the oxcart adorns one wall. On an even lower level is the beautifully proportioned Lower Church, laid out around the tomb of St. Mungo himself. One of the columns here may be a relic of the 1197 building which Bishop Jocelin had erected after the first cathedral burned down. On the hill behind the church, the **Necropolis** offers a wealth of old and interesting tombstones, including a monument to the Reformers with a statue of John Knox; the hilltop commands a nice view out over Glasgow.

Before the dark church is a spruced-up square where the old gas lamps bear a fish, a bell, and other symbols from the city's coat-of-arms, all associated with St. Mungo. On one side is the newish **St. Mungo Museum of Religious Life and Art**, which prides itself on its cross-confessional displays of the world's religions, ranging from personal statements to major works of art (attractions include Dali's *Christ of St. John of the Cross* and a Japanese Zen garden). Across the street is the oldest house in Glasgow: **Provand's Lordship** dates from 1471, built as home to the priest in charge of nearby St. Nicholas Hospital. It also claims to have sheltered Mary, Queen of Scots for a night, when she visited the ailing Darnley shortly before he went to Edinburgh and his murder (see "History," page 27).

City Centers

Originally the center of Glasgow, the cathedral area also saw the beginnings of the city's University, founded in 1451; the first classes convened in the cathedral crypt before relocating to High Street. The University moved across town to

Church) date from the 13th century, while the nave, where you enter, is of 15th-century vintage. The most striking Upper Church area is the Choir, used now as the High Church, which is separated from the nave by an ornate rood screen adorned with carvings of the Seven Deadly Sins without, and angels bearing family coats-of-arms within. High windows pierce the walls of both choir and nave, flooding them with light. In the mid-19th century, a Munich workshop fitted out the church with a set of new stained-glass windows, but their *oeuvre* proved not to withstand the test of time, and most of the windows had to be replaced again scarcely a hundred years later.

Kelvingrove in 1870, and the modern campus buildings grouped near the cathedral belong to a different institution, the technically-oriented University of Strathclyde. Before higher education had arrived in Glasgow, the area around High Street used to be called Bell o' the Brae; in 1300, it was the site of a William Wallace victory over the English.

By the 17th century, **Glasgow Cross** (further down High Street) had supplanted the Cathedral district as the center of town. There's still a cross here, although it's a 20th-century replica of the original; in the 1600s, there was also a Tolbooth (of which the steeple remains, now called **Cross Steeple**) and the Tontine houses. Another steeple further down the main artery of Trongate leading toward the present town center, the **Tron Steeple**, is all that's left of St Mary's Church (1637), which burned down in

Above: A face from the past in St. Mungo's Cathedral. Right: Figures from the present: variety is part and parcel of city life.

the 18th century; today, it stands before the **Tron Theatre**, one of Glasgow's most popular venues for Scottish fringe drama (and with a good cafe to boot).

In those days, Glasgow's modern "center" was unbuilt swampland; it wasn't until the city's glory days in the 18th century that **George Square** was laid out. This is an expanse of green and asphalt littered with statues of forgotten worthies and, in clement weather, Glaswegans trying to catch some rays. What's lacking is a statue of the eponymous George (the III); pride of place is granted to Sir Walter Scott, who stands perched atop George's pedestal, but so high (80 feet/24.5 m) in the air you could be pardoned for mistaking one for the other. Flanking the square are the Copthorne Hotel and Queen Street Station on one side, the Post Office on the other, and the **City Chambers** dominating one whole end with its Italian-Renaissance style facade. This 1880s building, home to the municipal administration, has as marvelous a "neo" effect within as without, with ornate

wood panelling; murals depicting Glasgow's rise, WPA-style; a banqueting hall; you name it (guided tours available).

GLASGOW TODAY AND YESTERDAY

In 1996, George Square hosted a contemporary Art Fair, which proved an unexpected success. Certainly the area has seen less successful endeavors with modern art, such as the **Gallery of Modern Art** on nearby Ingram Street, which opened the same year. Ambitious but scatter-brained, the new museum groups a range of international and Scottish contemporary art under the headings Earth, Air, Fire and Water. It's one of the few missteps in a city which generally has a very good sense of the modern.

But this part of Glasgow is more about business than art. South and east of George Square is the area known as **Merchant's City**, with a number of monuments to Glasgow's prosperous past: the **Trades House** on Glassford Street, built

by master architect Robert Adam in 1794; on Ingram Street, **Hutcheson's Hall** (1805/1876), which actually started out as a charitable institution, now the headquarters of the National Trust of Scotland; and the **Royal Exchange**, now a library, which developed out of a tobacco lord's 1780 mansion in what were then the suburbs. At the intersection of George and Buchanan Streets, at the center of what's now known as Nelson Mandela Place, stands another building of approximately this vintage: **St. George's Tron Church**, built in 1807. The present-day Stock Exchange is also on this square, as is the Athenaeum, which used to house the Royal Scottish Academy of Music and Drama (now on Renfrew St.).

Buchanan Street leads into the city's commercial center; it, together with Argyle Street, is a main drag for shoppers. Located here is the hands-down leading shopping mall in Glasgow: **Princes Square**. With palms, wrought-iron railings, and glass elevator, the architecture signals (as it's meant to) that this is a

place with class, equipped with legion designer boutiques, restaurants, and (sign of a distinguished mall) a really good bookstore. After this, the shops on Argyle Street are something of a comedown. Linking the bustling hub of Glasgow's **Central Station** and Glasgow Cross, Argyle Street also passes **St. Enoch's Square**, graced with a huge newish indoor shopping mall which includes an ice-skating rink. Die-hard shoppers will wait for the weekend and head down Argyle Street to Gallowgate and the **Barrows**, or Barras as it's better known, a mammoth flea market (founded in the 19th century) that takes over the whole area on Saturdays and Sundays.

Another popular venue that dates from the end of the last century is the **People's Palace**, situated near the Barras (and the notable, Venetian-style edifice of **Templeton's Carpet Factory**) on **Glasgow**

Above: Everything can be bought at the Barras flea market. Right: Purity of line: the style of Charles Rennie Mackintosh.

Green, Glasgow's oldest city park, which stretches along the river. The Palace is actually a museum of city history, presenting a comprehensive view of social and cultural history from Glasgow's official founding in 1175 to the present, in the form not merely of names and dates, but through photos, paintings, and documents which are particularly illuminating about the last two centuries. Stretching out behind the palace is the Victorian-looking glass conservatory of the **Winter Garden**, where you can take tea among the tropical plants in view of the Green's green lawns. Glasgow's women still have the legal right to hang out laundry to dry on the Green, though few avail themselves of it. A footnote for science buffs: it was while strolling across the Green in 1765 that James Watt solved the problem of the separate condenser – the dawn, one might say, of Glasgow's industrial age.

A central feature of that age runs past Glasgow Green: the **River Clyde**, once the setting for the city's thriving shipping and shipbuilding industries. But Clyde shipping slumped at the end of the 1920s, and has never really recovered. Today, there's a deserted feel to the piers and buildings along the river, and the new pedestrian **walkway** leading along part of it has little to offer in the way of sights, apart from street performers in summer or the bridges to the South Bank. Scottish artist Ian Hamilton Finlay has transformed the piers of the railway bridge into works of art, carving simple sentences into the stone.

Glasgow Arts

Art is scattered throughout the city of Glasgow. Take well-known **Sauchiehall Street**. At first glance, Sauchiehall seems to be a showplace of Glasgow's daily life. Its eastern end is a pedestrian zone with a full complement of chain stores (Marks & Sparks, Boots the Chemist, etc.). Nearby, on parallel Buccleuch Street, there's testimony to the daily life of the average Glaswegan in the **Tenement House**, a private apartment where Ms. Agnes Toward lived from 1911 to 1965 without making much concession to the progress of modernity. The apartment has been preserved just as she left it: virtually unchanged since she moved in, as if time had stood still.

Yet Sauchiehall is also the backbone of an area known for arts and theatre. At one end of it is the **Royal Concert Hall**, which presents a range of music events (check local listings) and includes a restaurant on the upper story open to non-concert-goers. A bit north of Sauchiehall, on Hope Street, is the ornate **Theatre Royal**, which has been beautifully restored to its former Victorian splendor. And anyone with an interest in the visual arts will be better served here than in the Gallery of Modern Art. Located on Sauchiehall are the **McLellan Galleries** of contemporary art, which host rotating exhibits; and the **Glasgow School of Art** is

one block north, on Renfrew Street. And this school is of note not just because it trains Scotland's artistic future, but because of its building, a masterpiece by Glasgow master Charles Rennie Mackintosh.

Mackintosh and the Glasgow Style

What Art Nouveau was to the French, Sezession to the Viennese, and Jugendstil to the Germans, the Glasgow Style was to the Scots. It wasn't merely derivative of Continental trends: it had a very particular, individual expression, largely due to Charles Rennie Mackintosh.

Yet the Glaswegan Mackintosh (1868-1928) never won as much acclaim at home as on the Continent. Together with his wife, Margaret Macdonald (her sister Frances married Mackintosh's friend and fellow designer Herbert McNair), he took part in the Vienna Sezession exhibition of 1900 and were prominently featured in many German exhibits and publications. In Glasgow, however, Mackintosh was less popular than other, less

radical designers who made more concessions to popular taste. It wasn't only that Mackintosh's straight lines were in deliberate contrast to the organic swirls of Jugendstil; he also had an uncompromising holistic approach, and it was hard to find clients willing to let him design not only a building's architecture, but also every detail of its interior, down to wallpaper and book bindings (as exemplified in the marvelous **Hill House**, in Helensburgh, some 40 miles west of Glasgow, built for publisher Walter Blackie). Frustrated by his lack of recognition, Mackintosh withdrew to France and spent his last years painting watercolors, dying not, as is often reported, of alcoholism, but of cancer of the tongue.

Heralded as Mackintosh's greatest achievement is the **Glasgow School of Art** on Renfrew St., built between 1897-1909. Sober in appearance, with straight lines and flat planes, the building's facade proves, on closer inspection, to incorporate a wealth of ornamental detail: take the wrought-iron railings. As this is still a working school, visiting hours are limited, but there are guided tours.

Equally famous is the **Willow Tea Room**, on Sauchiehall Street, where you can still take tea on an upstairs floor. Tea rooms became tremendously popular in Glasgow toward the end of the 19th century, and they were designed in appropriately modern style. Empress of the city's tea world was Miss Catherine Cranston, who had Mackintosh design several interiors for her various establishments (none has survived) before commissioning him with an entire building on Sauchiehall Street (Sauchiehall means "Alley of Willows," hence the tea room's name). Today, the downstairs floor is occupied by a jeweler, and the upstairs floor is partly a reconstruction, but you can still see the original facade and stained-glass double doors, and take tea in something like an original Mackintosh interior.

Above: Holistic design: Mackintosh was both architect and decorator of Hill House.
Right: Afternoon break in a Glasgow pub.

Once you've been bitten by the Mackintosh bug, there are further sites of pilgrimage – all likely to be increasingly crowded in future as a result of the massive Mackintosh show that traveled from Scotland to the States in 1996-7. Headquarters of the Mackintosh Society is **Queens Cross Church** (northwest part of town), the only church Mackintosh designed which was actually built. Two Glasgow schools of his design still stand: the **Martyrs' Public School** (1895) on Parson Street, and the **Scotland Street School** (1904) on Scotland Street; the latter is now a museum of education.

You get a more "insider" feel of Mackintosh's work from walking through the interior of a building. One of Mackintosh's signatures in many of his designs are small square inlays of colored glass set jewel-like into a wall or door. His interiors also featured gesso paintings by his wife, Margaret. These elements can be seen in the abovementioned Hill House; in the **House for an Art Lover**, completed in 1996 after designs from

1901; and in the **Mackintosh House**. This latter proves that Mackintosh practiced what he preached, living by his own designs: the rooms he lived in have been painstakingly reconstructed in the Hunterian Art Gallery in the University of Glasgow, proving once and for all how genuine and all-embracing was his talent as artist, architect, and interior designer.

GLASGOW MUSEUMS

There's more to the Hunterian than Mackintosh. The **Hunterian Museum and Art Gallery** is one of two Glasgow museums born of a private collector's bequest (see the Burrell Collection, below); it's also the oldest in Scotland, having opened in 1807. The other key name in the Hunterian is James McNeill Whistler; there's a fabulous collection of paintings, prints, and even personal objects by or belonging to this 19th-century American-born artist. There are also paintings by everyone from Rembrandt to the Glasgow Boys, a group of some 25 artists

who in the late 19th century broke away from traditions of academic painting to develop their own style, depicting non-traditional rural themes in a freer, naturalistic idiom. One of the "Boys'" ideas was to found a number of artists' collectives in rural settings; most successful of these was that founded by E. A. Hornel in Kirkcudbright (see p. 96), although there were also colonies in Brig O'Turk, Cambuskenneth, and Cockburnspath, among others.

Another good place to see the work of the Glasgow Boys, and to get a sense of what Glasgow Style was all about, is located across Kelvingrove Park from the University's towered and towering neo-Gothic headquarters: the wonderful **Kelvingrove Art Gallery and Museum**. This very visitor-friendly institution only has room to display parts of its extensive collection of Old Masters at any one

Above: Victorian gentility in the Royal Botanic Garden. Right: The Glasgow Rangers: another city trademark.

time, which means you can get a good look at a few masterpieces and a number of interesting lesser works without exhausting yourself (one of the best works is of uncertain authorship: *The Adultress Brought Before Christ* is either by Giorgione or by Titian). Other rooms take you through 19th-century Scottish painting before depositing you firmly in the 20th; the permanent Glasgow Style exhibit gives you a context for Mackintosh's work by presenting other designers of his day. There are also displays of natural history and Scottish history, including one set up to debunk venerable and exaggerated stereotypes of Scotland.

Across the street from this is the **Museum of Transport**, which includes, among its ship models and locomotives, a complete model of a cobblestone Glasgow street from 1938.

Museums may be the hallmark here; but it's the university that's made its mark on the area. Glasgow's **West End** is traversed by the artery of Byres Road, where fun shops and greasy student dives are cheek by jowl with some of Glasgow's hottest new restaurants, catering to a considerably better-heeled clientele. This mix reflects the part-student, part-yuppie population of Glasgow's "in" neighborhood. In the Victorian age, the West End was a refuge for the upper classes fleeing the increasingly crowded, lower-class city center. To fulfil their leisure needs, they built themselves exclusive recreation sites, such as the domed greenhouse of Kibble Palace in the **Royal Botanic Gardens**. But with the advent of tram lines, these gardens, too, became available to the masses, who came out to stroll among the tropical plants in the glasshouses or through the fragrant herb garden.

The Burrell Collection

Glasgow has plenty of cultural attractions, plenty of sights, and plenty of mu-

seums, but the **Burrell Collection** is in a class by itself. Since it opened in 1983, it's been the city's leading attraction. And it's a perfect museum for Glasgow: it manages to be at once a major collection of art and artifacts from Antiquity to the 19th century, and yet as quirky and individual as the city it's housed in.

Actually, the Burrell Collection isn't in Glasgow at all, but about 3 miles (5 km) out of town, in the green estate of **Pollok Country Park**. Glasgow had trouble finding a site, since the individuality (not to say eccentricity) of the collection's donor, Sir William Burrell, outlived that individual's demise. Burrell (1861-1958), a shipowner by profession and collector by obsession, gave his collection to Glasgow in 1944, and kept expanding it until his death; but when he made the donation, he stipulated that the collection was to be housed in a building located near Glasgow, yet in a rural setting. A site matching these conditions wasn't found until 1967, when Mrs. Maxwell McDonald offered the Pollok estate.

Perhaps one of the most remarkable features of the collection is that these 8,000-odd objects were all amassed by a single man. Burrell lived for years in Hutton Castle in the Borders, which was a fittingly magnificent setting for his objects; three rooms of the castle have been reconstructed here in the museum to give visitors an idea of how the other half lived.

The rest of the museum is an attractive modern building which affords vistas of the outdoors as well as of the objects on display. Main strengths of the collection are Oriental art – Chinese porcelain, bronze and jade; Japanese prints and Arabian rugs – and the so-called "Medieval and Post-Medieval European Art" works, which range from actual church portals to arms and armor. Included here as well are some gorgeous medieval tapestries and a world-famous collection of stained glass.

There's also a section of paintings and drawings, which is more standard, measured by the tastes of other Scottish

castle owners for whom Rembrandt and the Dutch school belonged as a matter of course to the family picture gallery. The collection culminates in a number of French works, including some by the Impressionists.

The high quality of private painting collections is also demonstrated in **Pollok House** itself, also located in the park, and also open to visitors. For those who are still able to take in such things after a visit to the Burrell, the walls of Pollok House's furnished rooms sport canvases by Spanish and English greats – Goya, El Greco, William Blake, and Hogarth – as well as interesting furniture and family objects. The house itself, the Maxwell family home, dates back to 1750, and is surrounded by attractive formal gardens in the middle of the huge park which is also home to a herd of genuine Highland cattle.

Above: Medieval treasures in the Burrell Collection. Right: Paisley's looms were once central to the town's livelihood.

AROUND GLASGOW

Anyone arriving in Glasgow by plane arrives not in Glasgow but in **Paisley**, home of Glasgow Airport, but about 10 miles/16 km out of town. At first glance, Paisley seems merely an industrial suburb, but few other industrial suburbs can boast a 12th-century abbey comparable to **Paisley Abbey**. The abbey has been going up and down ever since the English first did a job on it in 1307, so bears some notable testimony to architectural styles of the intervening years; the bulk of the first reconstruction took place after 1450. However, the tower collapsed even before the Reformation, and the church gradually declined in the years after; in the early 19th century, shops moved in, including a pawnshop. Renovation work began toward the end of that century, and continues today. The tower is safe enough that visitors are allowed to go up it from time to time; the glass has been replaced in the windows of the nave, and the choir contains tombs of the Bruce line, including Robert III. At one end of the nave is an early Christian cross, the **Barochan Cross**, dating from the end of the 1st millennium A.D.

Paisley's other claim to fame, the reason the town's name is familiar around the world, is the Paisley shawl. Originally, "Paisley" was the term for a kind of material rather than a pattern; the pattern we call "paisley" today was simply the most common design on the shawls produced here, which were an attempt to emulate the fine shawls imported from Kashmir, India. The development of improved looms allowed a leap in shawl production, which was a mainstay of the town – although Paisley was equalled in output by Norwich and Edinburgh – until a change in fashion ushered in a decline in the shawl trade around the 1880s. (See "From Tartan to Tweed," page 227.) The **Paisley Museum and Art Galleries** has a display devoted to Paisley shawls, al-

though to see the museum's huge shawl collection you have to make arrangements at the desk to speak to the shawl curator. Not far away, the restored **Sma' Shot Cottages** are the former homes of workers at the mills where the shawls were produced.

Dumbarton, 17 miles (27 km) from Glasgow, offers a foray into a more distant past; it's said to have been the birthplace of St. Patrick around 390 A.D., and the place where he was captured by the pirates who later sold him into captivity in Ireland. But the place is better known for the ancient **castle** which graces a hilltop overlooking the Clyde. Supposed to be one of the oldest fortifications in Britain, it's perhaps most commonly associated with Mary, Queen of Scots, who lived here as a five-year-old before setting sail for France in 1549. Three centuries earlier, it was also a stopover for William Wallace, a prisoner on his way to London and ultimate execution.

Dumbarton also features the **Denny Shipping Tank**, an outpost of the Maritime Museum in Irvine; providing a closer look at the methods by which ship hulls were designed and tested, it gives interesting insight into Dumbarton's shipping past.

Not far from Kilsyth, about 14 miles (22 km) north of Glasgow, you can walk up **Bow Hill** to see, not only a view over Glasgow, but the remains of a fort from the **Antonine Wall**. Like the earlier Hadrian's Wall, this wall was a Roman attempt to fence off the "safe" occupied territory of their province of Caledonia from the "half-naked savages with reddish hair and large limbs," who, according to Tacitus, dwelt in the North. Made of earth piled on stone foundations, with forts at regular intrevals, the wall, built across the narrowest part of Scotland, couldn't be held long; it was abandoned again within 20 years. This is one of its best-preserved sections; the remains of a fort can also be seen at **Croy Hill**, a mile or so further on. Some of the carved slabs and milestones from the wall are on display in the Hunterian Museum.

GLASGOW
Telephone area code 0141
Transportation

Glasgow is the only city in Britain besides London with its own Underground line, which is also distinguished by having originally been known, American-style, as "the subway." The Underground runs in a circle route around the city center; tickets are 60 p. Its hours, however, are fairly limited: from around 6:30 am to 11 pm on weekdays, and 11 am to 6 pm on Sundays. There's an "Underground Heritage Trail" for visitors; £1.80 gives you unlimited travel for one day plus a brochure outlining 17 walks from the Underground's 15 stations which give different views of various sides of Glasgow.

The Underground is part of the extensive network of Strathclyde Transport, which includes local regional trains servicing a large number of destinations in the area. Its main information office is the St. Enoch Travel Centre, St. Enoch's Square, tel. 2264826.

Accommodation

EXPENSIVE: **One Devonshire Gardens**, Great Western Road, tel. 3392001, fax 3371663. Glasgow's number-one hotel has sumptuously renovated Victorian town houses, each room decorated differently, constantly redecorated. Fabulous restaurant. **The Devonshire Hotel**, 5 Devonshire Gardens, tel. 3397878, fax 3393980. Another Victorian townhouse, next to but no relation to the above, also lovely and luxurious but not quite as expensive. **The Copthorne**, George Square, tel. 3326711, fax 3324264. Right on George Square, the heart of Glasgow (meals or drinks served on glassed-in terraces overlooking it). A bit of an old-style flavor, without the modern chrome gleam of, say, the Hilton. **The Glasgow Hilton**, William Street, tel. 2045555, fax 2045004. But of course, there is a Hilton, and it's one of the best places in town, health club and all.

MODERATE: **The Ewington**, 132 Queens Drive, tel. 4231152, fax 4222030. At the upper edge of "moderate" price range: lovely homey terrace house, elegant and comfortable. Meals. Not too central, but on the bus line, near the Burrell Collection. **Cathedral House**, Cathedral Square, tel. 5523519. Old, comfortable hotel in the oldest part of Glasgow. **St. Enoch Hotel**, 44 Howard St., St. Enoch Square, tel. 2212400. Central and reasonably priced, with cafe, run by a friendly young couple. **The Town House**, 4 Hughendon Terrace, tel. 3570862. Warm, family-run, in a row of terraces in the West End.

BUDGET: **Lomond Hotel**, 6 Buckingham Terrace, Great Western Road, tel. 3392339, fax 3395215. In the West End, in a row of terraces full of similar small hotels. Friendly, not far from the town center and right on the Underground. **McLays Guest House**, 264/276 Renfrew Street, Charing Cross, tel. 332 4786, fax 353 0422. Right behind Sauchiehall Street and down from the Glasgow Art School, clean, no-frills, and remarkably cheap. **University of Glasgow**, Conference and Vacation Office, 52 Hillhead St., tel. 330 5385, fax 334 5465, offers B & B accommodation at reasonable prices.

Restaurants

EXPENSIVE: **The Ubiquitous Chip**, 12 Ashton Lane, tel. 3345007. Tucked away inconspicuously in a former mews on a cobblestone side street in the West End, the "Chip" spearheaded the Scottish culinary renaissance. 25 years on, self-taught chef Ronnie Clydesdale is still serving things like Loch Fyne kipper pate or pan-fried Camas na Ceardaich scallops on a rösti. The downstairs dining room has an informal air, overgrown with greenery, but formal prices; upstairs, pub meals are more downscale. **The Puppet Theater**, 11 Ruthven Lane, tel. 3398444. Latest arrival on Glasgow's gourmet scene, this restaurant features striking interior decoration – dark walls, tasteful halogen lighting – and striking food by chef Iain McMaster. **The Buttery**, 652 Argyle Street, tel. 2218188. An enduring Glasgow tradition, and another place where you can explore the concept of fine Scottish dining. In an atmosphere determined by Victorian-style furnishings, you can sample things like highland venison, or the ubiquitous Scottish oat in a glaze for wild pigeon and blackberry pie. **Rogano**, 11 Exchange Place, tel. 2484055. Seafood restaurant from the 1930s with interior replicating that of the Queen Mary.

MODERATE: **Ashoka**, 19 Ashton Lane, tel. 3575904. Right across from the Ubiquitous Chip, it sends powerful clouds of spicy aroma out into the sedate little cobblestone alleyway. Reliable Indian food at moderate prices. **Yes**, 22 West Nile Street, tel. 2218044. Two-level dining, with standard pub fare upstairs, a wider and more eclectic selection below. **Mitchell's**, 157 North St, tel. 2044312, and 31/35 Ashton Lane, tel. 3392220. Bistro/restaurant with good food and drink. **Cafe Gandolfi**, 64 Albion St., tel. 5526813. Chic and beloved Glasgow cafe with heavy furniture and light meals.

BUDGET: **Fratelli Sarti**, 133 Wellington St., tel. 2482228, and 121 Bath St., tel. 2040440. Centrally located Italian trattorias (around the corner from one another) with lots of Italian atmosphere. **Tron Cafe-Bar**, 63 Trongate, tel. 5524267. Adjacent to Tron Theatre; cafe and informal hang-out restaurant with meals and snacks. **University Cafe**, 87 Byres Road. Famous student hang-out. **Insomnia**, 38 Woodlands Road, tel. 3325500. Glasgow's first 24-hour coffee shop. **The Granary**, 82 Howard St., tel. 2263770. Vegetarian food with great home-baked cakes. **The Unique**, 223 Allison St. Famous fish'n'chips on the south side of the city.

Pubs

The Drum and Monkey, 93 St. Vincent St. Downtown businessmen's meeting-place. **The Griffin**, 266 Bath St. For a real Glasgow pub experience, this down-to-earth pub is a perfect local hang-out. It also has good food; the menu is larger in its neighboring extensions, the **Griffiny** and the **Griffinette**. **The Horse Shoe**, 17 Drury St. Traditional pub (since 1888) with atmosphere, good pub grub, and teas served upstairs. **Uisge Beatha**, 246 Woodlands Road. Taste of the Highlands. **Blackfriars**, 36 Bell St. Spruced up for the 90s, but still cozy, with live music at night. **Babbity Bowster**, 16 Blackfriars St. Pub food, real ale, live music in Merchant City.

Tea Rooms

Many restaurants and hotels serve high tea in the afternoon. **The Willow Tea Room**, 217 Sauchiehall St. Famed for its interior design by Charles Rennie Mackintosh, it's better for this than for its eats, though you can't go far wrong with afternoon tea, and it closes at 4:30 pm anyway. **The Jenny Traditional Tea-Rooms**, 20 Royal Exchange Square. Tea, baked goods, and fudge in flowery ambience.

Museums

The Burrell Collection, Pollok Country Park, tel. 6497151. Originally a private collection, now Glasgow's leading museum: from Asian art to European Old Masters. Open Mon-Sat 10 am-5 pm, Sun 11 am-5 pm. **Kelvingrove Art Gallery and Museum**, Argyle Street, tel. 2219600. Good displays of Old Masters and natural history, armor and Glasgow Style. Free recitals on turn-of-the-century organ in the main hall some weekends. Open Mon-Sat 10 am-5 pm, Sun 11 am-5 pm. **Museum of Transport**, Bunhouse Road, tel. 2219600. Open Mon-Sat 10 am-5 pm, Sun 11 am-5 pm. **St. Mungo Museum of Religious Life and Art**, 2 Castle Street, tel. 5532557. Open Mon-Sat 10 am-5 pm, Sun 11 am-5 pm. **Gallery of Modern Art**, Queen Street, tel. 3311854. Opened in 1996. Open Mon-Sat 10 am-5 pm, Sun 11 am-5 pm. **Tenement House**, 145 Buccleuch St., 3330183. Open daily March-Oct, 1:30-5 pm. **Hunterian Gallery**, University Avenue, tel. 3305431. Glasgow's oldest museum: geology to the Mackintosh House. Open Mon-Sat 9:30 am-5 pm.

Theater, Music, Opera

You can reserve tickets for many events by phone from the **Ticket Centre**, Candleriggs, tel. 2275511. **Glasgow Royal Concert Hall**, Sauchiehall Street (behind Queen Street Station), tel. 2275511. International-caliber groups, from the Vienna Philharmonic to Celtic folk bands to Glenn Miller. **Theatre Royal**, Hope Street, tel. 3329000. The acclaimed **Scottish Opera** company, based in Glasgow, has a regular, if spotty, performance season in the Theatre Royal from October to June. Dates are sporadic, so don't count on anything just happening to be playing when you arrive. **Citizens' Theatre**, Gorbals St, tel. 4290022, the city's main venue for spoken theater, with stimulating productions of classic plays. **Tron Theatre**, 63 Trongate, tel. 5524267, contemporary fringe theater, mainly Scottish. **Tramway Theatre**, 25 Albert Drive, tel. 2275511, huge performance space, with tracks still running through, for avant-garde productions. **Glasgow Film Theatre**, 12 Rose St., tel. 3326535. Old-style two-screen house with a wide-ranging program of international and art films.

Night Life

Maxaluna, 410 Sauchiehall St, tel. 3321003. Sprawling, designer-style place, lots of plate-glass and black decor, with dancing in the so-called "Club Havana." **King Tut's Wah Wah Hut**, 272 St. Vincent's Street, tel. 2215279. Live music nightly, national as well as local bands. **Barrowland Ballroom**, Gallowgate, tel. 5524601, Glasgow's signature venue for real live rock and roll, with a seedy atmosphere to prove its purity of heart.

Festivals

Mayfest: City-wide festival with international theater and concerts, exhibitions, other events. **Glasgow International Jazz Festival**, end June-early July.

Tourist Information

Greater Glasgow Tourist Board, 11 George Square, Glasgow, tel. 2044400, fax 2213524. Also at **Glasgow Airport**: Tourist Information Desk, Glasgow Airport, Paisley, tel. 8484440.

AROUND GLASGOW
Accommodation

CLYDEBANK: *EXPENSIVE:* **Beardmore Hotel,** Beardmore St, tel. 9516000, fax 9516018. Large, modern luxury hotel toward Dumbarton. **PAISLEY (Glasgow Airport):** *MODERATE:* **Brabloch Hotel**, 62 Renfrew Road, tel. 889557. Pleasant, tree-shaded, near center. *BUDGET:* **Greenlaw Guest House**, 12 Greenlaw Drive, tel. 8895359. Clean, low-priced, 15 min from center.

Museums and Sights

HELENSBURGH: Hill House, Upper Colquhoun St., tel. (01436) 673900, designed by Mackintosh, daily Apr-Dec 1-5 pm. **PAISLEY: Paisley Museum & Art Gallery**, High Street, tel. 8893151, fax 8899240, Mon-Sat 10 am-5 pm. **Sma' Shot Cottages**, 11/17 George Place, tel. 8891708, open Apr-Sept, Wed & Sat 1-5 pm. **Coats Observatory**, 49 Oakshaw St. West, tel. 8892013. 1880s observatory, meteorological station since 1884. Mon, Tue, Thu 2-8 pm, Wed, Fri, Sat 10 am-5 pm.

Tourist Information

Tourist Information Centre, Lagoon Leisure Centre, Mill Street, Paisley, tel. (0141) 639467.

THE WEST COAST
Argyll and the Isles

LOCH LOMOND
INVERARAY
THE KINTYRE PENINSULA
ISLAY AND JURA
LOCH AWE TO OBAN
MULL AND NEARBY ISLES
GLENCOE AND POINTS NORTH

In the various administrative partitions of Scotland, Argyll has been the loser: first made part of the Region of Strathclyde in the 70s, it's recently been absorbed into a huge district called "Argyll, the Isles, Loch Lomond, Stirling, Trossachs." But the name lives on, and not just in argyle socks (so called because they were modeled on the tartan pattern of the local Campbell clan). Argyll means "coast of the Gaels," and this coast, with its bays, cliffs and beaches, splintering off into the start of the famous Western Isles, is one of the most beautiful and beloved regions of Scotland.

LOCH LOMOND

Driving to the Isles from Glasgow, you pass one of Scotland's most famous lochs. **Loch Lomond** is Britain's largest body of fresh water in area (if not in volume), extending more than 23 miles (37 km). At the heart of central Scotland, it marks the fault line between the mountain mass of the Highlands and the softer, younger red sandstone of the Lowlands; this Highland Boundary Fault is visible in the chain of islands that run like a

Preceding pages: The basalt "cathedral" of Fingal's Cave, Staffa. Left: A Scottish angler casts for trout.

dotted line across the loch's broader, southern end. But the real reason Loch Lomond is so well known is that a homesick prisoner in London, awaiting execution, immortalized the place in the song "By the Bonnie, Bonnie Banks of Loch Lomond," still sung in English-speaking countries around the world.

Today, visitors drawn to the loch by the song stay for its leisure possibilities. Windsurfers alternate with anglers: Loch Lomond contains more species of fish than any other loch in Scotland (including the protected fresh-water herring called *powan*, found in only one other Scottish loch). Its 38 islands didn't always fulfill a holiday role: in the 18th century, Inchlonaig and Inchmurrin were used as prison islands for people "disordered in their senses," or women bearing children out of wedlock. But the mountains around it have long been popular with hikers. **Ben Lomond**, east of the loch, is Scotland's southernmost Munro (see "Scotland on Foot," p. 234); while to the west are the four Munros known as the "**Arrochar Alps**," and **Ben Arthur**, christened "The Cobbler" by locals who found something vaguely cobbler-like in its distinctive craggy outline.

Driving up along the west bank of the loch, you pass **Wee Peter**, a statue of a small boy standing in the shallows a little

ATLANTIC

OCEAN

WEST COAST (SOUTH)

0   10   20 km

0   5   10 miles

124

way off shore. He's the work of a London-based stonemason, who placed him there around 1890, not far from his native village of **Luss**. Luss in fact needs little embellishment: it's a pretty town with low stone houses and pocket gardens bursting with flowers, all surrounding a lovely old church. It's the setting of a once-popular British television series.

"*Tarbet*," Gaelic for "isthmus," also translates as "place of portage," and Loch Lomond's **Tarbet** is one of many Tarbets or Tarberts in coastal areas. The portage in this case was from Arrochar at the head of the ocean inlet Loch Long, named not for its length but from the Gaelic for "Loch of the Ships" – although, as the ships in question were Viking longships, sailing up the loch and continuing over land to Tarbet, length did in fact have something to do with it. Viking graves still stand by Ballyhennan Church. Today, the Vikings might stay at **Arrochar**, a local holiday center.

The Cowal Peninsula

Between Loch Long and Loch Fyne, you get your first taste of Highland-like scenery. Winding through the high, steep fells, the road here roughly follows the course of an old military road; this was so difficult to build in these hills that during its construction, between 1746-8, a stone was placed at its side with the injunction to "**Rest and be Thankful**." Passing travelers generally obey, at least to snap a few pictures.

This stone is within **Argyll Forest Park**, which, founded in 1935, was the first Forestry Commission Forest Park in Great Britain. Its expanses of forests – not cultivated until the park was created – and high peaks (including Ben Arthur) make it a center for walkers, anglers, and wildlife lovers. But the Cowal Peninsula isn't only wilderness: to the south it offers beautiful beaches and bays to Glaswegan vacationers. A ferry brings them

from Gourock, south of Glasgow, to **Dunoon**, the region's main town, which bursts at the seams at the end of August with the Cowal Highland Gathering. Watching over the proceedings are the ruins of the 13th-century **castle** on Castle Hill, with a **statue of Highland Mary** at its foot, underlining the region's involvement with two highlights of Scottish history (Mary was born nearby). Dunoon stands near **Holy Loch**, supposedly so named because it saw the wreck of a ship bearing a load of soil from the Holy Land intended for Glasgow's cathedral.

Further south, Cowal has some beautiful beaches (notably around Kilbride and Ardlamont Bay) and scenery; especially lovely is the strait of the **Kyles of Bute**, separating Cowal from the island of **Bute**. In **Rothesay**, Bute's capital, the most notable feature is the distinctive circular 13th-century **castle**, which with-

stood Viking attacks to become a favorite residence of the Stewarts in their conflicts against the Isles.

Located on Bute is the **Mount Stuart Country House** with its gardens, open to visitors, one of a host of gorgeous gardens in the area. Farther up the peninsula, other gardens flourish like islands of domesticity in wild Argyll Forest Park. The Gulf Stream is kind to plants here, and brings some of them to surprising heights: **Younger Botanic Garden** is famed for giant California redwoods; while **Strone Gardens**, back up at the neck of the peninsula, claims to contain Britain's tallest tree, the "Grand Fir."

Before you reach Strone Gardens on the A815, a heart-shaped group of white stones mark the place where Argyll's tinkers, Britain's gypsy-like itinerant population, hold their wedding ceremonies.

INVERARAY

Above: A dusting of winter around Carrick Castle. Right: History of trial and error? Courtroom scene in Inveraray Jail.

Driving along the top of Loch Fyne, you see an arm of white houses reaching

out onto the surface of the water: **Invera-ray**. Inveraray Castle, home to the Campbells, Dukes of Argyll, is tucked out of sight in the trees off the road; when the 3rd Duke decided to build a new castle on the site of his 15th-century ancestral home in the 1700s, he moved the original settlement, clustered around the castle walls, to a planned village a little distance away. Surely the villagers couldn't complain: Inveraray is a white, tidy, compact lochside town, in keeping with a laird's vision of how the lower classes should live. Another side of life in Old Inveraray is preserved in **Inveraray Jail**, where costumed actors recreate the atmosphere of 18th-century lawcourts and prisons.

Inveraray Castle presents a taste of how the other half lived: opulently. There are family portraits by Gainsborough and his ilk, tapestries, luxurious furniture, and a forbidding collection of arms and armor, displayed in sunburst swirls of bristling muskets. Replacing the traditional rugged fortifications with manorial elegance, the castle heralded the advent of a new age, and it's moved with the Campbells into modern times: family relics range from a letter Rob Roy wrote to the 2nd Duke (he signed his name Campbell, as MacGregor had been proscribed) to color snapshots of the family today. This gentility belies the fact that the Campbells, whose name derives from the Gaelic *Na Caimbeulach*, "men of the twisted mouths," emerged as the villains time and again in many bitter battles.

Between **Loch Fyne** (known for its kippers) and the ocean, the land is bisected, at Lochgilphead, by the **Crinan Canal** (now used mainly by pleasure boats). In this area, the western shore of Scotland is particularly rich in testimony to prehistoric settlers: standing stones and stone circles (the two in **Temple Wood**, near Kilmartin, date from around 3,000 B.C.); Bronze Age cairns (for example, at **Dunchraigag**); or simply rocks perforated with distinctive cup-and-ring markings, whose origin is man-made if their significance has been obscured by time (there are some at **Kilmi-**

Above: The next generation learns the ropes of the fishing trade (Campbeltown).

chael, dating from around 1,500-1,000 B.C.).

An early settler within the memory of the history books was St. Columba, who preached and converted the Pictish heathen all along this coast in the 6th century. One of his early bases is **St. Columba's Cave**, a great cathedral-like opening in the rocky shore by Loch Caolisport, marked with a simple cross on one wall. Nearby **Castle Sween**, now a ruin, is one of the oldest stone castles in Scotland; the MacSweens (originally the Norse *Sueno*) built the keep in the 12th century.

A more striking site associated with Columba is **Dunadd Fort**, the first capital of the Dalriadic Kingdom which was the seed of today's Scotland. The rocky ruin still commands the flat landscape as it must have done in 574 A.D., when, some say, Columba crowned Aidan here in the first Christian coronation in Scotland. Even ruined, the site exerts a certain

magic. Four levels of protective ring walls encircle a hilltop where you can see a flat stone bearing the crude imprint of a human foot; a basin carved into another rock; traces of Ogham runic script; and great views.

The lasting effects of St. Columba's missionizing work are evident from medieval Christian sculptured stones, including crosses and tombstone effigies. **Kilmartin**'s church and churchyard house marvelous specimens: carved crosses are sheltered from the weather within the church, while some beautiful tombstones stand in the churchyard. In a lonelier seaside site stand the **Kilberry** stones, carved with ogival-headed warriors brandishing their swords.

KINTYRE PENINSULA

The Mull which Paul McCartney made famous in song is only the extreme tip of the **Kintyre Peninsula**, which extends pendulously from Scotland's western coast down into the North Channel. The peninsula is not heavily traveled, and therefore not heavily developed; sharing its 80-odd miles of empty beaches are occasional vacationers and a number of seals. And the passing Gulf Stream fosters explosions of blossoming rhododendrons and even palm trees. Steep, single-track roads winding around Kintyre's tip offer the most spectacular views of the peninsula's wild beauty – and of sharp drops from the meadows straight down to breakers on black rocks, many feet below.

The peninsula is moored to the mainland at **Tarbert** – but only barely moored. When the 12th-century Viking King Magnus Barfud (Barelegs) worked out a treaty granting him all the land he could sail around, he dragged his boats across the isthmus at Tarbert and laid claim to the Kintyre Peninsula, as well as the islands. Tarbert has been a fortified spot since the Iron Age; its first castle rose in the 6th century, and Robert Bruce expanded it in the 14th. Today, only castle ruins remain to survey the harbor of this picture-postcard fishing village.

In the 12th century, the Vikings were overcome by Somerled, who claimed the Lordship of the Isles and ushered in the reign of the Macdonalds. He's buried at **Saddell Abbey**, which he founded in 1160; it now stands ruined on Kintyre's eastern shore. Best preserved here are the sculptured stones, a specialty of the abbey until it closed in the 16th century.

Clan Macdonald's downfall came in 1647, when the enemy Campbells, led by the Marquis of Argyll, hunted them down to **Dunaverty Castle** at the peninsula's southern end. With their backs to the sea, the Macdonalds surrendered – and were promptly shot to all but one man in a massacre even more nefarious than that at Glencoe half a century earlier (see p. 137, below). The rock upon which the castle once stood looms jaggedly above the water, as if about to fall off the green meadows around it.

Past Dunaverty, by cliffs red and gold as brocade, are some depressions in the rock dubbed **St. Columba's Footprints**, supposedly the site where Columba first landed in 574 A.D. Beyond this, a glorious long empty sand beach stretches out to the actual **Mull of Kintyre**, which, for all the romance surrounding its name, is simply a beautiful point of land with a lighthouse built by the grandfather of author Robert Louis Stevenson (who left lighthouses dotted all around Scotland's coasts).

Another saint associated with Columba and Iona was St. Kieran: until the 17th century, Kintyre's main town was called Kinlochkerran, after him. After the Campbells' victory at Dunaverty, the town's name changed to **Campbeltown** in the Earls of Argyll's (dubious) honor. As Campbeltown, the town's claims to fame are more prosaic than religious. It's been called the birthplace of Scottish whisky, although only one of the area's forty distilleries survives. In the 18th century, it was a center for the Scottish herring fleet, a boom that abated after the herring, for reasons known best to themselves, mysteriously departed these waters for northern climes. Today, Campbeltown's most successful export are truckles, a kind of wax-encased cheese. At the center of town, where palm trees grow along the harbor, is a replica of the slender **Campbeltown Cross**, from which mileages on Kintyre are measured; tradition dictates that all weddings and funerals pass this site.

Campbeltown does have one religious attraction, on the tidal island of **Davaar**: a painting of the Crucifixion was found in a cave here in 1887. At first hailed as a miraculous image, it proved to be the work of the village schoolteacher, Archibald Mackinnon. Mackinnon left the town in disgrace: he had used the school's painting supplies for his work. As the painting gained in celebrity, the hapless teacher was restored to good odor; he returned, on request, to retouch it in the 1930s, when he was 80.

First Taste of the Western Isles

Kintyre is also a departure point for ferries to the islands. From Tayinloan, one runs west to tiny, lovely **Gigha** (pronounced GEE-a). Small though it be, Gigha has been populated for centuries, since the days of the prehistoric settlers who left the Holy Stone, later appropriated by the Christians as a preaching site. In 1493, the island came into the hands of the MacNeill family; Malcolm, the first MacNeill laird of Gigha, lies in the cemetery of the ruined **Church of Kilchattan**.

Gigha was always known for its fertile soil, which prompted Sir James Horlick to buy it in 1944; Horlick, passionate about rhododendrons, cultivated 50 acres of plants in **Achamore Gardens**, which he bequeathed to the National Trust of Scotland upon his death.

Above: Cute Scottish redhead. Right: The marvelous Celtic cross in Kildalton churchyard, Islay.

Scotland in Miniature

The island of **Arran**, off Kintyre's eastern coast, supposedly has every kind of terrain you encounter in mainland Scotland, but on a smaller scale. At one end of the spectrum are rugged Highland-like landscapes such as **Glen Sannox**, which H. V. Morton described as "three miles of the wildest Highland scenery that can be imagined." At the other are the cultivated grounds of elegant **Brodick Castle**, a building which grew from its 13th-century origins to a considerably expanded incarnation in the 19th century; its grounds in fact comprise Scotland's only island country park. There are prehistoric stone circles and standing stones scattered over **Machrie Moor**; there are ruined stone castles, like 14th-century **Lochranza Castle**. From the island's highest point, **Goat Fell**, you can survey the waters and the mainland around Arran; but Goat Fell is only one of ten peaks on Arran that are more than 2,000 feet high, making the island popular with walkers as well as with day-trippers out from Ardrossan.

ISLAY AND JURA

Islay (pronounced EYE-la) is the southernmost of the Inner Hebrides. Renowned for its cheeses almost as much as for its malt whiskies and countryside, Islay was long virtually an independent principality ruled first by the Norse and then, after the 13th century, by the Macdonalds, styled Lords of the Isles.

Geographically it is strange and delightful. Moorland lines its isolated east coast. Two waters, Loch Indaal and Loch Gruinart, slice into the island, while its western side rises to impressive cliffs.

In **Finlaggan**, a loch some 3 miles (2 km) southwest of Port Askaig, is the island of Eilean Mor. Here stand a ruined chapel and the castle where the Macdonalds lived in the 13th and 14th centuries.

Bowmore is Islay's unofficial capital. Laid out in 1768, its wide streets bespeak classicism, but its parish church of Kilarrow, built the following year, is an enchanting oddity, being round. Local architect Daniel Campbell asked Thomas Spalding to design it, perhaps inspired by Italian models; but local legend has it that the scheme was to afford the devil no corner to hide in.

In 1821, another Islay-born Campbell designed **Port Ellen**, the island's chief village. West of Port Ellen, don't miss the **Mull of Oa**, a peninsula with exhilarating cliffs. A monument on the peninsula commemorates 650 American soldiers and sailors who drowned here in 1918 when the *Tuscania* and *Otranto* were shipwrecked (one torpedoed, one driven onto the rocks).

Northeast of Port Ellen, **Kildalton Church**, begun in the 12th century, has a churchyard with one of the best Celtic crosses in Scotland, probably carved in the 9th century, and one of several dotted about the island. And the lighthouse near

Port Wemyss, built in 1824, was another work of Robert Louis Stevenson's grandfather.

Northeast of Islay, no more than 20 miles long, **Jura** is noted for its three splendid peaks (the **Paps of Jura**), the tallest 2,669 feet (816 m) high. Its west coast boasts lovely beaches and intriguing caves. Sparsely populated, its main village is **Craighouse**, whose harbor is so sprinkled with islands that it's known as Small Isles Bay. Craighouse also profits from a distillery founded here in 1884.

Between the island of Scarba and the north coast of Jura is a remarkable ocean whirlpool, created by the tides which are constricted by a couple of intruding juts of land. You can hear the whirlpool of **Corryvreckan** boiling from afar, and the small boats of local fisherfolk take care not to cross these waters when the pool is at its wildest.

Two small islands, 8 miles (13 km) west, are **Colonsay** (with a subtropical garden around Colonsay House at Kiloran, and another, Jura House Walled Gar-

den, of Australasian plants) and **Oron-say**, with a ruined 14th-century priory.

LOCH AWE TO OBAN

Some islands are closer to the mainland than others. **Seil** is actually joined to the mainland by the elegant stone semicircle of **Clachan Bridge**, built in 1791. By the bridge's Seil end is the inn **Tigh na Truish**, House of the Trousers. Restricted by post-Jacobite laws forbidding the wearing of kilts, the islanders used to stop off here on their way over to the mainland and change into a pair of the communal trousers that lay there for clients; on their return, they would again assume their preferred garments.

Back on the mainland, and indicating the direction toward the heart of the Highlands, is the snaking form of **Loch Awe**, once center of Campbell country; a

Above: Kilchurn Castle once defended Campbell interests around Loch Awe. Right: A gaggle of fishing boats in Oban's harbor.

clan slogan runs "It's a far cry to Loch Ow." The loch reflects like a slab of crystalline mirror laid at the foot of pine-forested hills. Ruins of two former Campbell strongholds pose photogenically against the scenic backdrop: 15th-century **Ardchonnel Castle** and the better-known **Kilchurn Castle**. Sir Colin Campbell built Kilchurn's keep in 1440; most of the rest of the building was added by a successor in 1693, before Hanoverians and the weather contributed to its literal downfall. The Campbells weren't alone; there were also Macdonalds about, living in **Fincharn Castle** (also ruined). In the loch, standing on a manmade islet or *crannog*, is **Innis Sherrich Chapel**, still reachable by means of stepping stones.

At the head of Loch Awe, by **Dalmally**, the monument on **Monument Hill** honors Duncan Ban Macintyre, an 18th-century Gaelic poet fondly called the "Burns of the Highlands." Interesting as his memory may be, the ascent here is really worthwhile for the views over the

loch and surrounding velvety hills, sun lying gold on the nap of their slopes.

Lovely Lorn

North of Loch Awe, you enter Lorn, a district named not for its desolation but for Loarn, one of three Irish brothers who captured this region in the 6th century A.D. Driving from Loch Awe to the coast, you pass a couple of rare pieces of testimony to industrialization in the Highlands. First comes the **Cruachan Pumped Storage Power Station**, a hydroelectric plant lying in a cavern at the heart of Ben Cruachan like something out of a James Bond film. A technological forbear is **Bonawe Iron Furnace**, founded in 1753; the National Trust has restored this site so that you can wander through the pastoral red-brick buildings, following the course of the iron ore as it was delivered and smelted into ingots. The furnace, a rare attempt to bring non-agrarian capital into the Highlands, operated until into the 19th century; one of its main outlets was the Navy, to which it furnished weapons and ammunition.

Nearing the coast, you pass the **Falls of Lora**, Europe's only seawater falls, by Connel Bridge on the way to **Dunstaffnage Castle**. This, too, was a Campbell holding, but one which they obtained from the MacDougalls. However, the castle was originally far more than just a clan seat. This site marked the capital of the Kingdom of Dalriada, replacing Dunadd in this role in the 9th century A.D. Believed to be the seat of Kenneth MacAlpine's court, it would have housed the Coronation Stone, or Stone of Destiny, before MacAlpine moved that object and his court to Scone. The extant castle ruins, however, stem from a later building of approximately 13th-century vintage. In the ruined chapel are a number of Campbell tombs.

Hard by is **Oban**, a hive of summer activity. Busy-ness has defined the character of the town, whose name means "little bay," through much of its history. Things may have been sleepier in the original

WEST COAST (NORTH)

Stone Age settlement, but in the 18th century, this was one of the busiest towns on the west coast, a droving center for cattle on their way to the Lowlands and British markets. And in the 19th century, tourist-laden excursion steamers puffing up from Glasgow and the brand-new railway helped convert the town into the vacation spot it is today.

Converging on the active harbor are a network of narrow streets filled with shops, fish restaurants practising for the annual Seafood Festival in September, and tourists. Towering over the whole thing is the odd neo-Classical circle of **McCaig's Tower**. This is sometimes described as a rich man's folly, but the word may be too pejorative, for the

wealthy local banker John Stuart McCaig came up with the idea of building it in 1897 partly as a way to create jobs in the depressed local economy. The building, however, was never finished. Pulpit Hill commands a marvelous view out over the harbor to the nearby islet of **Kerrera** (with the ruins of **Gylen Castle**, a 16th-century MacDougall tower house) and the "garden island" of **Lissmore**. In contrast to McCaig's Tower, Oban's oldest building is a complete ruin: 15th-century **Dunollie Castle**, a little way out of town.

One reason for Oban's busy-ness today is its role as a main ferry port for Mull, which lies just offshore, and other Western Isles.

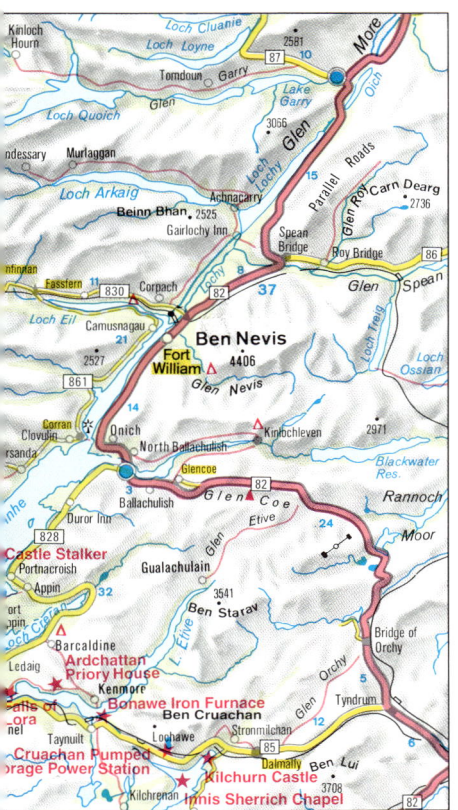

MULL AND NEARBY ISLES

Mull, the largest island of the Inner Hebrides, is enticingly varied. Around Loch Buie, Loch Don and Loch Spelve at its southernmost tip is a sharp headland. Dominating the center of the island is Ben More, 31,96 feet (977 m) high. The north is moorland. The island is cherished by hunters of deer and grouse, as well as all those who delight in peaceful fishing.

Tobermory, a fishing village founded in 1788 and the island's capital, is one of the loveliest anywhere. Its brightly-painted houses rise in tiers from the bay where, in 1588, a treasure-laden galleon of the Spanish Armada sank, blown up by a prisoner.

Passing through **Dervaig**, with its single street and the **Mull Little Theater** (the smallest professional theater in Great Britain), you come to **Calgary**, with its splendid white sands. A Highlander, Colonel J. F. Macleod, became chief of the Canadian Mounted Police and in 1876 named Calgary, Alberta, after this town.

Travel south to the overhanging **Gribun Rocks**, or the basalt caves and columns of the **Carsaig Arches** on the south coast. **Craignure**, a small port on the easternmost point of Mull, is guarded by two fortresses: **Duart Castle**, begun in the 13th century and much extended in 1633, and **Torosay Castle**, with its 12-acre formal garden and Italian statue walk. A miniature steam railway runs here from the ferry.

Surrounding Mull are other wonderful, smaller islands. Oval-shaped **Staffa**, with its basalt caves and awe-inspiring cliffs, lies off its west coast. The "Hebrides" Overture by Mendelssohn (who came to Mull in 1829) was inspired by the celebrated cavity here, and is thus also known as "Fingal's Cave." With its cluster columns, the cave resembles a natural cathedral.

Nearby **Ulva** supports scarcely 30 people these days, but once sheltered twenty times that number when the kelp industry flourished. Also rising off the west coast of Mull are the six **Treshnish Islands**, their shapes as bizarre as their names: Dutchman's Cap, Lunga, Fladda, and Cairn na Burgh More. Uninhabited, not often visited, the islands are a precious bird sanctuary.

Closer to the coast is **Inch Kenneth**, only half a mile long, yet bearing the remains of an abbey and an ancient cross, carved magically in the Celtic style. When Sir Allan Maclean and his two daughters entertained Boswell and Dr. Johnson here in 1773, Boswell crept out of the party to pray before this cross, clutching it and invoking St. Columba.

Once, 360 such elaborately carved crosses rose on an even holier spot, the

island of **Iona**, just off Mull's easternmost tip. Only three remain: 9th-century **St. John's Cross**, 10th-century **St. Martin's Cross**, and 15th-century **Maclean's Cross**. The first two stand near the abbey which St. Columba founded in 563, when he sailed from here with 12 companions to evangelize Scotland. The abbey was rebuilt in the 15th century and superbly restored after 1938 by a community formed by Presbyterian divine Baron George Macleod.

Maclean's Cross stands on the road to **St. Oran's Cemetery**, Scotland's oldest Christian cemetery and the last resting place of 48 Scottish kings (including Duncan, murdered by Macbeth). In **St. Oran's Chapel**, which dates from 1080, lies Lord Ronald, whom Walter Scott wrote about in his poem "The Lord of the Isles." And when Johnson and Boswell came here, the former observed, "That

Above: Devotional candles illuminate medieval Iona. Right: A lone farmhouse punctuates the emptiness of Glencoe.

man is little to be envied, whose patriotism would not gain force upon the plain of Marathon, or whose piety would not grow warmer among the ruins of Iona."

GLENCOE AND POINTS NORTH

On the mainland, in the former Dalriadic Kingdom, old buildings abound. On the shore of Loch Etive, north of Oban, is **Ardchattan Priory House**, the second-oldest inhabited house in Scotland, and notable as the site of the country's last Gaelic-speaking parliament – in 1308. Continue north through Appin and you'll come upon a vista dominated by the square form of the former Stewart keep of **Castle Stalker**, looking doughty, slightly sinister, and deserted (though it isn't) on its island in Loch Linnhe.

Glencoe

Tragic as the 1692 massacre that occurred here was, its events alone might not have been enough to confer legendary status on a mountain valley. **Glencoe** continues to capture the popular imagination because of its spectacular beauty. Tawny slopes sweep breathtakingly up from a narrow, burbling brook; the only sign of human habitation are the flecks of color of windbreakers of hillwalkers out to experience the scenery first-hand. If they don't feel like tackling the **Devil's Staircase** (a switchbacking trail over the glen's northern ridge, part of the West Highland Way) or ascending the **Three Sisters** (outcroppings of the highest mountain in Argyll, **Bideanh nam Bian**) and **Buachaille Etive Mhor**, the Great Shepherd of Etive, they may wander to **Ossian's Cave**, apocryphally held to be the birthplace of the 3rd-century bard, or penetrate to the **Hidden Valley**, where Clan Macdonald used to hide cattle stolen from the Lowlands before they were themselves reduced in

the infamous massacre at the hands of the Campbells.

One reason the Campbells continually emerge as villains is that they, the line of the Dukes of Argyll, were loyal to the King of England. Most clans in the 17th century didn't want to acknowledge the sovereignty of King William and Mary, remaining loyal to "Scotland's" James VII (known in England as James II), who had been forced to abdicate. In 1691, King William III offered a blanket pardon to all rebels prepared to swear loyalty to him by January 1; by this time, most of the clan chieftains felt able to comply. In winter, however, traveling conditions were poor, and so it was that Alasdair MacIain, the old clan chief of the Macdonalds, wasn't able to get to Inveraray to sign the oath until January 6. Too late. William III's Scottish representative had already ordered Argyll's troops, led by a Campbell, to go in and wipe the clan out. Marching into Glencoe, the "narrow glen," the men were met by the unsuspecting Macdonalds, who not only welcomed them heartily in true Highland fashion, but put them up for a good two weeks. This gave Campbell's men time to plan out the blocking of the passes, so that, when the signal came from **Signal Rock** on February 13, the Macdonalds were trapped like lambs for the slaughter. The slaughter wasn't as huge as it's been painted: many of the 200 clansmen did manage to escape, and the total death count was around 40. A museum in a thatched house in the village of **Glencoe** sheds further light on these events.

At the eastern end of Glencoe extend the impressively empty landscapes of **Rannoch Moor** and **Black Mount**, over which fled David Balfour and Alan Breck in Robert Louis Stevenson's classic novel *Kidnapped*.

Moidart and the Jacobites

Due west of Glencoe are even wilder climes: Moidart, Sunart, and the mountainous peninsula of Ardnamurchan. The latter, in particular, is scenically specta-

cular: *Ard na Mòr Chuain*, "Height of the Great Seas," dramatically juxtaposes mountains and water.

Bypassing the circuitous route through Fort William, a car ferry crosses Loch Linnhe to **Corran**. Here, a lighthouse stands by the southern access to the Caledonian Canal, which stretches across Scotland like a seam from here to Inverness (see p. 145). From here on in, nature holds sway. At **Strontian**, in whose lead mines the element strontium was discovered in 1790, the woods of **Ariundle Nature Reserve** are what Scotland's oak forests might have looked like before deforestation. Further on, the molded mountains around **Camas nan Geall** rise behind a curving beach, also marking the site of a prehistoric chambered cairn, **Cladh Chiaran**.

By Kilchoan, 13th-century **Mingary Castle**, long a stronghold of the Lords of the Isles, still contains a cannon from the Spanish Armada. From here, it's not far to **Ardnamurchan Point**, the westernmost point on mainland Britain. By its lighthouse, you can look out over the "Small Isles" all the way to the mountains of Skye. Perhaps an even more beguiling view is that of the stunning white beach at **Sanna Bay**. Behind this, the "ring dyke" around **Glen Drian** isn't a manmade barrier, but the geological term for the crater of a long-extinct volcano.

Sanna doesn't hold a monopoly on beaches: there are beautiful ones all along the stunning north coast, culminating in the "singing sands" of **Kentra**. The dominance of water is reflected in the boat-shaped ceiling which ship's joiners created in the church at **Acharacle**. Nearby **Mingarry** documents other traditional, if less honorable, crafts in its **Illegal Museum**, devoted to poaching and whiskey distilling. A little road from here leads to the romantic ruins of **Castle Tioram**, burned by its own chief in 1715 to keep it from falling into the hands of the Campbells.

Above: Highland reverie:monument at Glenfinnian to the uprising of "Bonnie Prince Charlie."

North of here is the cradle of the Jacobite Rebellion, the place where Charles Edward Stuart landed to win back the kingdom of Scotland for his father, and from which he fled a year later, utterly defeated. In July, 1745, "Bonnie Prince Charlie" sailed in from France to reach the Scottish mainland at **Loch na Uamh**, confident of French backing for his plan of regaining the throne. Planting trees at his nearby estate, Clan Cameron's chief Lochiel heard of Charlie's arrival and rode off to warn him against the attempt; the trees which he left lying in a row behind him are now known as the "Seven Men of Moidart," a symbolic reflection of Prince Charlie's handful of followers. In fact, there were more than seven followers, and there are only five trees left, but romance doesn't quibble about details. A **cairn** by the loch commemorates Charlie's landing.

A more striking memorial marks a more striking moment. Atop the monument at **Glenfinnian**, a Highlander gazes down Loch Shiel in quiet reverie. It was here that Charlie raised his standard and waited to see how many Highlanders would show up: after a hiatus, in marched the Camerons, bagpipes playing. Charlie's whole endeavor reads like a movie script, filled with symbolic gesture: by **Fassifern**, he placed a wild white rose from the roadside in his hat to become "The White Cockade," a symbol of his quest. Yet the real world won out in the end: even as Charlie was mustering the reluctant Highlanders, the minister of Ardnamurchan was sending word to the Duke of Argyll that the enemy had landed, setting in motion the forces that were ultimately to defeat him.

What's whitest between **Arisaig** and **Mallaig** are the beaches, such as the gorgeous **Sands of Morar**. At **Morar**, Britain's shortest river links the sea and Britain's deepest freshwater loch, supposedly home to its very own loch monster, Morag. The two towns are also ferry

ports. From here, you can get boats to the "Small Isles" of Rum, Eigg, Muck, and Canna. Loveliest and wildest of the islands, **Rum**, or Rhum, was completely depopulated in the Highland Clearances, when all the inhabitants left for America. Its turn-of-the-century **Kinloch Castle** is now the island's only hotel; its owner's mausoleum, a Doric temple, communes with nature in true Greek tradition across the bay. **Canna**'s **Compass Hill** is so named because its iron deposits distort the compass readings of passing ships. **Muck** is the smallest and most fertile island; its rather unfortunate name derives from a Gaelic word for "pig," denoting either the island's shape or the porpoises (sea pigs) that swim in its waters.

As well as being a departure point for ferries to the Outer Hebrides, Mallaig used to be the main port for Skye. The A830 between Mallaig and Fort William is still known as the "Road to the Isles." The railway line along here, crossing the viaduct at Glenfinnian, is one of the most beautiful in Scotland.

Any Fort in a Storm

There's no fort in **Fort William**. There was one in the 17th century, built as an outpost of civilization in a wild land; but it was sold off around 1867 and pulled down to make room for the railway. This paved the way for Fort William's growth as a tourist center.

"Every healthy man who visits Fort William climbs **Ben Nevis**. No one suggests that he should do so. It is just one of Scotland's unwritten laws of decent conduct." H. V. Morton's observation continues to hold true, at least in that Ben Nevis is Fort William's main tourist attraction. And the ascent isn't as daunting as some mountain climbs; after all, the mountain is only 4,406 feet (1,347 m) high. However, the variable weather can pose a risk: lives are lost on Ben Nevis every year, largely because of underpreparation. Take heed, precautions, and good shoes.

Transportation

TRAIN: Opened in 1894, ScotRail's West Highland Line, running from Glasgow to Oban or Fort William, is one of the most popular stretches of railway in Britain. A West Highland Rover pass allows 4 days' unlimited travel within an 8-day period for £39; if you want to take ferries to the islands, a Freedom of Scotland pass covers ferries as well. Information: (0345) 212282 (see "Guidelines" for more details). *BUS*: Scottish CityLink runs buses from Glasgow to destinations including Oban, Campbeltown, and Fort William. Tel. (0141) 3329191.

INVERARAY AND AREA
Accommodation

STRACHUR: *MODERATE:* **The Creggans Inn**, tel. 0136/9860279. Renowned family inn particularly well known for good Scottish cooking, from snacks to teas to the genuine article.
INVERARAY: *MODERATE:* **The Great Inn**, tel. 01499/302466, fax 302389. Large, creaky inn, decent food. **The George Hotel**, tel. 01499/302111, fax 302225. Comfy hotel, recommended pub.
DALMALLY: *EXPENSIVE:* **Portsonachan Country Club**, S bank of Loch Awe, nr Dalmally, tel. (in Scotland) (0800) 454393. Vacation complex with individual holiday apartments, a range of sports facilities, fine restaurant on banks of Loch Awe. *BUDGET:* **Glenorchy Lodge Hotel**, tel. (01838) 200312. Individually furnished rooms; great views, friendly staff, and a penchant for families.
FORD: *BUDGET:* **Ford Hotel**, tel (01546) 810273. Young owners have taken over this pub and created a lovely homey B&B with great cooking.
ARDRISHAIG: *MODERATE:* **Allt-Na-Craig**, Tarbert Road, tel. (01546) 603245. Old Victorian mansion with views of Loch Fyne.

Restaurants

EXPENSIVE: **Lock 16**, Crinan Hotel, Crinan, tel. (0154) 683261, fax 683292, fabulous rooftop restaurant, with water views and incredibly fresh fish.

Museums and Sights

INVERARAY: Inveraray Castle, ancestral seat of the Campbell family, with adjacent **Combined Operations Museum**, where invasion forces were trained in World War II. Open April-mid Oct Mon-Thu and Sat 10 am-1 pm, 2 pm-5:30 pm, Sun 1-5:30 pm (Jul & Aug no lunch pause), tel. 01499/302203 or 500218. **Inveraray Jail**, popular living museum, open Nov-Mar 10 am-5 pm, Apr-Oct 9:30 am-6 pm, tel. 01499/302381. **Arctic Penguin**, iron schooner with museums and a/v presentations, open Apr-Oct 10 am-6 pm, Nov-Mar 10 am-5 pm, tel 01499/302213. **Auchindrain Open Air Museum**, 5 mi/8 km S of Inveraray, restored original West Highland township, open Apr-Sept 10 am-5 pm, tel. 01499/500235.

Sports

FISHING: Loch Long is one of Britain's best places for sea angling. For fishing Loch Awe, you can rent boats and tackle at **Ardbrecknish Boating Centre** (B840 betw. Inveraray and Dalmally), tel. 081663/223 or 256. *RIDING:* **Castle Riding Centre**, Brenfield Farm, Ardrishaig:trail riding and courses for horseback riders of all levels. Mrs. Tove Gray-Stephens or Mr. Chris Hall, tel. 01546/603274, fax 603225. *WALKING:* For information about the Arrochar Alps, contact the **Ranger Service** in Tarbet, tel. (01389) 758216. Guided walks by **Compass Ventures**, Tarbet, tel. (01301) 702349.

KINTYRE PENINSULA
Accommodation

MODERATE: **Columba Hotel**, East Pier Road, Tarbert, tel. (01880) 820808. Victorian building by picturesque harbor; restaurant with local seafood and produce. **White Hart Hotel**, Main Street, Campbeltown, tel. (01586) 552440, fax 554972. Traditional hotel; locals find food "gorgeous."

Restaurants

North Beachmore Farm Restaurant, near Muasdale on the A83, locally beloved (often crowded), with great home cooking.

Museums and Sights

Glenbarr Abbey with Macalister Clan Visitor Centre, tel. 01583/421247, laird returned to his ancestral home trying to make ends meet by showing visitors around. Open daily exc. Tue 10am-6 pm. **Campbeltown Heritage Centre**, Lorne Street, open Mon-Fri 12-5 pm, Sat 10 am-5 pm, Sun 2-5 pm. Endearingly homemade, interesting displays.

Sports

GOLF: **Machrihannish** is one claimant to the title "birthplace of golf." Tel. (01586) 810213.

OBAN / AROUND OBAN
Accommodation

EXPENSIVE: **Glenfeochan House**, Kilmore, tel. 01631/770273, fax 770624. Victorian country mansion with gardens, lovingly restored by present owners; former Cordon Bleu teacher prepares meals for guests. *MODERATE*: **Barriemore Hotel**, the Esplanade, tel. (01631) 566356. Victorian house overlooking the bay. *BUDGET:* Ariogan Farmhouse, Upper Soroba, tel. (01631) 65257, family farmhouse 2 mi/3 km from town.

Restaurants

EXPENSIVE: **The Manor House Hotel**, Gallanach Road, tel. (01631) 562087, Scottish/French cuisine in elegant ambience. *MODERATE*: **Boxtree Restaurant**, 108 George St. Cozy and central, with good home cooking.

Museums and Sights

Oban Sea Life Centre, Barcaldine, Connel, tel. (01631) 720386. **Oban Distillery**, Stafford St., tel.

(01631 64262), open Mon-Fri 9:30 am-5 pm, also Sat Easter-Oct. **Cruachan Power Station**, 15 mi/24 km E of Oban, open Apr-Oct 9 am-4:30 pm, tel. (081662) 673. **Castle Stalker**, N of Oban; can be viewed by prior arrangement, tel. (018832) 2768.

GLENCOE / FORT WILLIAM
Accommodation
EXPENSIVE: **The Moorings Hotel**, Banavie, tel. (01397) 772797, fax 772441. Leading local hotel with nautical theme, individually decorated rooms, friendly staff, and excellent restaurant. **Inverlochy Castle**, Torlundy, tel. (01397) 702177, fax 702953. Live like a king. Complete with period dining room, fine cooking, the works. *MODERATE:* **King's House Hotel**, tel. (01855) 851259, as isolated as one could wish, and the oldest licensed inn in Scotland, with true country-style pub meals.

Restaurants
FORT WILLIAM: *MODERATE:* **Crannog Seafood Restaurant**, Town Pier, tel. (01397) 705589. Pleasant waterfront seafood restaurant.

Sports and Activities
CLIMBING / CANOEING: **Snowgoose Activities** offers courses in these and other sports, guided climbs and walks. The Old Smiddy, Station Road, Corpach, 4 mi/6.5 km W of Fort William, tel. (01397) 772467. *CYCLING:* **Off Beat Bikes** rents, sells and repairs. MacRaes Lane, Fort William, tel. (01397) 704008. *SKIING:* **Glencoe Ski Centre** is Scotland's oldest ski resort; spectacular scenery. Tel. (018556) 226 or (018552) 303. The **Nevis Range Ski Area** (Aonach Mor), some of the highest skiing in Scotland. Tel. (01397) 705825, fax 705854. *WALKING:* The **West Highland Way** extends 93 mi/150 km from Glasgow to Fort William.

Tourist Information
Argyll, the Isles, Loch Lomond, Stirling, Trossachs Tourist Board, Old Town Jail, St. John St., Stirling, tel. (01786) 470945. **Tourist Information Centre**, Boswell House, Argyll Square, Oban, tel. (01631) 63122, fax 64273. **Fort William and Lochaber Tourism**, Cameron Square, tel. (01397) 703781, fax 705184.

THE ISLANDS
Transportation
TRAIN: **Scotrail** runs day tours from Glasgow to Mull; tel. (0345) 212282. On Mull, a narrow-gauge railway operates between the harbor, Craignure & Torosay Castle, Easter-mid-October, Mon-Sat: **Mull & West Highland Narrow Gauge Railways**, Craignure, (01680) 812494. *FERRY:* **Caledonian MacBrayne** runs ferries to the Western Isles and Arran. For general information and schedule, contact the head office in Gourock, tel. (01475) 650100, fax 637607. Ferries leave from **Dervaig** and **Iona** for Fingal's Cave, **Staffa**.

Accommodation / Restaurants
ARRAN: *MODERATE:* **The Lagg Hotel**, Kilmory, tel. (01770) 870255. Comfortable inn in the S of the island; very good meals. **The Apple Lodge**, Lochranza, tel. & fax (01770) 830229. Former village manse. **Creelers**, near Brodick, tel. (01770) 302810. Local seafood restaurant so renowned it's opened a branch in Edinburgh. Open April-Oct.
GIGHA: Gigha Hotel, tel. (015835) 254, fax 282. Island's only hotel; restaurant, self-catering cottages.
ISLAY: *MODERATE*: **Kilmeny Farmhouse**, Ballygrant, tel. (01496) 840668, farmhouse with 2 B&B rooms, lovely evening meals with local produce. **Glenmachrie Farmhouse**, Port Ellen, tel. (01496) 302560, homey candlelit dining room with home cooking. **Kilchoman House**, Bruichladdich, tel. (01496) 850382, restaurant with self-catering cottages (advance booking needed).
JURA: *MODERATE*: **Jura Hotel**, tel. (01496) 820243, fax 820249. Jura's only hotel: family-run, with good Scottish cooking and views.
MULL: *MODERATE:* **Strongarbh House**, Tobermory, tel. (01688) 302328, fax 302238. Victorian stone country house, Taste of Scotland restaurant. **Calgary Farmhouse Hotel**, near Dervaig, tel. (01688) 400256, in a restored farmhouse near Calgary's gorgeous beach, with restaurant in converted barn. *BUDGET:* **Ardrioch Farm**, Dervaig, tel. (01688) 400264. Working farmhouse with cozy rooms and very good cooking.

Museums and Sights
ISLAY: Bowmore Distillery, tel. (0146) 681871, visits by arrangement. Other distilleries, including **Laphroaig**, also offer tours. **Finlaggan Visitor Center**, by the castle ruin, tel. (0149) 684644, open Apr-Oct Thu & Sun 2-6 pm, May-Sep also Tue 2-6 pm. **Museum of Islay Life**, Port Charlotte, tel. (0149) 605358, open Apr-Oct Mon-Sat 10 am-5 pm, Sun 2-5 pm, Nov-Mar Mon-Wed 10 am-1 pm.
JURA: Jura House Walled Garden, open Mon-Sat 9 am-5 pm, tel. (0149) 682213.
COLONSAY: Kiloran Gardens, tel. (0195) 12312, open daily during daylight hours.
MULL: Duart Castle, tel. (01688) 2309, daily May-Sept 10:30 am-6 pm. **Mull Little Theater**, Dervaig, tel. (01688) 4250. **Tobermory Distillery Visitor Center**, tel. (01688) 2119, Apr-Oct Mon-Fri 10 am-4 pm. **Torosay Castle and Gardens**, daily mid-Apr-mid-Oct 10:30 am-5:30 pm; gardens 9 am-7 pm in summer, daylight hours in winter.
IONA: Worship at 2 pm weekdays, Holy Communion Sun 10:30 am. Island open Mon-Sat 10 am-5 pm. Tel. (0141) 55287391.

Tourist Information
Tourist Information Center, Bowmore, Islay, tel. (01496) 810254.

THE HIGHLANDS
Scotland's Rugged Northwest

CALEDONIAN CANAL
INVERNESS
BLACK ISLE
THE NORTHWEST
SKYE

For many people, the Highlands are synonymous with Scotland. Steep, majestic mountains framing wild glens; moors dotted with sheep and grouse; isolated white sand beaches reached along single-track roads like ribbons of concrete laid tenuously down in the purply heather. Here are some of Scotland's best hill walking, fishing, windsurfing, and nature-watching opportunities: you can spot puffins and dolphins, seals and skuas around the waters off these shores, even if the waters themselves are generally too cold to make one's own entry into them a desirable option.

The chill of the weather, and the ruggedness of the landscape, is offset by the genuine warmth of the people. Scotsmen themselves will point out the friendliness of their compatriots (and tell you that it's something that distinguishes them from their English neighbors to the south), and nowhere is that more in evidence than in the Highlands. After conversing with a peasant woman near Inverness, Samuel Johnson was so favorably impressed that he observed, "Civility seems part of the national character of Highlanders" – which still holds true today.

Preceding pages: Blue waters and the "Black Cuillins": the view from Elgol (Skye). Left: Young Highlanders show their stuff.

CALEDONIAN CANAL

Slashing across the northern section of Scotland like a knife-cut is the line of the **Great Glen**. Running down the middle of this geological fault line are three arrow-straight lochs – Linnhe, Lochy, and Ness – pointing the way to the north, and traversing some of the most beautiful landscape in Scotland along the way. In 1822, engineer Thomas Telford saw the fruition of his plans to link them with the opening of the **Caledonian Canal**, the first canal in Britain to run from one coast of the country to the other. Today, although it can still handle heavy shipping, it's used predominantly by pleasure craft. "If I were asked to indicate the most romantic inland voyage in Europe, I would vote for the journey up or down the Caledonian Canal," H. V. Morton wrote. "The Rhine cannot hold a candle to it."

One of the canal's most striking sections, technically at least, is the series of locks by **Banavie**, just north of Fort William. Dubbed **Neptune's Staircase**, these 8 lochs negotiate vessels over a 64-foot (20 m) drop in altitude between the canal and sea level on the western end.

Branching into the artery of the Great Glen are parallel side glens with their own spectacular scenery. During World War II, this secluded wilderness area

HIGHLANDS

0   10   20 km
0   5   10 miles

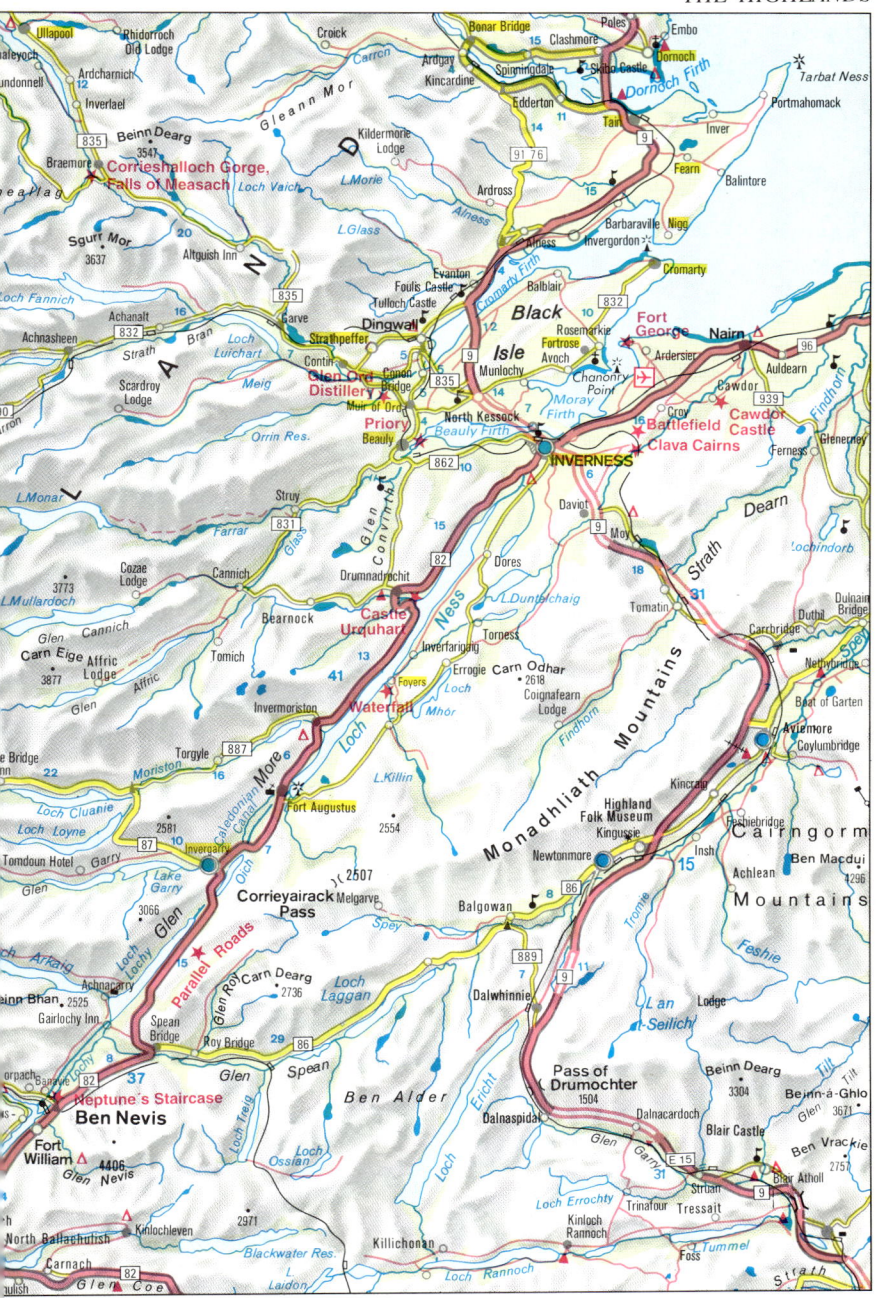

served as a training ground for commando forces. Three of these soldiers, frozen in bronze, form the **Commando Memorial**, gazing out from their roadside plateau over a stunning view of Ben Nevis.

An older history is reflected in the **"Parallel Roads"** of nearby **Glen Roy**, the work not, as locals used to believe, of the giant Fingal, but of retreating waters at the tail end of the Ice Age. A mere 10,000 or so years ago – yesterday, to geologists – ice had dammed up water in this valley; when the ice melted and the lake began to drain, it left behind it a series of shelves, some 30 feet wide, along the hillsides.

This dramatic scenery calls for more dramatic stories, however, and the Highlands oblige with centuries worth of tales of clan feuds and discord. In July, 1544, the area around **Laggan** saw the largest

clan battle ever fought: the Battle of the Shirts involved some 1,000 men, and almost, but not quite, managed to wipe Clan Fraser off the map. Near this site is testimony to a smaller-scale but no less grisly bit of Clan MacDonell history. After the two sons of a newly-deceased 17th-century laird were killed in a piece of uncontrolled family infighting as they were celebrating their accession to their heritage, another branch of the family (some say the family bard) determined to avenge them, marched on the perpetrators – a father and his six sons – and did away with them. Having cut off their heads, they decided to wash them off before presenting them to the clan chief at Glengarry. A monument still stands over the **Well of Seven Heads**, recounting a version of this story.

The MacDonells continued to provide local color until into the 19th century. The last clan chief at Glengarry, Colonel Alastair Ranaldson MacDonell, conducted himself as if he were a 16th-century Highlander, attiring himself in full

Above: Through the locks of the Caledonian Canal. Right: "Nessie" in an unusually photogenic mode.

Highland garb and traveling about with a host of retainers. Today, beautiful, deserted **Glen Garry** seems to await his return; driving through here, you'd never suspect that it was home to several thousand people before the infamous Highland Clearances emptied the land. Even the seat of the clan, **Invergarry Castle**, was destroyed by the Duke of Cumberland in 1746, punishment for the supporters of the Jacobite rebellion. Today, its ruins stand near the Glengarry Castle Hotel, which dates from the Victorian period during which the little village here was also planned out.

The other lasting memories of this whole region are of Bonnie Prince Charlie, who marched through in triumph only to retreat in bitter defeat a matter of months later. One reminder is the **Roderick Mackenzie Memorial**, erected to a supporter of Charlie's who, mortally wounded by pursuing British troops, led them to believe that he was the prince they sought. His head was brought to "Butcher" Cumberland at Fort Augustus;

many people were ready to swear that it was, in fact, Charlie's head, and the search for Charlie briefly let up, which perhaps helped the prince to get away.

What a Ness

Fort Augustus was in fact named for Cumberland, christened William Augustus, although General Wade built the fort at the intersection of two of his military roads when William Augustus was still a boy. The fort's military function was relatively brief: built in 1729, it was turned over to the Benedictine Order in 1876, presumably following the Bible's swords-into-plowshares dictum. A Heritage Center in the abbey records the area's history, from earliest times (also documented by **Cherry Island**, an Iron Age *crannog*, or manmade island, in the loch nearby) to the most famous local denizen of these parts, the Loch Ness Monster.

Alas, the image captured in the famous photograph of "Nessie" surfacing above the misty waters was in fact a manmade

149

device; one of the perpetrators confessed to the hoax, in writing, a year before his death. Yet the legend of the Loch Ness Monster persists, backed up by dozens of near-sightings (one of the brothers in the monastery insists that he saw it). And hope springs eternal for would-be Nessie seekers on passenger boats up and down the loch, or peering out from vantage points along the road. One theory about the origins of the legend makes the "monster" a sturgeon, which have achieved tremendous sizes (one caught in Russia was 9 meters long and weighed 2 1/2 tons). Scotland's waters seem to function as the bastion for the legends of sea monsters and creatures of the deep that used to accompany the ocean in general; monsters also dwell or have dwelt in Loch Morag and Loch na Beiste on the west coast, and Gavin Maxwell recounts a convincing reported sighting in his book *Ring of Bright Water*.

If Nessie doesn't choose to put in an appearance, there's still plenty to see along the shores of Loch Ness. Most famous lookout point is **Castle Urquhart**, a largely 16th-century structure blown up in 1692 to save it from the evil Jacobites; its ruins, lounging along the shore, seem veritably to echo a monster's form. At **Foyers**, on the opposite bank and to the south, the river Foyers cascades into the loch in a foaming waterfall. Turning off from Loch Ness on the A381 through Glen Urquhart, you'll eventually come to the head of **Glen Affric**, a beautiful wild valley which shelters a section of the original Caledonian Forest.

INVERNESS

The prefix *inver* means river mouth; hence the town at the mouth of the Ness is **Inverness**, unofficial but widely acknowledged "Capital of the Highlands."

Right: A tame aspect of Inverness, "Capital of the Highlands."

Inverness has won this title more by virtue of its geographical position than by its own merits, though it's a pleasant enough town. Gone is the castle which Mary, Queen of Scots took from defiant rebels; gone is Cromwell's fort; today's **castle** is a bright, 19th-century edifice in pinkish stone, as is the 19th-century **St. Andrews Cathedral**. Even the **Mercat Cross**, near which, in bygone days, townswomen used to rest as they carried water from the river, is a replica. Truly old, by contrast, is **Abertarff House** with its "turnpike" spiral staircase, built in 1594. One unusual feature is the town park of the **Ness Islands**, linked to each other and the mainland by means of little footbridges.

For true history, you have to leave the town and drive east to **Clava Cairns**, beautifully haunting stone mounds pitted with enigmatic cup-and-ring markings, with an adjacent group of sentinel-like standing stones. Some of the most important cairns on mainland Britain, these date from somewhere between 2000 and 1500 B.C., and still exert an aura so profound that dogs have been known to refuse to go near them.

A more recent, and more infamous, site is **Culloden Moor**. On this expanse of scrub heather, dotted with stones and clan flags, the last battle on British soil was fought on April 16, 1746. If Prince Charlie symbolizes all romantic notions of Scottish independence, Culloden Moor symbolizes the dashing of that dream. It was here that Charlie – whose Highland troops had advanced almost to the gates of London, but then, fearing the cutting off of their supply lines, retreated back to Scotland – was finally confronted by the Duke of Cumberland, who had promptly marched north after them to exact retribution. Charlie was doomed from the outset: facing his 5,000 tired Highlanders were 9,000 fresh, better-armed troops. Cumberland earned his sobriquet of "butcher" for his order after the battle to spare no wounded; even in-

jured men who surrendered were mercilessly killed.

After the original "incident," the British decided they needed a better military outpost in this area, and built **Fort George**, which was completed in 1769. Still in use, this moated, star-shaped fortification on a spit of land jutting out into the Moray Firth is one of Europe's finest pieces of military architecture. An older fortification stands inland: **Cawdor Castle**. The name survives from the 11th century, when Macbeth had King Duncan murdered here, but no trace remains of that original building; today's attractive castle dates back "only" to 1372, and bears the stamp of additions and renovations from the 16th and 17th centuries.

THE BLACK ISLE

Just north of Inverness, Black Isle is neither black nor an island, but rather a promontory jutting out to carve the Cromarty, Firth from the Moray Firth. Its profile is not altogether unlike that of one of the local dolphins: the Moray Firth is home to one of the last populations of bottle-nose dolphins in the world, and dolphin tours depart from a variety of points along the shore. One theory about the name is that it's a translation of a corrupted Gaelic form of "Saint Duthus's Island," after a holy main who died around 1065. His church and chapel in Tain, dating from the 14th and 11th centuries, respectively, were for centuries a place of pilgrimage. Others postulate that this mild peninsula remains black and snowless even when the rest of the area is buried under a blanket of snow.

Popular with sailing aficionados, **Fortrose** also boasts a lovely, albeit ruined, cathedral. At **Chanonry Point** here is a plaque commemorating one of the area's most famous sons: a man variously called Coinneach Odhar or Kenneth MacKenzie, better known as the Brahan Seer. Those of his prophesies which weren't fulfilled when he made them in the first half of the 17th century have been steadily coming true ever since: among other things, he foresaw the advent of the Caledonian Canal ("Ships will sail at the back of Tomnahurich," a hill by Inverness). But his clarity of vision led him to a bad end, or so goes the story: asked by his patroness, a local countess, to tell her what her husband was doing at that moment on his travels abroad, the seer replied that he was in the arms of a woman, and the countess was so furious that she had the seer placed in a barrel of tar and burned to death on this spot.

Local Hero

Local tales of this sort were a particular interest of another local, Hugh Miller, who lived in **Cromarty**, the main town of the Black Isle. Born and raised here, Miller went on to become a noted geologist, but never lost his fascination for his country; and he collected local legend in his book *Scenes and Legends of the North of Scotland*. His writing style is notable for its lucidity and clarity, even in his scientific works; in the period he wrote them, in the first half of the 18th century, some of his books saw as many as 24 printings. His thatched-roof residence is now a **museum** preserving original furniture and manuscripts.

Cromarty is a lovely town in itself, with a **Court House** that's now a museum of local history with "living" exhibits and a Mercat Cross dating back to the 15th century. Guarding one side of the narrow entrance to Cromarty Firth, the town has been known for its excellent harbor since about the same period. At the other side of the strait, **Nigg** houses a construction yard for oil platforms; when they're not in use, the platforms are parked in a row down the length of the firth, an elephantine and incongruous

component in an area that also houses a bird reserve.

At the neck of the Black Isle is the **Muir of Ord**, historically a center for cattle-driving; its annual, one-day Black Isle Show is one of the leading agricultural events in Scotland. The distillery at **Glen Ord** is the last survivor of what used to be nine distilleries availing themselves of the water of the Allt Fionnaidh (White Burn). Good water is a resource around here: the town of **Strathpeffer** came to prosperity when the healing properties of its sulphur springs were discovered. Dr. Morrison opened his pump room around 1820, and with the advent of the new railway Strathpeffer became a booming Victorian spa. Its buildings still give some evidence of its heyday, and you can take the waters in a sampling pavilion. Above the railway station stands the **Eagle Stone**, a Pictish relic with carvings of horseshoe and eagle figures.

Monuments to the region's early Christianity abound north of the Black Isle. There's 13th-century **Fearn Abbey**, which was used as a parish church until 1712, when the roof fell in, killing several parishioners, just as the Brahan Seer had prophesied (the church is now restored, completed with a sturdier roof). Then, at **Tain**, "Ross-shire's bonniest town" and one of Scotland's oldest royal burghs, with a charter supposedly dating back to 1066, there are the abovementioned church and chapel of St. Duthus, as well as a charming turreted **Tolbooth**. Just north of town is the distillery of **Glenmorangie**, whose copper stills are the tallest in the Highlands.

THE NORTHWEST

Sutherland

The farther north you push, the more you have a sense of discovering virgin territory, even if this is belied by the cars of other travelers. Past Bonar Bridge,

Right: The immigrants: the Highlands' human population was cleared out to make room for sheep in the 18th and 19th centuries.

you're in Sutherland, a (former) county which stretches like a band across the middle of northernmost Scotland, leaving room for Caithness at the northeastern tip. This was the "southern land" of the Viking kingdom, hence its name; and Viking presence is still reflected in modern place names ending in suffixes like "ster" and "wick." Sutherland embraces much of what's loveliest on the Highlands' coasts, but there aren't many people, off season, to enjoy it: this area has the lowest population density in all of Europe. It's said the region doesn't boast a single traffic light. What people there are tend to gather on the coasts; inland, much of the empty country is occupied with the Flows, the largest expanse of peat moor in Europe, with a rich and distinctive avian population.

One reason the land is so empty are the infamous "Highland Clearances." Starting in the late 18th century, local lairds decided it would be more profitable to use their lands for sheep than rent it to cattle-raising small farmers, or crofters,

who often paid their rent in services rather than cash. To make room for the former, they set about evicting the latter. Whole villages were brutally uprooted and homes burned; those inhabitants who stayed around were unceremoniously moved to coastal locations with no infrastructure and poor soil, where they tried to eke out a living as farmers and novice fishermen. Others departed on overcrowded ships for the United States and Canada – 20,000 of them between 1763 and 1775. The bitter irony is that the sheep gradually ate away at the fabric of the ecosystem; where cattle graze gently, sheep overgraze relentlessly, tearing the grass away to the roots and ruining the pastureland. Furthermore, there was enough competition from other wool centers, such as Australia, that sheep proved less economically successful than had been hoped. At least one landowner recognized the problem, and tried to bring back cows, but the people never returned; the Highlands have been empty ever since. You can still see the founda-

153

tions of long-abandoned houses in roadside meadows; the whole deserted village of Achanlochy stands near **Bettyhill**, on the north coast, where a **Museum of Clearances** documents the Strathnaver clearances that began in this area.

Long the center for Highlands life and a transportation hub for visitors was **Lairg**, at one end of Loch Shin. Since displaced by more active vacation centers, such as Ullapool, Lairg remains a bastion for traditional crofters, or small farmers, who convene at the annual crofters show in August, the last of its kind in Britain. A **Croft Museum** near Dunbeath, further up the coast, illuminates the local farming lifestyle which remains central to the area. Highland schools even have a two-week "Tattie Holiday" in November, upholding the time-honored tradition of freeing children to help their families with the annual potato harvest. Today, when even working farmers supplement their incomes with B&Bs or some other tourist-trade activity, these two off-season weeks may be the only chance a family has to take a vacation.

Loch Shin itself is a reservoir made by damming the River Shin; watching salmon scale the salmon ladder, built to enable them to continue natural migratory patterns despite the dam, is popular in summer. Further downstream, at the **Falls of Shin**, the river cascades in swirls of Guinness-colored foaming water.

Seals sun themselves on the sand banks of Dornoch Firth; and wildflowers grow along the pastoral shore of what's actually a military bombing range, across the firth from the town of **Dornoch**. Many people admire sea and sun from the links of one of the best golf courses in Britain, the **Royal Dornoch**. This pleasant town also boasts a 13th-century **cathedral**, where a couple of old tombstones present the emblem of a local clan:

Right: Stones of the North: sea stacks at Duncansby Head.

a severed hand. A squabble was going on over a plot of land, and the agreement was that whoever touched it first should claim it; when the clansman saw that his rivals were ahead of him, he cut off his own hand and cast it ahead of him, and them, onto the land in question. Dornoch was also the site of the last witch execution in Britain; an unfortunate woman named Janet Horne was burned in 1722 for, among other things, turning her daughter into a pony. More peaceful is **Dornoch Castle**, a 16th-century bishop's palace, where you can take tea in the gardens of a cozy hotel.

Knowing about the Clearances, it may not be very p.c. to sympathize with one of the aristocratic families that brought them about, but **Dunrobin Castle**, ancestral home of the Dukes of Sutherland, is eminently worth a visit. Built in three stages, it was shaped into its present form in the 19th century, though the core dates from the 17th century and a part of it goes all the way back to the 13th – a combination which, as one might expect, has left a legacy of ghosts and unexplained bumps in the night. The castle was built to be approached from the water; a visitor would thus see the full expanse of its facade before passing through the lovely formal gardens, and possibly stopping off to admire the stuffed tigers' heads and weapons among the trophies in the hunting lodge. Garibaldi was a friend of one of the Dukes, and received the loan of his yacht for his Italian campaign; he wrote him every day as he sailed about Italy.

No one who's lived in the castle has ever wanted to give it up; the second wife of a late Duke, barred by his heirs from continuing her residence, promptly built nearby **Carbisdale Castle**, known to some locals as "Spite Castle," today (she would be horrified to know) a very posh youth hostel.

Brora is famous for its wool; Hunter's Woollen Mill is one of the best outlets for

tweeds and knits in the country. North of Brora, a stone by the road commemorates the death of Sutherland's last wolf. A closer look at the history of the area is presented in **Helmsdale**, where local residents, seeking new ways to bring in business, have erected a small but appealing **Heritage Center;** it may not be as popular an attraction as the discovery of gold which sparked a small gold rush here in the 1860s, but it does its bit. This town is also one of the few places where, on a clear day, you can spot an offshore oil rig; most of these lie far out of sight of land. This whole coastline was graphically depicted in the novels of Neil Gunn, who was born in nearby **Dunbeath**.

Caithness: Stone Diaries

Caithness, the northwestern tip of Scotland, is a rocky place. It's not just that its coastal cliffs rise mightily out of the Pentland Firth (once the Pictland Firth), splintering off into towering sea stacks and outcroppings. And it's not just that this area is one of the richest in prehistoric stones in Scotland. It's also that stone was long a cornerstone of the local economy. In the 19th century, Caithness flagstone was shipped throughout the world: after the industry's launch in 1824, Caithness flags were used in pavements from Canada to Calcutta.

First sight of Caithness's stones is the **Hill o'Many Stanes** near Mid Clyth, a Bronze-Age arrangement of more than 200 stones arranged in 22 fanning rows, their purpose a mystery. Hard by, the **Grey Cairns of Camster** rank with Clava Cairns as some of the best on the British mainland; dating from the Stone and Bronze Ages, they include a famous long, "horned" cairn.

Near the once-prosperous harbor of **Wick** are more stones: the twin ruins of **Castle Sinclair** and **Castle Girnigoe** thrust up from the shore as if echoing the forms of natural sea stacks elsewhere along the coast, such as the three at **Duncansby Head**.

The North Coast

John o'Groats, famous as the northernmost point on mainland Britain, is not, in fact, the northernmost point on mainland Britain. Its curious name derives from Jan de Groot, a Dutchman who settled here during the reign of James IV and, some say, operated a ferry service up to Orkney (a passenger ferry still runs from here); perhaps a more noteworthy local daughter today is the Queen Mother, sometime resident of the **Castle of Mey**. Then comes the actual northernmost point, **Dunnet Head**. This may be identical with the Cape Oras which Greek chronicler Diodorus Sicilus mentioned in 50 B.C., making it the first place in Scotland to be mentioned by a writer.

Like many Highland regional centers, **Thurso** is a hub for the area by virtue of being the only sizable town around, rather than for its own charms, though it's attractive enough, with a restored fishermen's quarter called Fisherbiggins. It also hosts surfing championships; this coast enjoys some of the best waves outside of Hawaii. The actual harbor is **Scrabster**, a little distance away, from which ferries depart for Orkney; the name of this northernmost harbor on the British mainland derives from the Norse *Skarabolstadr*, "standing on the edge."

From Thurso, the road along the north coast is a lesson in Highlands driving, a one-lane ribbon of concrete through bare and beautiful country. The muted hues of its landscape, punctuated with an occasional crofter's cottage, are brought into sharper relief by an active sky which sheds now sun through the clouds, now iron-gray rain. One sharp contrast to the natural beauty is the nuclear power plant at **Dounreay**, a local employment center until fairly recently. But the overwhelming majority of high points in this region are literally high places: Munros and

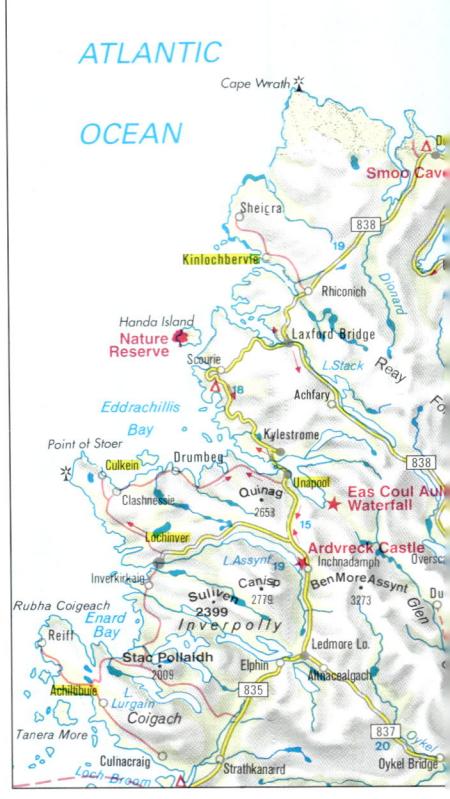

other mountains, enticing hill-walkers and photographers. Even some of their names are inspiring: **Ben Loyal** and **Ben Hope** are two of the most majestic, although their names in fact derive not from virtues but from *Ben Laoghal* and the Norse word *hop*, meaning bay. The former is a stunning backdrop to the village of **Tongue**, a commanding presence behind the Kyle of Tongue's metallic, reflecting waters; the latter stands behind beautiful **Loch Eriboll**, the north coast's deepest natural anchorage, and a shelter to Allied convoys in World War II. When a German submarine fleet surrendered here at the end of that war, it fulfilled the Brahan Seer's prophecy that a war would end at Eriboll.

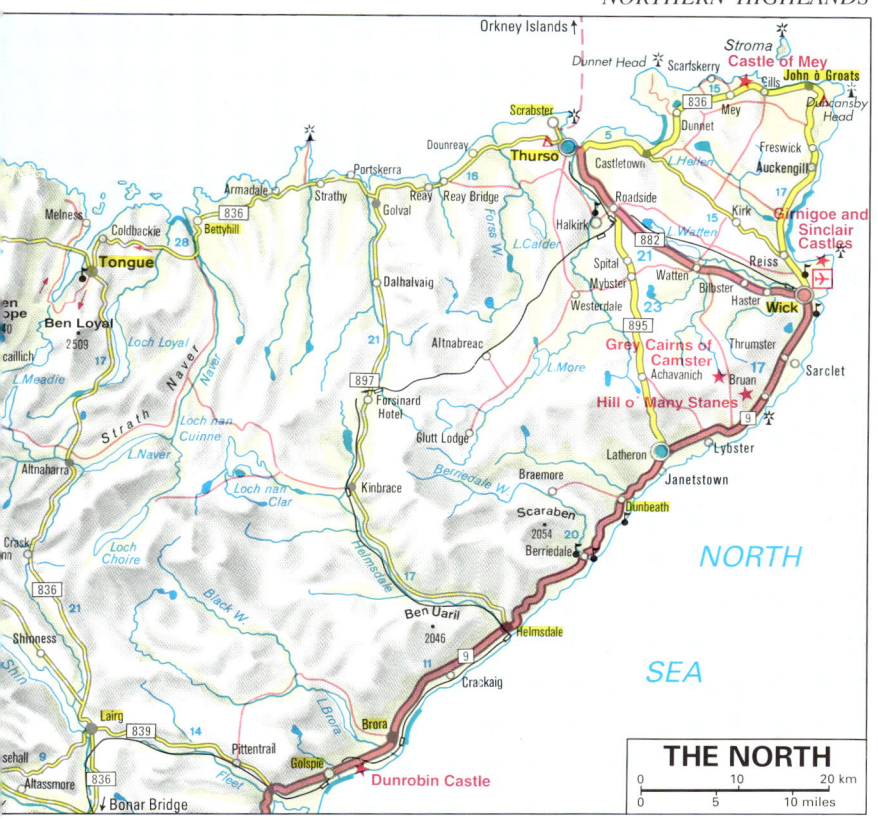

At **Durness**, with the wind whipping off the sea, white sand beaches worthy of the Caribbean, in ambience if not in temperature, pose coyly between dark rocks. Below the cliffs is **Smoo Cave**, a huge three-chambered cavern; above them is the new, small, and very popular Durness Golf Course. From here, a minibus and ferry bring you the 12 or so miles to **Cape Wrath**. Angry as the sea can get along here, especially in winter – something attested to by the sea stacks of eroded cliff – the cape's name actually derives from the Norse word *hvarf*, point of turning, which the cape has been for generations of coastal sailors. Today, it's a home to birds, who nest on the cliffs of **Clo Mor**, the highest in Great Britain.

For the Birds

Mermaids are supposed to dwell in the waters all along the northwestern coast of Sutherland. However, you'll probably have more success if you're looking out for birds. This area so poor in human life is rich in avian fauna. One of Britain's few puffin colonies has taken up residence not far from the magnificent beach at Sandwood Bay, which is quite a long walk from the road, but well worth it. Boat cruises bear the two-footed over the water to the bird sanctuary of **Handa Island**.

Other natural attractions are more fixed: the large stack of the Old Man of Stoer (not to be confused with Skye's

157

Ferry Pool

Old Man of Storr) at the end of a hairy single-track road out to Culkein, or **Eas Coul Aulan**, supposedly the highest waterfall in Britain, which you can visit on boats departing from **Unapool** (also known as Kylesku).

By **Lochinver**, near beautiful **Loch Assynt**, two mountains of character dominate the countryside: the gray sugarloaf of **Suilven**, and the distinctive spiky crown of **Stac Polly** (originally Pollaidh). You'll pass both on the "mad road" from Lochinver to **Achiltibue**, presumably thus designated because of its extreme narrowness and steep gradients, which passes through a vivid range of stunning countryside, from woods to marshes to beautiful seaside, on its winding way. Achiltibue itself boasts the bizarre **Hydroponicum**, a greenhouse, called the "Garden of the Future," where plants grow without soil.

Above and right: Tropical colors in a cold climate: the inlet by Smoo Cave, Durness, and rhododendrons in Inverewe Gardens.

The true town center along this coast is **Ullapool**, which began rather unceremoniously as a fishing station founded in 1788 to provide locals with employment; Thomas Telford stepped in to take over the urban planning in 1790. Today, the boat traffic from here includes ferries to the Outer Hebrides, and the place is filled with vacationers and crafts shops. Further on, pedestrian footbridges girdle the deep gash of **Corrieshalloch Gorge**, where plunge the **Falls of Measach**.

Not all local authorities were as insensitive to the plight of the poor as the Clearances might indicate. For all its bleakness of name, "Destitution Road," as the A832 is called between Corrieshalloch and Poolewe, was built as a way to create employment during the potato famine in 1851, and indeed occupied more than 1,000 people. Along it, you can see nine Munros, notably the beloved **An Teallach**, to the south. Once the road

reaches the seaside, you're rewarded with some great beaches: turn off at **Laide** to find the white sands of **Mellon Udrigle**, facing a panorama of mountain silhouettes across the water. On the way you pass Loch na Beiste, where a dread loch monster dwelt until the 19th century, when the local laird called in some sailors to pour lime into the mouth of its supposed cave (none of the locals would go near the place to do the job). An older relic at Laide are the remains of a chapel built around the time of St. Columba, in the 6th century.

Poolewe's beaches aren't its only attraction: there are also the grounds of **Inverewe Gardens**, incongruously lush in this northern climate. Landowner Osgood Mackenzie determined that he would transform the wild land spit of his property into a garden, aided by the passing Gulf Stream, and set about draining bogs, planting pine windbreaks, leveling and cultivating the land. The National Trust now tends the beautiful gardens that attest to his success.

Past **Gairloch**, another pleasant town with a heritage center to orient visitors, is **Loch Maree**, one of the loveliest lochs in Scotland. Certainly it was beautiful enough to attract Queen Victoria; on its southern shore, Victoria Falls commemorate her visit. The "Maree" comes from St. Maelrubha, a 7th-century Celtic missionary who built a chapel on an isle here as well as a monastery on the coast at Applecross. The pine forests here are part of **Beinn Eighe Nature Reserve**: a now-rare example of the kind of pine woods that used to be common in Scotland. At **Torridon**, displays in the Countryside Center shed light on the natural riches both of the nature reserve and of the Torridon Estate.

Turn off to **Shieldaig** and you descend a steep hill to a neat row of stone houses lined up along the water like eager schoolchildren to face Shieldaig Island. Shieldaig derives from the Viking *sil-vik*, herring bay; on the island, not fish but trees are cultivated, one of several efforts to recreate the area's original forestation.

SKYE

Skye is perhaps the most beautiful of all of Scotland's islands. Lounging in the blue waters near the mainland of the west coast, it raises tawny flanks to breathless, rocky heights: a chunk of the Highlands set adrift in the ocean. Its crowning mountain range, the Cuillins (or Coolins), are among the highest – and most dangerous – peaks in Britain; most of the country's serious mountain climbers train here preparatory to scaling Everest or similar heights. "The islands afford few pleasures, except to the hardy sportsman, who can tread the moor and climb the mountain," noted Dr. Johnson. Today, the less athletic can take in the panoramas from laybys on the single-track roads.

Skye is also bound up with the romance of Scotland's past. "Carry the lad who's born to be king / Over the sea to Skye" runs the "Skye Boat Song." The "lad" in question was Bonnie Prince Charlie, escaping to safety (diguised as a woman) after the debacle on Culloden Moor had ended his dreams of reclaiming the throne of Scotland. Assisting him in his flight was local girl Flora MacDonald, who was later arrested for her complicity and imprisoned for a period in London; her bravery and loyalty have been magnified through the lens of history to make her as popular a figure as Charlie himself. Other Skye hosts to the Young Pretender were the MacKinnon family, to whom he entrusted the recipe for Drambuie (see p. 226).

And yet, "It may be almost as disappointing to see Skye as to meet in later life the girl you wanted to marry when you were eighteen," writer H.V. Morton observed in the 1920s. Too true. There's no question that Skye is one of the most stunning places in Scotland. But the wave of visitors has clearly left its mark in restaurants, hotels, and shops scattered like

Above: Life reduced to its elements: a Skye-scape in red, white, blue, and green. Right: Music-making at a ceilidh.

sores in the valleys. With the advent of the Skye Bridge from Kyle of Lochalsh in 1995, furthermore, Skye became effectively a peninsula: gone is the lyrical romance of the trip "over the sea to Skye," replaced by the prose of traversing a concrete arch over the blue water. One thing the bridge has definitely destroyed is the little island of Eilean Ban, upon which it rests; now that the bridge is completed, the government is trying to sell the island, but the attractions of its little house and lighthouse are considerably less with the presence of a four-lane concrete behemoth in the back yard. High bridge tolls are another cause of local controversy.

The advent of the bridge has ushered in quieter times for the town of **Kyleakin**, formerly the main ferry port. It's the main town in the gentler, southern part of the island, the Sleat peninsula, also called the "garden of Skye;" **Armadale Gardens** surround the **Clan Donald center** .. Nearby, the renowned cookbook author-Claire MacDonald of MacDonald oper-

ates her well-known restaurant and hotel.

More stunning is the scenery on the side road to Elgol; **Torrin**, on this road, is where Skye marble is quarried. At the end of the road, a breathtakingly steep descent deposits you by a shingle which commands perhaps the most stunning view of the Cuillins, sultry and jagged across the water of Loch Scavaig.

Exploration along the shoreline here reveals honeycomb cliffs and a larger opening known as **Bonnie Prince Charlie's Cave**, where the MacKinnons feted the Prince before his return to the mainland. The same family later entertained Dr. Johnson and Boswell on their Hebridean tour; the traveling pair also met Flora MacDonald, personal highlights unfortunately not available to the legion modern tourists anxious to follow in Prince Charlie's footsteps. Perturbed at the slowness of their progress, Boswell commented that "the computation of Skye has no connection whatever with real distance."

The main A850 leads you past the **Cuillins**, as well; those nearer the road here are the Red Cuillins, which are gentler than the Black Cuillins you see from Elgol. Red or black, they frame the road with a hypnotic, other-worldly beauty. One of the nearest heights to the road, by Sconser, is **Glamaig**, which people not only walk up, but run up in a Hill Race every July.

By proceeding due west from the head of Loch Sligachan you come to the road to **Glenbrittle**, which hikers use as a base for Cuillin walks; a fork will bring you to Skye's only distillery, **Tallisker**. From **Sconser** itself, ferries depart for another beautiful, and much less visited, island, **Raasay**, which lies curled in Skye's protective shelter.

Main town on Skye is **Portree**, named "King's Port" (*righ*, pronounced "ree," is Gaelic for king) in honor of a long-past

Above and right: Both sides now: the opulence of Dunvegan Castle, and a woman spinning at the Skye Croft Museum.

visit from James V. Experienced in catering to visitors, Portee has everything one could wish for in a holiday center: parking, shops filled with local crafts and outdoor gear, restaurants, beautiful views of its sheltered harbor, and roads out.

Dunvegan and northern Skye

From here, the lobster-shaped island spreads out into the claws of its two northern peninsulas. At the neck of the western one is the modest village of **Dunvegan**; highlight here is the **castle**, with elements from every architectural style through the ages, since it was begun in 1200. This is the seat of Clan MacLeod, and a doughty seat it is, for all of the ameliorating ornamentation added by its colorful gardens. It sits perched by the water – seal tours depart from its dock – guarding family heirlooms such as the ancient **Fairy Flag**, which can protect the clan when it is unfurled, but preserves its efficacy for three uses

only (and two of these have already been used up).

Trotternish, the northeastern peninsula, is veritably a claw of volcanic rock, clutching at water and sky with abrupt formations of gray stone. Along its coast, the carved cross of **Flora MacDonald's grave** stands in Kilmuir Cemetery; an old crofter's home has been converted into the **Skye Museum of Island Life**; and **Duntulm Castle**, home of the MacDonalds, Lords of the Isles, guards the island's northern tip.

Even more impressive is the central part of Trotternish's long rock ridge. The rock here is in fact in an ongoing process of slippage, and the imperceptible movement has caused a riot of bizarre rock formations, stacks, and needles emerging from the greensward in an area called the **Quiraing**. After these formations, which comprise some of the most striking scenery on Skye, the seaside cliff of **Kilt Rock** (so called because its red-orange striated cliffs supposedly resemble the plaid of a tartan) or the

brooding form of the rocky stack dubbed **Old Man of Storr**, above the road, seem relatively pale by comparison.

Road from the Isles

In seasons when Skye is overcrowded, the mainland may offer consolations: **Kyle of Lochalsh** and, even more, **Plockton** are charming little villages (though Plockton has become over-popular after having served as setting for a television sitcom called *Hamish Mac-Beth*).

Another highlight, on a spit of land not far from Skye, is the forbidding-looking castle **Eilean Donan**. The current edifice was rebuilt in this century after a turbulent history beginning in 1220, when it was raised to withstand the Vikings; in the 18th century, it was even garrisoned by Spanish for a time. Today, it's more famous as a subject for photographers than for the displays which you can see inside.

THE GREAT GLEN AND INVERNESS
Accommodation
INVERNESS: *EXPENSIVE:* **Dunain Park Hotel**, Dunain Park, tel. (01463) 230512, fax 224532. Secluded country-house hotel with comfortable rooms and suites, famous for its restaurant with herbs and vegetables from its own walled garden. *MODERATE:* **Glenruidh House Hotel**, Old Edinburgh Road South, tel. (01463) 226499, fax 710745. Wonderful family-run country-house style hotel, set in greenery and with a very good Scottish-oriented dining room, but only a short distance from the town center. **Moyness House**, 6 Bruce Gardens, tel/fax (01463) 233836, excellent small central family-run hotel, in house once inhabited by author Neill Gunn. *BUDGET:* **Clach Mhuilinn**, 7 Harris Rd., tel. (01463) 237059. Quiet B&B. **Inverness Student Hostel**, Culduthel Road, tel. (01463) 236556. Private hostel, pleasant atmosphere.
INVERGARRY: *MODERATE:* **Glengarry Castle**, tel. (01809) 501254. Country house hotel near ruin of seat of Clan MacDonell.
FORT AUGUSTUS: *BUDGET:* **Fort Augustus Abbey**, tel. (01320) 366233, fax 366228. Hostel-type accommodation in clean double and single rooms in former abbey; meals available.

Restaurants
INVERNESS: *EXPENSIVE:* **Number One**, 1 Greig St., tel. (01463) 716363. Bistro with some of Inverness's best food.

Museums and Sights
FORT AUGUSTUS: Fort Augustus Abbey and **Heritage Center**, tel. (01320) 366233. Open daily 10 am-5 pm, summer 9 am-6 pm.
INVERNESS: The Eden Court Theater, Bishops Road, tel. (01463) 234234. Leading theater complex presenting music, drama and cinema. **Museum and Art Gallery**, Castle Wynd, Mon-Sat 9 am-5 pm, Jul-Aug also Sun 2-5 pm.

Sports and Activities
BOATING: **Jacobite Cruises** runs boats along Loch Ness, with docks at Inverness and Castle Urquhart. Tel. (01463) 233999. The luxury barge **M. V. Vertrouwen** operates week-long trips along the Caledonian Canal, with full fabulous meals and side trips. Contact Trevor Jones, The Coach House, North Trekeive, St. Cleer, Cornwall PL14 6SA.
WALKING: The trail from gorgeous **Glen Affric** to **Kintail** is 20 mi/32 km of difficult but beautiful walking; there are easier routes in Glen Affric itself.

EAST COAST
Accommodation
BEAULY: *MODERATE:* **The Lovat Arms**, tel. (01463) 782313. Tartan prevails in the individually decorated bedrooms, each representing a different local clan; warm, pleasant establishment.

DORNOCH: *MODERATE:* **Dornoch Castle**, Castle Street, tel. (01862) 810216, fax 810981, in a real old castle, but cozily attractive rather than chillingly elegant, and with the best restaurant in the area. *BUDGET:* **Khuzistan**, Mrs. B. Fraser, 9 Poles Road, tel. (01862) 810552, pleasant B&B.
BRORA: *MODERATE:* **The Links Hotel**, Golf Road, tel. (01408) 621225. Comfortable hotel overlooking golf course, with good restaurant.
CULRAIN: *BUDGET:* **Carbisdale Castle** is the most elegant youth hostel you're likely to find; it's an actual converted castle, complete with reception rooms and art works. Tel. (01549) 421232.

Museums and Sights
Groam House Museum, High St., Rosemarkie, Black Isle, tel. (01381) 620961, has relics of early Pictish settlement and film about the Brahan Seer. Open May-Sept Mon-Sat 10 am-5 pm, Sun 2-4:30 pm, Oct-Apr Sat & Sun 2-4 pm. **Black Isle Wildlife and Country Park**, Drumsmittel, tel. (01463) 731656, open March-Oct 10 am-6 pm. **Anta**, near Fearn, tel. (01862) 832477, cottage manufacturing of tartan ceramics and hand-woven rugs. **Glenmorangie Distillery**, Tain, tel. (01862) 892477, visitor center open Apr-Oct Mon-Fri 10 am-4 pm, 2 daily tours, Nov-Mar Mon-Fri 2-4 pm, 1 daily tour. **Dunrobin Castle**, near Golspie, tel. (01408) 633177, open May-mid Oct Mon-Sat 10:30 am-4:30 pm, Sun 1-4:30 pm, until 5:30 pm June-Sept, or by appointment. **Timespan Heritage Center**, Helmsdale, tel. (01431) 821327, open daily Easter-mid Oct 10 am-5 pm, Sun 2-5 pm. **Laidhay Croft Museum**, Dunbeath, tel. (01593) 731244, open Easter-Oct. **Caithness Glass Visitor Center**, Wick, tel. (01955) 602286.

Sports and Activities
GOLF: The **Royal Dornoch Golf Club** course is one of the best in the world. Tel (01862) 810219.
FISHING: **Caithness and Sutherland Angling Services**, Reay, tel/fax (01847) 811470. Fly fishing for trout, equipment hire, information.

Tourist Information
Sutherland: The Square, Dornoch, tel. (01862) 810400 (24 hours), fax 810644. **Caithness**: Information Center, Whitechapel Road, Wick, tel. (01955) 602596 (24 hours), fax 604940.

THE NORTH AND WEST COASTS
Accommodation
TONGUE: *MODERATE:* **Ben Loyal Hotel**, tel. (01847) 611216, fax 611212. In one of the emptier parts of the Highlands with stunning views of the Kyle of Tongue and photogenic Ben Loyal, a homey hotel with very good food.
KINLOCHBERVIE: *MODERATE:* **Kinlochbervie Hotel**, tel. (01971) 521275, fax 521438. Some expensive rooms, but a budget annex; all the

amenities, including a Taste of Scotland-recommended restaurant.

KYLESKU (UNAPOOL): *MODERATE*: **Kylesku Hotel**, tel. (01971) 502231, fax 502313. Low-key, *simpatico* little hotel on the loch shore, where the boat leaves for cruises down Lochs Glendhu and Glencoul; excellent but not expensive food in dining room or outside, with water views.

LOCHINVER: *EXPENSIVE:* **Inver Lodge**, tel. (01571) 844496, fax 844395. Abundant creature comforts, including fine food, in the "wilderness."

ULLAPOOL: *EXPENSIVE:* **Altnaharrie Hotel**, tel. (01854) 633230. One of the Highlands's finest, with (at one time) a Michelin star for fine cooking. Guests are met in hotel boat and brought over the bay from Ullapool. *MODERATE:* **The Ceilidh Place**, 14 West Argyll Street, tel. (01854) 612103. Great, casual atmosphere; restaurant/cafe is popular hangout for region. Also bunkhouse, £10 a night. *BUDGET:* **Tir Aluinn Hotel**, Leckmelm, nr Ullapool, tel. (01854) 612074. Country house *au naturel*. **The Shelling Guest House**, Garve Road, tel. (08154) 612947, modern, on the shore.

SHEILDAIG: *MODERATE:* **Tigh an Eilean Hotel**, tel. (01520) 755251, fax 755321. Warm, homey, newly-renovated hotel with loch views, cozy lounge, formal dining room, and pub.

Restaurants

LOCHINVER: *MODERATE:* **Lochinver Larder & Riverside Bistro**, Main Street, tel. (01571) 844356. Delicatessen with adjacent restaurant.

LAIDE: *MODERATE:* **Old Smiddy**, Laide, tel. (01445) 731425. Hot tip: this family business has mushroomed, and no wonder, with Kate Macdonald's wonderful cooking supported by a warm ambiance. Tea room for lunches and snacks; book ahead for dinner. Also two rooms for B&B.

Museums & Sights

BETTYHILL: Strathnaver Museum of the Highland Clearances, tel. (01641) 521418. Open Easter-Oct Mon-Sat 10 am-1 pm, 2-5 pm, Nov-Mar Mon, Wed, Fri 2-4 pm, Tu & Th also 10 am-1 pm.

DURNESS: Balnakeil Craft Village, 3/4 mi/1 km W of Durness. Former military base now housing a handful of craftsmen creating leatherwork, pottery, etc. Open daily (some shops close Sun) Easter-Oct. **ACHILTIBUE: Hydroponicum**, tel. (01854) 622202, "garden of the future." **ULLAPOOL: Ullapool Museum**, 7/8 W. Argyle St., tel/fax (01854) 612987, local history.

Sports and Activities

GOLF: The Kyle of Lochalsh's course, overlooking Skye, is one of the cheapest in Britain. *WALKING:* Guided walks by North West Frontiers, Strathkanaird, Ullapool, tel/fax (01854) 666229.

Tourist Information

The Highlands of Scotland Tourist Board, Tourist Information Center, Aviemore, tel. (0990) 143070, fax (01479) 811063.

SKYE
Transportation

As of 1996, you can drive to Skye over a new toll bridge; the bad news is the high toll: £4.30 in winter, £5.20 in summer. Caledonian McBrayne still operates ferry service from Mallaig to Armadale (30 min): passengers only in winter, vehicles in summer; tel. (01687) 462403, fax 462281 (Mallaig). Ferries from Sconser to the island of Raasay (15 min). Portree office: tel. (01478) 612075, fax 613090. Skye Car Rental, Broadford, tel. (01471) 822225.

Accommodation

MODERATE: **Flodigarry Country House Hotel**, Staffin, tel. (01470) 552203, fax 552301. Imposing castle-like hotel on the water by the Quiraing and adjacent to Flora MacDonald's cottage. **Rosedale Hotel**, Beaumont Crescent, Portree, tel. (01478) 613131, fax 612531, in former fisherman's house on the water. **Viewfield House Hotel**, Portree, tel. (01478) 612217, great old faded family house. *BUDGET:* **Quiraing Lodge**, Staffin, tel. Kate Money (01470) 562330, cozy coastal B&B with vegetarian cooking.

Restaurants

EXPENSIVE: **Three Chimneys**, Colbost, 7 km W of Dunvegan (turnoff to Glendale), tel. (01470) 511258. In an old stone house, with low ceiling beams, fireplaces, and wood panelling; local specialties, from salmon to red deer to Skye strawberries. Book ahead. **Kinloch Lodge**, Sleat, tel. (01471) 833214, fax 833277. Luxury hotel best known for its restaurant, run by cookbook author Claire Macdonald of Macdonald in the 17th-century family home.

Museums & Sights

Talisker Visitor Centre on the B8009, tel. (01478) 640314. Skye's only single malt distillery. Open year-round, but afternoons only off-season, and not always weekends. **Clan Donald Visitor Centre**, Armadale Castle, Sleat, tel. 844305. Headquarters of Macdonald clan. Open Apr-early Nov, 9:30 am-5:30 pm. **Dunvegan Castle**, tel. (01470) 521206, open daily March-Oct 10 am-5:30 pm. **Skye Museum of Island Life**, Kilmuir, open Mon-Sat 9:30 am-5:30 pm, old crofter's home.

Sports and Activities

RIDING: **Skye Riding Center**, 4 mi/7 km N of Portree, tel (01470) 532233 or 532439. *WALKING:* NTS Ranger Service & Guided Walks, Balmacara Estate, tel. (01599) 566325.

Tourist Information

Tourist Information Centre, Bank St., Portree, tel. (01478) 612137.

OUTER

HEBRIDES

St. Kilda

Scarp
Hushinish
Forest
of Harris
1887
Ardyourlie
Tolmachan
Ardhasig
Taransay
Luskentyre
HARRIS
Tarbert
Carnach
Borvemore
Manish
Northton
Leverburgh
Rodel

L.Langavat
859
21
Balallan
Gravir
Lemreway
Kebock
Head

Sound of Shiant
Shiant I.

THE LITTLE MINCH

RubhaHunish
Kilmaluag
Kilmuir
Uig
855

Pabbay
Berneray
Boreray
Newton
Vallay
Ard an
Runair
865
Sollas
Tighary L.Scadaway
Balranald
Nature Reserve
North Uist
867
Lochmaddy
Barpa Langais
Locheport
Eaval
Baleshare
Carnish
Aird
Ine
Ronay
Benbecula
Liniclate
Creagorry
Carnan Inn
Loch Druidibeg
Nature Reserve
Lochskipport
Hecla
1988
Howmore
South
Flora MacDonalds
Birthplace
Beinn Mhor
2034
865
Uist
Stuley
Daliburgh
Lochboisdale
Ludag
Pollachar
Eriskay
Saligarry
Barra Cille
Borve
Barra
Ersary
Castlebay
Kisimul Castle
Vatersay
Flodday
Muldoanich

Monach I.
Sound of Monach

Sound of Harris

Sound of Barra

Bagh nam Faoileann
Wiay

Waternish Point
Geary
Dunvegan
Head
Milovaig
Dunvegan
Castle
Edinbain
Dunvegan
Glendale
Roskhill
Loch
Snizort
Kensaleyre
Bernisdale
863
Bracadale
Coillore
Carbost
Drynoch
Fiskavaig
Carbost
Glenbrittle
850

SEA OF THE

HEBRIDES

INNER

HEBRIDES

Cuillin

Sound

Canna
690
Kinloch
Castle
Rhum
Askival
2663

Mull, Oban

THE OUTER HEBRIDES
The Long Islands

ST. KILDA

BARRA

SOUTH UIST, BENBECULA,

AND NORTH UIST

HARRIS AND LEWIS

Hebrides derives from the Norse word *havbredey*, which means "islands that border on the sea." The Outer Hebrides certainly do. Comprising more than 200 islands, they lie 40 miles (64.5 km) or so west of the Scottish mainland, curving northeastwards for some 130 miles (210 km) in a line that's led to their local nickname, "the long islands." Beginning with a sprinkling of little islands at the southernmost tip, the chain of islands, as it stretches northeast, bear colorful, evocative names: Barra, Eriskay, South Uist, Benbecula, North Uist, Harris and Lewis.

Place names here are almost all Norse in origin, for after the 9th century the Vikings held sway in the Outer Hebrides. Ultimately, they ceded them to Scotland, along with the other Western Isles, with the 1264 Treaty of Perth, signed after their resounding defeat at Largs.

The landscape is bare and windswept. The west coasts, exposed to the Atlantic and eroded by the harsh sea, can be strikingly beautiful. For all their similarities, each island has its own character: Lewis and Harris, for example – though they are technically one island – vary dramatically. Lewis consists mainly of flatlands, with rolling moors and an abundance of

Preceding pages: Between sea and sky: the windswept Outer Hebrides.

lochs; while North Harris boasts unadorned hills and rugged mountains which reach their highest point in the 2,662-foot-high (814 m) peak of An Clisham. Some of the islands have splendid, white sandy beaches, others nature reserves, including four National Nature Reserves. In addition, they're sprinkled with monuments dating back to the Stone Age.

A mere 29,500 people inhabit the Outer Hebrides; 80% of them live on the two largest, Lewis and Harris. Only a handful of the other islands – Baleshare, Barra, Benbecula, Berneray, Eriskay, Grimsay, North and South Uists, and Vatersay – are inhabited at all; the rest are devoid of human beings entirely.

Naturally, the inhabitants of the Outer Hebrides earn their living in part from fishing (for mussels and crabs, as well as for trout and salmon); but they also farm smallholdings, known as crofts, like their mainland counterparts. Many of them still speak Gaelic among themselves, kindly switching to English for tourists; the islands' remoteness has kept the language alive. Note that many signposts are in Gaelic only; visitors should take the precaution of obtaining a Gaelic-English map from local tourist offices.

Strikingly, the islands vary in their religious beliefs. South Uist and Barra are mainly Roman Catholic (demonstrated

169

with imposing statues of the Madonna on South Uist and on the highest point on Barra, **Heaval**); whereas the people of North Uist, Harris and Lewis are almost all members of the Free or the Free Presbyterian Church. They follow the Old Testament injunction that the Sabbath, Sunday, be kept holy; no one, therefore, journeys far or works save when absolutely necessary. Instead, they worship, singing psalms in Gaelic.

Take care, therefore, to fill up your gas tank on Saturdays, for on Sundays nearly all gas stations are closed. So are many public houses, hotel bars and restaurants, particularly on Harris and Lewis (though you might find a meal in a hotel). On Wednesday afternoon, too, many shops are closed and bus services curtailed.

ST. KILDA

Symbol of the isolation of the outer islands is the remote archipelago of **St.**

Above: Abandoned St.Kilda in a wreath of cloud.

Kilda, which lies 50 miles (80 km) west of Harris. In 1772, when Dr. Samuel Johnson – already temperate in his praises of Scotland – learned that Boswell was thinking of buying the island, his response was sardonic; "Pray do, Sir; we shall go and pass a winter amid the blasts there. We shall have fine fish, and we shall take some dried tongues with us,and some books. We will have a strong-built vessel, and some Orkney men to navigate her," and, Johnson added, a clergyman as well. Certainly inhabitants of the outer islands were faced with scant entertainment in the long winter months, and certainly they tended to be both pious people and skilled navigators. Ultimately, the pleasures envisioned by Dr. Johnson weren't enough for St. Kilda's inhabitants: in 1930, they asked the government to evacuate them, and were resettled on the mainland. Today, anyone who arranges a visit through the Tourist Information Center discovers an enthrallingly beautiful island, its cliffs rising grandly from the sea,

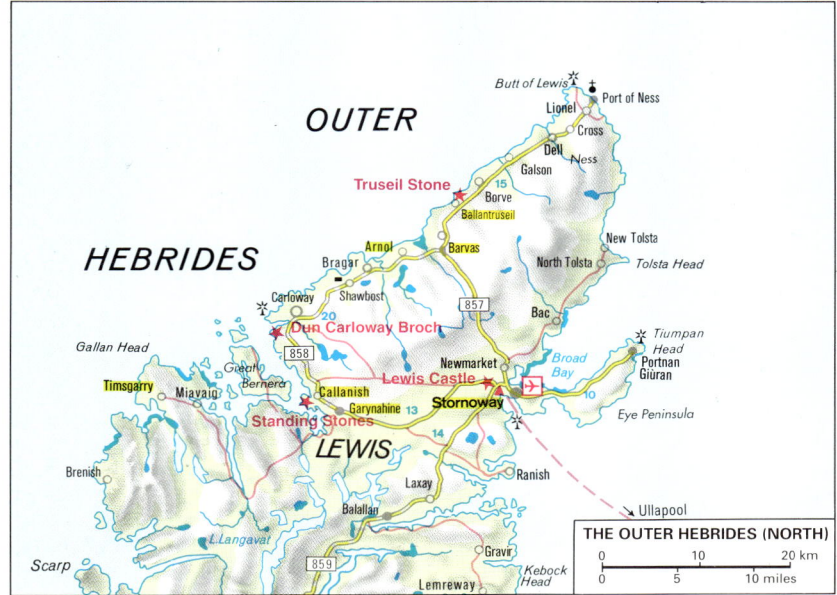

THE OUTER HEBRIDES (NORTH)

its abandoned village poignant. St. Kilda is also one of the prime centers for sea birds in Europe; its cliffs are alive with gannets, puffins, and fulmars.

BARRA

Barra (*Barriagh* in Gaelic) is the southernmost and scenically gentlest of the main islands. A causeway connects it to the little island of **Vatersay** (*Bhatarsaigh*), with its gentle beaches, just to the south. Here, you find a memorial to a ship which was swept onto the rocks and lost its company of islanders on their way to America during the Highland Clearances of the 19th century.

Only 1,300 people live on Barra; their crofts are scattered throughout the island. They're almost outnumbered by the plant life: some 1,000 different species of wildflower have been identified here. The island's four lochs abound with brown trout and sea trout. And even technology is subject to the forces of nature: Barra's airport is renowned for the fact that its

runway is flooded by the tide twice daily.

An ancient spot, Barra derives its name from an early 7th-century saint, Finbar (or St. Barr), whose name means "white head." Finbar came from Ireland to proselytize Scotland, and such was his sanctity that when he died, in 633 or thereabouts, the sun – legend has it – refused to set for two weeks.

Capital of Barra, and of local lobster-fishing, is **Castlebay**, whose name indicates that in the bay rises **Kisimul Castle**, built between the 12th and 17th centuries. Perched quaintly on a little island off the coast, it is still formidable even in its ruins, with narrow slits for windows and a forlorn keep built in 1120. Most of the rest dates from the 15th century and was once home to the chiefs of the MacNeil clan.

At its north end, at **Barra Cille**, Barra has no fewer than three 12th-century chapels. Here, the author Compton Mackenzie is buried under a plain rough-hewn cross. Mackenzie, born in England in 1883, lived on the island during World

War II. In 1947, his novel *Whisky Galore* (and a subsequent film based on it) brought new fame to a neighboring island, inhabited by a mere 200 islanders and a mere 3 miles by 1.5 miles (5 by 2.5 km) in size: **Eriskay** (*Eiriosgaigh*), northeast across the Sound of Barra. Mackenzie's yarn mirrors the real-life shipwrecking of the *Politician*, whose cargo, 24,000 cases of whisky, was gleefully rescued and imbibed by the islanders, deprived of whisky through wartime privations.

Until this glorious moment, Eriskay was most famous for **Prince's Strand** on its west coast, where the Young Pretender, Bonnie Prince Charlie, first arrived in Scotland on July 23, 1745.

SOUTH UIST, BENBECULA AND NORTH UIST

Fewer than 2 miles (3 km) to the north is the southern tip of the island of **South Uist** (*Uibhist a Deas*), home to just under 3,000 islanders. Some 22 miles (35 km) from north to south and no more than 7 miles (11 km) across, it is cooled by more than 190 fresh-water lochs. Here, in quiet **Milton**, the celebrated Flora MacDonald was born in 1722. Her island has superb beaches, as well as peat bogs and mountains, the two highest **Ben Mhor** (2,034 feet/622 m) and **Hecla** (1,988 feet/608 m). Delightful **Lochboisdale** is the village landing spot of ferries; nearby, on the south coast, is the **Pollachar standing stone**, planted around 3,000 years ago. South Uist is also noted for the **Loch Druidibeg Nature Reserve**, where corncrakes are among the protected birds and graylag geese breed in peace. And at **Tobha Mor** are ruined 13th-century chapels and the graveyard of the Clan Ranald chiefs. Another local Flora, Flora Johnstone, has earned renown for the pat-

Right: Dream beach on wild Harris (Sound of Taransay).

terns of seashells she's affixed to an abandoned school bus in her yard and, when she ran out of room there, on her house, as well (on the road to Eochar).

From South Uist, a causeway leads to **Benbecula** (*Beinn na Faoghia*). Lochs festoon its eastern side; most of the population of 1,800 is concentrated along the western coast, with its lovely beaches – the finest is **Culla Beach** – and **Borve Castle**, a magical 14th-century ruin, once the home of the MacDonald family, with walls 10 feet (3 m) thick.

After his defeat at Culloden, Charles Edward Stuart landed at Benbecula in May, 1746; hiding in a cave, he saw government troops patrolling the waters in search of him. Though no Jacobite, Flora MacDonald is supposed to have saved him by perilously bringing the Young Pretender (who was disguised as a serving-woman) in a rowboat from Rossinish, on the northwest corner of Benbecula, to Portree on the isle of Skye.

Nature-lovers will relish **Loch Bee**, home of countless mute swans, rivaling the Loch Druidibeg Nature Reserve.

The road over Benbecula continues on, by means of another causeway and bridge, to **North Uist** (*Uibhista Tuath*), which has a mere 1,800 inhabitants. This is another island sprinkled with estuaries and trout-filled lochs. Its sole, diminutive village, **Lochmaddy**, receives ferries on the eastern coast. But the island is exquisite. Its living attractions include the **Balranald Nature Reserve**, haunt of the red-necked phalarope. And relics of the past abound in the form of ancient sites: standing stones at **Blashaval**; the ruins of an old pottery manufacturer, dating back to the Stone Age, on the peaceful islet of **Eilean-an-Tighe**; **Barpa Langais** on the slope of Ben Langais, where you can see a Stone Age chambered cairn and, not far away, the standing stone circle of **Pobull Fhinn** (which means Fingal's People). And as far as purely natural attractions go, North Uist offers both hill country to

the east – its highest hill, **Eaval**, rises to 1,138 feet (348 m) – and, on the western coast, extensive beaches of white sand.

HARRIS AND LEWIS

Although they regard themselves as separate, the two main islands of the Outer Hebrides, **Harris** (in Gaelic *Na Hearadh*) and **Lewis** (*Leodhas*), are physically united, save in terms of their differing landscapes. **South Harris**, connected to North Harris by a narrow isthmus at **Tarbert**, and blessed with delightful beaches, retains the memory of Lord Leverhulme, an entrepreneur and soap-manufacturing king who bought Harris and Lewis in 1918. Determined to modernize fishing and farming techniques, he set out to build a fishing port at **Leverburgh** in 1923; but the town, at first successful, was abandoned upon his death in 1925. Earlier monuments from the past remain. In particular, at nearby **Rodel** do not miss the splendid 16th-century **church of St. Clement**. Inside, in

1532, Alastair Macleod, or Alastair Crotach (which, in Gaelic, denotes his crooked back), commissioned a magnificent sculpted tomb, in which his mortal remains were laid to rest 15 years later.

Many of the rugged hills of North Harris afford entrancing views of Skye. And inside the crofters' cottages, looms incessantly weave the prized Harris Tweed. By an Act of Parliament, only tweed handwoven by the islanders in their homes, finished on the islands, and of guaranteed quality gains the celebrated Orb trademark (see p. 227).

While only 2,500 people live on Harris, **Lewis**, some 30 miles long and 14 miles wide (48 by 22.5 km), has a population of more than 20,000. Its unofficial capital, **Stornoway**, is the only town of any size in the Outer Hebrides, though peopled by a mere 8,000 islanders. Even the Pakistani community here is fluent in Gaelic. The parish church of St. Columba dates from 1794. In Francis Street, a memorial marks the site of the house where the explorer Alexander MacKen-

Above: Peat-cutting for winter fuel on the Outer Hebrides.

zie was born around 1755. He became a fur-trader in Canada, and in 1789 discovered the Canadian river which is named after him. On the same street stands the Episcopalian chuch of **St. Peter**, in which are preserved an ancient sandstone font and the prayer book of explorer David Livingstone.

Stornoway's harbor is thronged with visitors hoping to see the seals (hence Stornoway's sobriquet *Portrona*, port of seals), who usually obligingly appear. Overlooking the harbor is the 19th-century **Lews Castle**, where Lord Leverhulme lived for a time during his Hebridean experiment. East of Stornoway, on the arm of the Eye Peninsula, the ruined 14th-century **Ui Church** contains some notable carved tombstones.

If it's stones you want, the **standing stones** at **Callanish** are some of the most remarkable prehistoric remains you'll find. Seeming at first to be planted in a random thicket, these ancient megaliths prove, on closer inspection, to be arranged in a circle around a central, taller stone, and in rows radiating out from this nucleus. There are other stone circles in the immediate area, as well as a chambered cairn, almost certainly a later insertion. Not far away, the 2,000-year-old circular drystone fortified tower of **Dun Carloway** is a hilltop Iron Age broch some 30 feet (9 m) high. A road bridge leads from Lewis to the peaceful island **Great Bernera**, whose waters are a breeding ground of lobsters.

Farther up this western coast of Lewis is the town of Barvas, dominated by 908-foot (278 m) Ben Barvas. Early man was here, as well. The towering **Truseil Stone** (pronounced Thrushel), a prehistoric monolith, rises at **Ballantruseil**, north of Barvas; further north is the stone circle and burial cairn at **Steinacleit**. The island culminates in natural stone: if you travel a few miles further north to Swainbost, your reward is a stunning view of the rocky pinnacles and cliffs close by the **Butt of Lewis**.

THE OUTER HEBRIDES
Transportation

BY PLANE: **British Airways Express** flies from Glasgow and Inverness to Stornoway, Benbecula and Barra most weekdays; there are also inter-island flights (tel. 0181/8974000 or 0345/222111).

BY BOAT: **Caledonian MacBrayne** runs ferries from the mainland and the Isle of Skye to ports at Barra, North and South Uist, Harris and Lewis (some service seasonal); tel. (01475) 650000 (head office) or (01851) 702361 (Stornoway). The trip from Ullapool to Stornoway takes about 3.5 hours. Caledonian MacBrayne also runs ferries between the islands, and there are smaller, private ferries, as well: a passenger ferry from South Uist to Barra and Eriskay (**Eriskay Enterprises**, tel. 01878/720233) and car ferries from South Uist to Eriskay (tel. 01878/720261), Berneray to North Uist (**Sound of Harris Ferry Service**, tel. 01876/540230), and Scalpay to Harris (tel. 01859/540266).

Accommodation

HARRIS: *MODERATE:* **Ardvourlie Castle Guest House**, Aird A Mhulaidh, tel. (01859) 502307, actually a Victorian hunting lodge in the middle of open county; Taste of Scotland dining. **St. Kilda Guest House**, Leverburgh, tel. (01859) 520419: little house with big ocean view and home cooking. **Allan Cottage Guest House**, Tarbert, tel. (01859) 502146, cottage-style, near ferry terminal, personal accommodation, good dinners.

LEWIS: *MODERATE:* **Baile Na Cille Guest House**, Timsgarry, Uig, tel. (01851) 672242, fax 672241. Remote, surrounded by open country and sea, homey and friendly. **Park Guest House**, 30 James St., Stornoway, tel. (01851) 702485; Victorian house in the middle of town, with good food. *BUDGET:* **Stornoway Backpackers Hostel**, 47 Keith St., Stornoway, tel. (01851) 703628. Central and practical.

BENBECULA: *MODERATE:* **Dark Island Hotel**, Liniclate, tel. (01870) 603030, fax 602347; large, rambling hotel, Taste of Scotland.

BARRA: *MODERATE:* **Castlebay Hotel**, Castlebay, tel. (01871) 810223; overlooks town, friendly owners and nice restaurant. **Isle of Barra Hotel**, Tangasdale Beach, tel. (01871) 810383, fax 810385, friendly, on the beach.

NORTH UIST: *MODERATE:* **Lochmaddy Hotel**, tel. (01876) 500331, fax 500210. Newly renovated traditional hotel, on water, near ferry.

Restaurants

LEWIS: Tigh Mealros, Garynahine, by Callanish, tel. (08151) 621333. Unpretentious, warm and cozy; family-run, featuring local specialties, seafood. **Copper Kettle Tearoom**, 5a Dalbeg, tel. (01851) 710592.

HARRIS: First Fruits, Pier Road Cottage, Tarbert, tel. (01859) 502369; cottage tea room.

ERISKAY: Am Politician, 3 Baile, Eriskay, tel. (01878) 720246. Eriskay's only bar, named for the wreck immortalized in Whisky Galore.

Museums & Sights

LEWIS: Calanais Standing Stones Visitor Center, tel. (01851) 621422, open Apr-Sept Mon-Sat 10 am-7 pm, rest of year til 4 pm. **Western Isles Museum**, Francis St, Stornoway, tel. (01851) 70772, open in season Mon-Sat 10 am-1 pm, 2-5 pm; archaeology, social history, and the history of the Western Isles. **Bernera Museum**, Bernera, Uig, tel. (01851) 612275, open in summer. **Gearranan "Black House" Village,** no. 3, Garenin, tel. (01851) 710652, ongoing restoration of village. **Lewis Loom Center**, Point St., Stornoway, tel. (01851) 703117, Harris tweed: guided tours and shop.

SOUTH UIST: Kildonan Museum, Kildonan, tel. (01878) 710343, open in summer.

BARRA: Barra Heritage Center (opened 1996, information not yet available). **Kisimul Castle**, Castlebay, tel. (01871) 810336: boat runs out to the family home of Clan Macneil; call for times.

ST. KILDA: Ask at the tourist information center for details on organized tours.

Sports & Activities

FISHING: Stornoway Angling Association, Stile Park, Willowglen, Stornoway, tel. (01851) 703248, offers brown trout fishing. For sea angling, contact the Sea Angling Club on South Beach St., Stornoway, Lewis, tel. (01851) 702021. On Harris, Finsbay Fishings (tel. 01859/530318) offers a range of fishing, plus self-catering cottages.

GOLF: Lewis's golf club is at Willowglen Road, tel. (01851) 702240. Harris has a nine-hole course at Scarista, tel. (01859) 520214. Eriskay also boasts a six-hole course.

WALKING: A new network of ten walking trails are currently being laid out on the islands. For guided walks, as well as climbing and all manner of water sports, contact the Uist Outdoor Center, Lochmaddy, tel. (01876) 500480.

Festivals

There are **mods** (Gaelic festivals) on Harris, Lewis, and South Uist, generally in the month of June. In addition, July and August see **Blasad den Iar** ("a taste of the West") evenings, devoted to Gaelic culture and music on North and South Uist, Harris, and Barra. Contact the tourist office for details.

Tourist Information

Western Isles Tourist Board, 26 Cromwell St., Stornoway, Isle of Lewis, tel. (01851) 703088. **South Uist Tourist Office**, Pier Road, Lochboisdale, tel. (01878) 700286, open Easter-Oct.

ORKNEY AND SHETLAND
Northern Highlights

ORKNEY MAINLAND
HOY / SCAPA FLOW
OTHER ISLANDS
SHETLAND

First of all, get it right. It's not *the Orkneys*, never has been, never will be. The 70-odd islands of the archipelago six miles north of Scotland are collectively known as "Orkney." The "ey" says it all: the suffix comes from the Old Norse word for "islands." To confirm their status as single places, both Orkney and Shetland have a mainland and a number of islands. If an Orcadian says "Mainland," he's referring to the largest island in Orkney; the main body of Scotland is termed "Scotland" or "the South."

Orkney and Shetland have reason to think of themselves as a world apart; they didn't become Scottish until the relatively recent date of 1472. And they didn't join the country as conquests of war, either, but rather because Christian I of Norway couldn't afford a complete dowry when his daughter Margaret married the extremely young James III. The Earldom of Orkney and the Lordship of Shetland were offered as collateral until the dowry was paid in full; but the money couldn't be found, and the islands were therefore annexed to the Scottish crown.

For a group of islands buffeted by the Atlantic, lit by the Northern Lights, and

Preceding pages: The cliffs of Yesnaby, Orkney. Left: "God's clowns": puffins are one ethnic group in Orkney's diverse sea bird population.

with a history reaching back into the Stone Age and associated with the Vikings, Orkney is surprisingly tame in aspect. The bulk of Mainland is gently rolling farmland, broad fields sloping around sky-colored lochs, rising to a maximum elevation of a friendly 876 feet (268 m). None of your Highland peaks here. What places the seal of "wildness" on this area are the standing stones, sloping mounds of cairns, or ruins of stone brochs set like brooches in the landscape, pinning the country to a history before the dawn of history, almost beyond imagination.

And at the fringes of the springy green meadows, at a place like **Yesnaby** on Mainland's Atlantic coast, the pastureland abruptly drops in sheer cliffs to the thrashing surf below. Thrust out from the cliffs are the fingers of "stack" formations or natural bridges carved by the pounding water. Orkney's signature stack, the **Old Man of Hoy**, is the highest in Britain; on **Stronsay**, the stack formations are topped with hermitages where men lived alone for years in proximity to the elements and their God. Living on the cliffs today are huge flocks of sea birds: thousands upon thousands of gulls and gannets, skuas, shags and puffins cling to the face of the rock or rise to whirl like clouds of snowflakes over the foam. This is Orkney at its wildest.

179

ORKNEY MAINLAND

Islands, even pastoral, have something elemental about them. Orkney is a place of earth and water and stone. Five thousand years ago, men and women piled up the stone and covered it with earth to create dwellings, connected by narrow subterranean passages. They lived here for hundreds of years before the elements rose against them and a sandstorm, Pompei-like, blanketed all traces of their town. Millennia later, another storm came and uncovered part of the Stone Age settlement of **Skara Brae**. A century of subsequent excavation has brought to light ten dwellings, some still fitted out with storage shelves and closets, grinding stones, fireplaces, and beds. Mushroom-like, as if grown from the earth, the low rounded dwellings seem almost like cartoon homes, Fred Flintstone's Bedrock

Above: Daily life in the Stone Age: a house at Skara Brae. Right: "Circle of the Sun": the enigmatic Ring of Brodgar.

come to life, under the legs of curious full-sized 20th-century visitors. Only off season, or on a gray day when you're alone with Skara Brae and the sea, can you start to invoke the ancient past.

Burial mounds are easier to comprehend: houses of the dead, built to last, used for generations. **Maes Howe**, 3000 BC, is one of the most spectacular prehistoric cairns in Europe. Its evenly layered stones form, within, a high chamber; from without, a gently mounded barrow. The doorstone that sealed its narrow passage can only be closed from inside: evidence that the living had something to do with it. Also pointing to ceremonial intent is the fact that the entrance corridor lines up with the midwinter sun; if the sun penetrates through the clouds on the winter solstice, a ray of its light shines straight in and illuminates the entire chamber. Maes Howe contained many generations of prehistoric bones before the Vikings descended through its roof, and used it for shelter. To pass the time, they overlaid the rudimentary Stone Age

carvings with Viking runes, Norse graffiti. "I carved this up high," "Ingebjorg is the most beautiful woman there is," an elaborate doodle of a dragon. Some of the runes speak of treasure, but as Stone Age man had nothing the Vikings would have recognized as treasure, one can only surmise that earlier Vikings had also used this as a place of burial.

More ambiguous is the purpose of the prehistoric standing stones. Those at **Stenness** guard the road, or shelter sheep during rainstorms; for rain is frequent on Orkney, where the locals say you can experience all four seasons in a single day. Despite this, the name of the **Ring of Brodgar** means "Circle of the Sun." Not quite half of this perfect ring of standings stones are still *in situ*. The menhirs here are flat, hard-edged, geometric: modern art, when compared to the softer forms of Stonehenge or Brittany.

At the very tip of **South Ronaldsay**, connected to Mainland by a series of causeways, the **Tomb of the Eagles** stands near the edge of a sea cliff. There are still a few sea eagles riding the ocean winds here; talons and remains found in this grave gave the site its name. The farmer who owns the land discovered the first artifacts here one day when he was digging; complete excavations in 1976 unearthed bones, simple stone tools, pottery shards. Nearby, a Bronze Age house is fitted out with a flagstone floor, a stream diverted into the house for "running water," a central hearth, and beds so short it's generally concurred that these people slept curled or sitting up.

Norse by Northwest

Later, the Vikings came. The *Orkneyinga Saga* recounts the feudings of 11th- and 12th-century Viking lords. It mentions **Orphir**, where are the remains of the only extant medieval round church in Scotland, built in the 12th century, next to the foundations of a Viking drinking hall. There are more foundations on the tidal islet **Brough of Bursay**, linked by a sand bar to Mainland's northern tip. The

green velvet of its flat sloping top sports the shapes of Viking longhouses like enigmatic runes, patterns without an immediately evident meaning. Gray among them are the foundations of the 11th-century **St. Magnus Church**, where the body of St. Magnus, the island's patron, supposedly lay after his murder in 1116. The Vikings also lived in the **Broch of Gurness**, the best-preserved of Orkney's brochs, heart of a settlement that continued into the 1st century A.D.

One of the most spectacular Viking finds was made by the sea. On the island of **Sanday** in 1991, the waves uncovered a boat tomb with three bodies and lavish funerary objects. The whalebone plaque curling up into twin dragon heads, which lay at the feet of the woman, has already become an Orkney hallmark; it, and other relics of the tomb, are now in Kirkwall's **Tankerness House Museum**. The sea has since finished its job, washing away

Above: Old tombstones line the walls of St. Magnus Cathedral (Kirkwall).

every trace of the land where the boat was originally buried.

Church Bay

All things on Orkney – roads, ferries, Viking treasure – eventually lead to **Kirkwall**. Mentioned in the *Orkneyinga Saga* by its name, which means "church bay," the town is dominated by the great soft weathered **St. Magnus's Cathedral**. Red and white stone gently melt into one another as if they'd grown together: there's none of the geometric precision of Siena in these organic arches. Inside, the walls are lined with old 16th- and 17th-century tombstones, on which skulls and angels commemorate the dear departed. Like sentries, the relics of Saints Magnus and Rognvald are walled into the pillars at either side of the altar. The building's age – it was founded in 1137, completed in the 15th century – is most evident in the animal heads supporting the arches of the vaulting, which could almost be the figureheads of Viking ships.

There's more old stone in the ruins of two castles across the street: the 12th-century **Bishop's Palace**, with its 16th-century round tower, and the Renaissance **palace** of Earl Patrick Stewart. Few rulers have been so bitterly hated; the Earl's beautiful palace, built with forced labor, was a kind of symbol of its patron's cruelty. When Stewart was finally arrested and condemned to death for revolt against the government (his lands had been confiscated because of his debts), execution was postponed for a week so that he would have some chance to "better himself" before his demise.

Today, Kirkwall's past lives on in extant traditions, from the **Orkney Library**, Scotland's oldest public library (1683) to the **Highland Park distillery**, the northernmost malt whisky distillery in Scotland (and one of the best). Another old tradition, revived every Christmas and New Year's Day, is the **Ba'**, a game

that involves all of Kirkwall's men. The principle is that of soccer: two teams, the Uppies and the Doonies, vie to get the eponymous ball to their respective goals, the waters of the harbor or a town square. The ball may be propelled by any means you can get away with: feet, hands, head, even smuggled under one's shirt.

A highbrow pendant to this riotous mass spectacle is June's **Saint Magnus Festival**, brainchild of composer Sir Peter Maxwell Davis, whose residence of choice is a house on Hoy. One of the most acclaimed composers working today, Davis writes a kind of heathery Orkneyan music, both in his symphonies (the 6th premiered in 1996) and his many operas.

Backbone of Mainland's other main town, **Stromness**, is its port; and indeed, the town is shaped not unlike a backbone, consisting mainly of a single curving street following the line of the water. To the Norse, Stromness was *Hamnavoe*, "haven-bay," and a haven it remained to Orkney's shipping, from the ships of the

Hudson's Bay Company, which stocked up on water from **Login's Well** before transatlantic crossings, to the P&O ferries running to the Scottish mainland today. This town's cultural highlight is the **Pier Arts Centre**, which has an exemplary collection of contemporary art overlooking the water.

HOY

Heay, High Island in Old Norse, has yielded **Hoy**, the name of Orkney's highest island. Closer cousin to Scotland's Highlands than any other part of Orkney, Hoy's silhouette towers over Mainland, and from atop its peaks you can see almost all of Orkney. Less populated than Mainland, it's great country for hill walkers, who traverse the fells on their way to the Old Man of Hoy (now, alas, apparently crumbling) or **St. John's Head**, one of the highest vertical cliffs in Britain.

Hoy's most famous manmade monument is the **Dwarfie Stane**, a block of red sandstone with chambers hewn into the rock. It's loosely described as a tomb – the only rock-cut tomb in Britain – but in fact its purpose is uncertain. Like Maes Howe, it bears graffiti, including an inscription in Persian by a 19th-century eccentric laird who spent a few nights in the tomb. Of later vintage are the two **Martello towers** flanking the harbor; they were built in 1813 as protection against the American navy.

SCAPA FLOW

But the waters between Mainland and Hoy, the channel of **Scapa Flow**, have played a central role in wars since British ships used it when avoiding the dangerous English Channel in the days of Napoleon. In World War I, as well, this was a naval base; although the British forces weren't able to prevent the torpedoing of the *H.M.S. Hampshire* in 1916. The ship sank with most of its crew, including Lord Kitchener, *en route* to a secret mission in Russia. A **monument** to Kitchener from the people of Orkney now stands guard on Mainland over the formidable cliffs of the Atlantic coast, a square windowless tower turning a blank facade to the site of the tragedy atop the striated, bird-laden rocks of **Marwick Head**. The conclusion to Orkney's role in World War I came in 1919, when the captured German fleet, detained in Scapa Flow, sank itself in a gesture of resistance on Midsummer's Day.

Other wrecks later joined these on the floor of Scapa Flow, today a paradise for divers. In World War II, a number of ships were deliberately scuttled to block the eastern access to the waters. This didn't keep a U-boat from penetrating in October, 1939, and sinking the *H.M.S. Royal Oak* with 833 hands on board. Winston Churchill determined to take action and block the access once and for all:

Right: Spoils of war? Italian POWs transformed a Nissen hut into the Italian Chapel.

hence the **Churchill Causeways**, which still link Mainland to South Ronaldsay via two other islets. Brought in to furnish the requisite labors were Italian POWs, who left behind them a different kind of monument: in their spare time, they built the **Italian Chapel**, which still stands near the first causeway from Mainland. It takes close inspection of this simple Catholic chapel to realize the whole thing is trompe-l'oeil painting and metalwork adorning a simple Nissen hut; since the war, it has stood as a sign of reconciliation and enduring faith triumphing over the division of war.

OTHER ISLANDS

Just north of Mainland lies green **Shapinsay**, so close to the center of Orkney's action that it's been dubbed "suburbia," although its **Balfour Castle** is more stately than suburban. Mainland's other closest neighbor is **Rousay**, where the archaeological finds crowd closely together. Enjoying pride of place here is **Midhowe**, which boasts the best-preserved broch in all of Orkney as well as the twelve-chambered prehistoric tomb called "the great ship of Death."

The cliffs of **Red Head** on **Eday** bring to view the red sandstone which was quarried on the island and used to build Kirkwall's St. Magnus's Cathedral. From this vantage point, you can see over to the large northern island of **Westray**, an exception in Orkney in that its population is growing. Not just its bird population, although **Noup Head** is one of Europe's most important seabird breeding grounds; the human population is also doing fine. One Westray export are Orkney chairs with their arched basketweave backs; Orkney presented two of these as a wedding present to Prince Charles and Lady Diana Spencer.

Stronsay, to the west, also used to be a hub of business: for a few weeks each season, it was the base for Scotland's her-

ring fleets. The harbor at **Whitehall** was so crowded with ships that on a Sunday, when fishing was forbidden and the boats were in port, you could walk from the harbor town of Whitehall over to Papa Stronsay on the decks of the ships at anchor. Relics of past industry are the remains of "kelp-kilns," where seaweed was burned to produce a major export in the 18th century. At the cliffs at **Vat of Kirbister** is a fine natural stone arch.

Sprawling **Sanday**, like a crab with outstretched claws, seems appropriately named: its sand beaches are exemplary. But its soil wasn't sandy; in fact, land was valued more highly here than in the rest of Orkney on medieval tax registers. Today, knitwear, beaches, and golf number among its attractions, as does the chambered cairn at **Quoyness**. To the north – the most northerly island of Orkney – is **North Ronaldsay**, known for its sheep. A stone wall excludes these animals from the green inland pastures, confining them to the shore, where they live on seaweed and thus produce a dar-

ker, more strongly flavored meat than their pampered mainland cousins.

SHETLAND

Comparing the people of Orkney with those of **Shetland**, 60 miles (100 km) further north, poet Hugh MacDiarmid declared, "The Orcadian is a farmer with a boat; the Shetlander is a fisherman with a croft." His observation also serves to differentiate the terrains of the two islands: where Orkney is gently pastoral, windswept Shetland is far wilder.

Yet though the waves can crash against Shetland's shores, the wind makes it difficult for trees to take root, and the rainfall can be prodigious, this is gentle country. **Ronas Hill**, Shetland's highest peak, reaches no more than 1475 feet (450 m). Washed by burns and tumbling streams, the land has no river, but many lochs, lochans and voes (as the penetrating arms of the sea are called). At midsummer, these waters are fished for brown trout; in August and September,

185

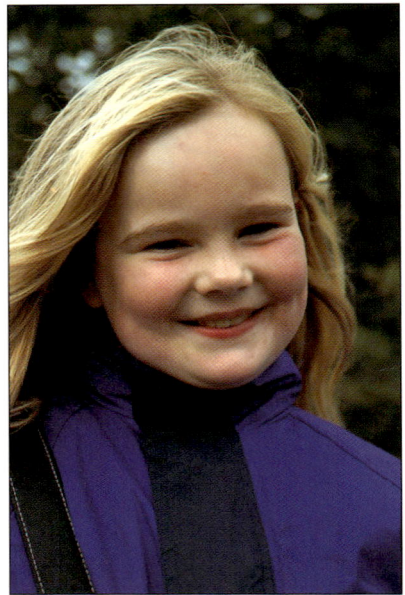

for sea trout. Another harvest of Shetland's waters is oil: the discovery of lucrative Brent Field, in the North Sea, gave Shetland an important economic boost. Visible signs of industrialization, however, have remained largely confined to the area around the waters of **Sullom Voe**, one of three points in Scotland where oil from the rigs comes ashore. Still, the risk of oil spills, such as that following the wreck of the tanker Braer in 1993, is a constant underlying threat to the environment.

Fewer than 20 of the 100 Shetland Isles are inhabited; in fact, sheep outnumber people by eight to one. The largest island, **Mainland**, has a population of 19,000. Not far from Sumburgh airport is its southernmost tip, **Sumburgh Head**, where the cliffs rise about wild waves and puffins rest. Sumburgh Head is north of the **Roost**, a tidal current whose roars can be heard inland.

Above: Viking genes? Shetland was Norwegian for seven centuries.

Nearby **Jarlshof** is accounted among Europe's finest archaeological sites, encompassing three villages which themselves incorporate distinct Stone Age, Bronze Age, Iron Age and Viking settlements. Here, too, is a medieval farmhouse, and the 16th-century home of Earl Robert and Earl Patrick Stewart.

At the Loch of Spiggie, the Royal Society for the Protection of Birds has a sanctuary. Nearby, the **Shetland Croft House Museum** is a 19th-century thatched cottage typical of many on the islands, its exhibits displaying the traditional lifestyle of Shetland folk.

Farther north, offshore by Sandwick, is the little island of **Mousa**, grazed by sheep and ponies, and fascinating for a fortified round tower (or broch) some 2,000 years old, the best-preserved Iron Age tower in Scotland. More than 40 feet (12 m) high, its parapet is reached by means of a staircase running between the inner and outer walls.

Center of Shetland is its capital, the sea port of **Lerwick**. Britain's northernmost town has preserved not only its stone piers but also such traditions as **Up Helly Aa**, a no-holds-barred January festival when the citizens, dressed in winged helmets and armor, burn a Viking longboat before feasting and celebrating through the night. Geographically, Lerwick is nearer Bergen, Norway than to any comparable British town.

Lerwick's harbor is sheltered to the east by the island of Bressay. Because of this protected position, King Haakon of Norway rested his fleet here on his way to making his unsuccessful attack on Scotland in 1263. Cromwell's men built **Fort Charlotte** here in the 16th century; although the Dutch, who took over the town for a time, partly destroyed it, the fort was restored under King George III. The town center has picturesque stone streets flanked by granite houses, nestling together as a defence against the gales that sometimes rage from the sea.

At Lower Hillhead, Lerwick, a **Museum of Shetland Life** sets out the history of the islanders from prehistoric days to the present, covering archaeology, art and textiles, everyday life and shipping. But even more of a Lerwick highlight is **Clickhimin Broch**, a well-excavated Iron Age site on the outskirts of town. The settlement itself dates even farther back: the broch was built within a Stone Age fort. Though partly ruined, the remains of this fortified tower still reach 17 feet (5.2 m).

Bressay itself, off Lerwick's shore, has a cave with a remarkable echo as well as Lerwick's golf links. On its seaward side is the even smaller **Isle of Noss**, to which an inflatable dinghy transporrts visitors when weather conditions allow. Beyond spectacular scenery, with 600-foot (183-m) cliffs, the island's attraction is that it's the **Noss Nature Reserve**, sheltering gulls, auks and gannets. Noss also has a Shetland pony stud farm; these miniature ponies were once used to pull cartloads of coal through Britain's mines.

Opposite Lerwick, on Mainland's western side, is **Scalloway**, once the capital of Shetland and still evoking the past with the ruins of **Earl Patrick's Castle**, built in 1600. Its bay is enticing, and fishermen ply for brown trout in the Tingwall loch, in the midst of which is a tiny island where long ago the Norse parliament sat. In **Scalloway Museum**, visitors learn the story of how small boats from the town kept in touch with the resistance movement in Nazi-occupied Norway during World War II; escaping from Norway to Shetland was known as "taking the Shetland bus."

North of Mainland is **Yell** (pop. 1,100), and, east of Yell, **Fetlar**, where the Royal Society for the Protection of Birds has a sanctuary and where you can sometimes see otters playing in the water as you stroll along the coast.

Still further north, **Unst** is the most northerly island of Britain – indeed, there

is no land between Unst and the North Pole. Shetland is a mere 400 miles (645 km) from the Arctic Circle, and while it isn't truly a land of the midnight sun, midnight in summer is not dark but merely twilit. Unst, 11 miles long and 4 wide (18 by 7 km), is the smallest of the main Shetland Isles. Its population, some 1,000 crofters and fisherfolk, is supplemented by numerous Shetland ponies grazing on its common land, and by more than 100,000 sea birds nesting on the cliffs of **Herma Ness**, one of Scotland's most important nature reserves. At the southeast corner of the island is **Muness Castle**, built at the end of the 16th century for Lawrence Bruce, half-brother of the Earl of Orkney, whose chief aim as local sheriff was to line his own pocket.

Two of the Shetland Islands lie far from the Mainland group; each of them is some 27 miles (44 km) distant, isolated in the ocean. Better-known of the two is

Above: Shetland's trademark ponies were used in 19th-century coal mines.

Fair Isle, once of Britain's most isolated inhabited islands, now owned by the National Trust. Fair Isle knitwear, with its geometric patterns, is world-famous and still exported from here (see p. 229), but the island's spare population also spins, weaves, makes traditional wooden boats, stained-glass windows, straw-backed chairs, spinning wheels, and fiddles. Fair Isle is also beloved of birdwatchers; an observatory for studying the myriad rare birds that flock to the island can accommodate 34 of them.

Then there's **Foula**, with forty islanders and the little harbor of Ham Voe, which is the most westerly of the Shetland Isles. Five peaks rise on Foula, the highest – 1,373 feet (420 m) – the **Sneug**. The island's cliffs are spectacular, especially the **Kame** on the northwest coast, the second-highest cliff in Britain, 1,200 feet (367 m) above the sea. From here, you can spy on Arctic terns, stormy petrels, great skuas, red-throated divers, fulmars, and kittiwakes, as well as the occasional porpoise.

ORKNEY
Telephone area code 01856 (except where noted)
Transportation
BOAT: **P&O Ferries** runs the main car ferry line from Scrabster to Stromness, as well as from Aberdeen to Stromness; tel. (01224) 572615. **Orkney Ferries** run from Kirkwall to the smaller islands; tel. 872044. *CAR RENTAL:* in Kirkwall, from W.R. Tullock, Castle St., tel. 876262, fax 874458, or Scarth Car Hire, Great Western Road, tel. 872125. *AIR:* British Airways flies to Orkney from London, Glasgow, Aberdeen, Inverness, other cities; tel. (0345) 222111. **Loganair** flies from Kirkwall to 5 other islands, with combination packages letting you visit several islands at reduced rates. The flight from Westray and Papa Westray is the shortest commercial flight in the world (1 minute). Tel. 872494.

Accommodations
KIRKWALL: *EXPENSIVE:* **Foveran Hotel**, St. Ola (2.5 mi W of Kirkwall on A964), tel. 872839. Comfortable hotel with acclaimed dining room. *MODERATE:* **West End Hotel**, Main St., tel. (01856) 872368, fax 876181. Pleasant family-run hotel at a quiet end of the main street, with good food. **STROMNESS:** *MODERATE:* **Stromness Hotel**, tel. 850298, fax 850610, traditional stone hotel overlooking town and harbor. **FINSTOWN:** *BUDGET:* **Linnadale B&B**, Mrs. A. Tait, tel. 761300. **HOY:** *BUDGET:* Mrs. L. Budge, **Stoneyquoy**, Lyness, tel. 791234, B&B in comfortable farmhouse, with sun room. **SHAPINSAY:** *MODERATE:* **Balfour Castle** offers accommodation for guests. Tel. 711282, fax 711283. **WESTRAY:** *MODERATE:* **Cleaton House Hotel**, tel. (01857) 677508, comfortable hotel; meals.

Restaurants
KIRKWALL: *BUDGET:* **Trenabies Cafe**, 16 Albert Street, tel. 874336. On the main street, crowded local hangout for tea, snacks, or full meals. **STROMNESS:** *EXPENSIVE:* **Hamnavoe Restaurant**, 35 Graham Place, tel. 850606. Not actually all that expensive for this high caliber of cooking. *BUDGET:* **The Cafe**, 22 Victoria St., tel. 850368. Good food, with changing daily specials; waterfront terrace. **ST. MARGARET'S HOPE:** *EXPENSIVE:* **Creel Inn and Restaurant**, Front Road, tel. (01856) 831311. Orkney's finest restaurant; try fish cakes in sorrel sauce or Orcadian Fish Stew. Also a few rooms to let. *MODERATE:* **Murray Arms**, Back Road, tel. 831205. Pub meals, dinners, rooms.

Museums & Sights
KIRKWALL: Highland Park Distillery Visitor Centre, Holm Road, tel. 874619. Has informative film about Orkney. **Tankerness House Museum**, Broad St., tel. 873191. Local history, Stone Age to present. Mon-Sat 10:30 am-12:30 pm, 1:30-5

pm; also Sun May-Sep 2-5 pm. **STROMNESS: Pier Arts Centre**, tel. 850209, open Tue-Sat. **HOY: Scapa Flow Visitor Centre**, Lyness. History of naval base in World Wars. Mon-Fri 9 am-4 pm, also May-Sep, Sat & Sun 10:30 am-3:30 pm.

Sports and Activities
DIVING: The many wrecks scattered around the ocean floor have made Scapa Flow, especially, a paradise for divers. A local outlet is **The Diving Cellar**, 4 Victoria Street, Stromness, tel. 850055, fax 850395. *FISHING:* Because an ancient Norse law is still in effect here, you don't need a permit to fish in Orkney's lochs; courtesy dictates that visiting anglers join the Orkney Trout Fishing Association (Mr. J. Purvis, 19 Bridge St., Kirkwall, tel. 875858).

Festivals
The Ba', Kirkwall, Mainland, traditional game held on Christmas and New Year's Day. **St. Magnus Festival**, Kirkwall, Mainland, international June music festival initiated by composer Sir Peter Maxwell Davis. **Festival of the Horse**, South Ronaldsay, August, features children's costume competition; some costumes go back several generations.

Tourist Information
Orkney Tourist Board, 6 Broad Street, Kirkwall, tel. 872856, fax 875056.

SHETLAND
Accommodation / Restaurants
LERWICK: *EXPENSIVE:* **Kvelsdro House Hotel**, tel (01595) 692195, fax 696595, Shetland's stab at *grand luxe*, overlooking the harbor. *MODERATE:* **The Noost Restaurant**, 86 Commercial St., tel. (01595) 693377. **BRAE:** *EXPENSIVE:* **Busta House Hotel**, Busta, tel. (0180622) 506, fax 588. Supposedly the oldest continuously inhabited house in Shetland; sea views, very good restaurant. **HILLSWICK:** *MODERATE:* **St. Magnus Bay Hotel**, tel. (0180623) 372, fax 373. This hotel was built in Norway and floated across the North Sea; appropriately, dining room specializes in seafood. **SUMBURGH:** *MODERATE:* **Sumburgh Hotel**, Sumburgh, tel. (01950) 460201, fax 460394. Redone laird's house at island's S tip.

Museums & Sights
Böd of Gremista Museum, N of Lerwick, open June-Sep Wed-Sun 10 am-1 pm and 2-5 pm, in 18th-c. fishing booth. **Crofthouse Museum**, Voe, Dunossness, open daily May-Sept 10 am-1 pm and 2-5 pm. For boat trips to **Mousa**, contact Tom Jamieson, Leebitton, Sandwick, tel. (01950) 431367.

Festivals
Up Helly Aa, Viking fire festival, Lerwick: last Tue in Jan. Visitors were long discouraged, now allowed.

Tourist Information
Shetland Islands Tourism, Market Cross, Lerwick, tel. (01595) 693434, fax 695807.

THE NORTHEAST
Fish And Flowers:
Grampian & Aberdeen

STRATHSPEY
ROYAL DEESIDE
ABERDEEN
THE MORAY COAST

When you're looking at a map of Scotland and find the country's northeastern corner, shouldering its way into the North Sea, flowers might not be the first thing that come to mind. Surprise. To bring brilliance to the land under the luminous gray skies, locals from Aberdeen to Forres have planted their towns with a wealth of bloom, from borders in town parks to whole flower sculptures.

Northeastern Scotland is full of contrasts and surprises. Its western side is technically part of the Highlands: here are some of Britain's highest mountains, the Cairngorms and the isolated Grampian Highlands, which foster an active community of hillwalkers and skiers. Then, you have Royal Deeside, where Prince Albert, after studied consideration of sites throughout Scotland, selected Balmoral as the summer home of Queen Victoria. Balmoral is just one of the area's legion castles, which reflect everything from the need for defense in the 15th century to the desire for manorial elegance in the 19th. The River Spey is an artery for one of Scotland's main whisky-producing areas; distilleries abound. And the northern boundary of this region

Preceding pages: "Tossing the caber," an 18-foot tree trunk, at a Highland Games. Left: Copper kilns at the Royal Lochnagar Distillery.

is the coast of the Moray Firth, where charming fishing villages look out over bottle-nosed dolphins toward the (invisible) oil platforms in the North Sea.

STRATHSPEY

The wildest, roughest part of this section of Scotland are the **Cairngorms**: the largest mountain range in Britain, they're also some of the oldest, comprised of rock hundreds of millions of years old. Taming the area is the resort town of **Aviemore**, where a leisure center provides activity even off-season – off *ski* season, that is; with the high mountains nearby, this is one of Scotland's leading ski areas (Victorian **Grantown-on-Spey** is another popular base). In summer, there's compensation in the form of walks in **Glen More Forest Park**, with its resident reindeer herd; and some of the chair lifts are still in operation to bring you to the great views. At lower altitudes, the **Strathspey Railway** runs steam trains from Aviemore to **Boat of Garten,** where ospreys nest in spring. Nearby **Carrbridge** focuses on forestry; its Forest Tower commands a fine view of the Cairngorms.

South of Aviemore is **Kingussie**, where the **Ruthven Barracks**, built to control the Highlanders in 1718, were blown up by Prince Charlie's men after

they realized their dreams were dashed in the wake of Culloden. A **Highland Folk Museum** illustrates what they went back home to.

The name of this area is **Strathspey**. *Strath* is Gaelic for valley, and *Spey* is the river that runs from here to Kingston, where it empties into the Moray Firth. This is Scotland's fastest-flowing river, popular with salmon anglers and whiskey drinkers. Half of Scotland's distilleries are supposedly located in this area. These range from well-known names like **Glenlivet** and **Glenfiddich** to the more exotic-sounding **Tamdhu** and **Cardhu** (the latter originally opened by a woman); the "Malt Whisky Trail" extends over to **Strathisla Distillery** at Keith. At **Craigellachie**, you can visit the **Speyside Cooperage**, one of the last places in Scotland where the oak barrels in which whiskey is matured are still made by hand.

Above: Roll out the barrel: hard at work at the Speyside Cooperage. Right: Living like a king, Victorian style: Balmoral Castle.

ROYAL DEESIDE

Another kind of trail begins at **Braemar**, across the Grampians from Aviemore: the Castle Trail. Scotland's northeast is truly well fortified: there are more than 70 castles scattered throughout the region. The one at Braemar, dating from 1628, was originally used for military purposes, though later converted into a residence. It replaced the earlier **Kindrochit Castle**, now a still-visible ruin.

Castles are associated with royalty, and one reason the Northeast's castle heritage has remained alive is the continued presence of royalty in the region. Braemar marks the start of "Royal Deeside." The castellated banks of the River Dee were obviously popular with aristocrats from time immemorial, but they truly came into fashion in the mid-19th century, when Queen Victoria, Prince Albert and their family took up summer residence at **Balmoral**, buying the place outright in 1852. Albert brought his zeal for city planning and landscaping to his "majestic village" (from the Gaelic *bail*, village, and *moral*, majestic), laying out the grounds (razing a 16th-century tower in the process) and bringing in Aberdeen's city architect, William Smith, to redesign the castle. In the summer months, visitors can peruse the Royal collections of porcelain and pictures – if no member of the Royal Family happens to be in residence.

Ever since Victoria's day, the towns and hamlets of this quiet, forested region have been elevated with the conferral of royal attentions. Little **Crathie Church** is known as the place where the royals attend services; the local distillery is the ***Royal* Lochnagar**. And **Ballater**, the nearest town, has visible signs of the Queen's patronage in the form of coats-of-arms over the doors of grocers' and butchers' shops, signifying that they operate "By Appointment" to Her Majesty. It was here that Victoria disembarked when she traveled by train, for Ballater was the end of the line; she had forbidden the railway to extend any farther west and sully her beloved countryside. (The porcelain toilet fixtures of the now-defunct station's Royal Waiting Room today grace a local hotel.) One of Victoria's favorite haunts was **Glen Muick**, south of the village; after Albert's death, she used to withdraw to a cottage at one end of it – dubbed "the Widow's House" – to be alone.

Highland Games

Victoria and Albert played a large role in popularizing what has become a trademark event of the Highlands: Highland Games. These events began hundreds of years ago as a sort of clan Olympics, village festivals with dancing, music, and men tossing about rocks and tree trunks as part of the entertainment. One reason they've reached their present established – and popular – state was Victoria's support. A fan of traditional Scottish dress and customs, she was quite taken with her first Braemar Gathering in 1848. The

Royals still often attend today, and this Gathering, on the first Saturday in September, remains the queen of the numerous Gatherings and Games held in the Highlands throughout the summer.

Highland Games involve everything from traditional dance competitions to athletic events practiced by the aptly-named "Heavies," who vie in throwing the Weight over the Bar or Tossing the Caber. The "Caber" is a tree trunk some 18 feet (almost 6 m) long – Braemar's is 19 feet 9 inches – which athletes try to throw end-over-end. But there are also lighter events like bagpipe contests, or, at Braemar, a footrace to the top of the hill Creag Choinnich. Tradition holds that the first games here were held in the 11th century when King Malcolm was looking for a footrunner, and came up with this method of selecting one.

A Man's Home is his Castle

From here on, you can easily wear yourself out moving from one elegant

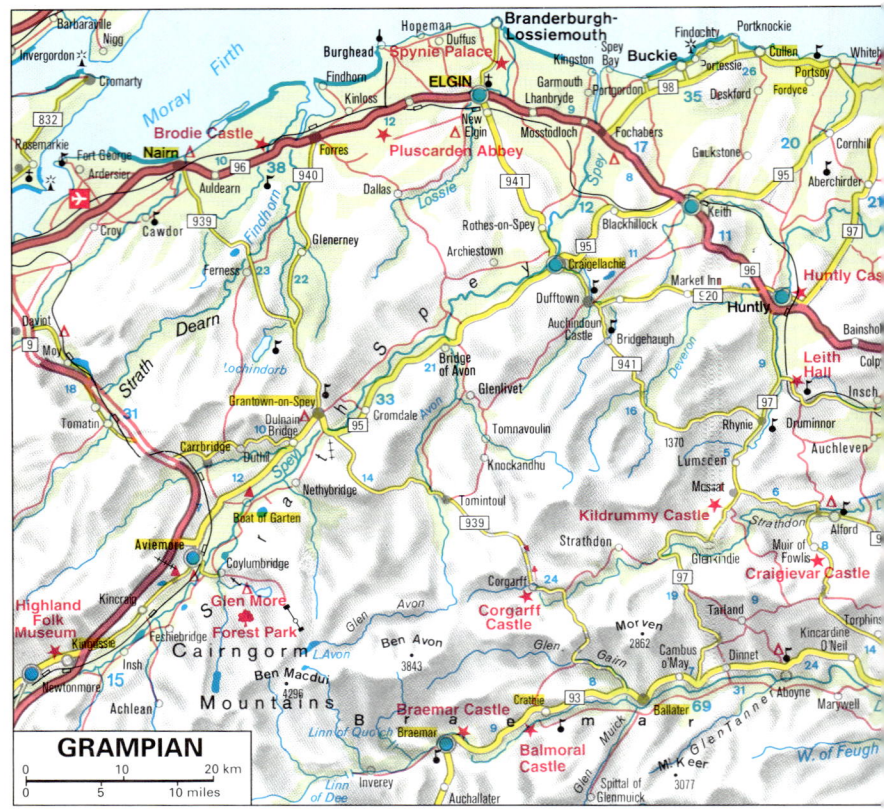

GRAMPIAN

| 0 | 10 | 20 km |
| 0 | 5 | 10 miles |

castle to the next medieval ruin along the signposted **Castle Trail**. Each castle is associated with one or several families, clan strongholds or military outposts before being converted into lavish residences or left to the mercies of the elements. There's a castle here for every taste, from the remains of **Kildrummy Castle**, the best-preserved 13th-century castle in Scotland, to elegant baronial **Fyvie Castle**, owned by five families between the 14th and 20th centuries, and running the gamut from 16th-century towers (with the castle's famous wheel stair running from top to bottom) to 18th-century luxury. Fyvie's village church echoes this variety on a smaller scale, with Celtic stones in one gable and Tiffany stained-glass windows.

Near Fyvie is **Haddo House**, an elegant William Adam residence built for the Gordons, who also owned Fyvie for a time. Haddo is all elegant 17th-century symmetry and plasterwork: one of its greatest hits is the Burne-Jones stained glass in its 1880 chapel. The house is also known for its musical performances, with its own Choral and Operatic Society. As the Gordons were the leading family in this area, they had several castles scattered about: **Huntly Castle** is an earlier one, now partly ruined. Its main body dates from the 16th and 17th centuries, and it includes a satisfyingly grim-looking 15th-century dungeon.

But other families made their way here, too. The Forbes family didn't have

An even earlier castle remnant survives in Inverurie in **The Bass**, a huge mound created in 1160 as the base for a wooden defensive palisade and tower. Pictish symbol stones in the adjacent churchyard are signs of life from a millennium or so earlier; the Picts also left symbols and Ogham runes on the **Brandsbutt stone**, at the edge of Inverurie, and the elaborate **Kintore** symbol stone in that nearby town's churchyard.

But even the Picts were late arrivals on the scene. Long before castles, before Picts, earlier builders were active in northeastern Scotland. This region contains one-quarter of all prehistoric standing stones in the British Isles. Seen here is the recumbent stone circle, a formation of standing stones alternating with horizontal ones. Examples can be seen near Inverurie at **Easter Aquhorties** or **Loanhead**, by Daviot; they are thought to date from around 3000 B.C.

The press of castles doesn't abate as you approach the east coast. The Burnett family castle is **Crathes**, which has marvelous wooden ceilings painted with classical heros, legends, and poetry, and fabulous gardens surrounded by drunkenly ballooning yew topiary. **Drum Castle**, dating from the 13th century, was the Irvine family seat for 653 years; its 16th-century chapel includes a font imitating a Saxon one in Winchester Cathedral and a replica of a silver Madonna from Augsburg. One of its walled gardens is devoted entirely to historic roses.

Stonehaven is where the castles meet the sea. Just south of the picturesque harbor, with a museum in its 16th-century **Tolbooth**, the remains of **Dunnottar Castle** sprawl over the top of a cliff thrusting out into the ocean. This dramatic site has had a dramatic history, withstanding attacks by William Wallace (when it was in English hands) and later by the dreaded Montrose, who ravaged the countryside in frustration when he was unable to take it. Later, 167 Cove-

to wait to get to America to make their fortune: 15th-century **Tolquhon Castle**, the family tower house, is rare in that it's preserved many of its original furnishings, while 17th-century **Craigievar Castle**, another Forbes home, has retained its graceful, turretted exterior. The **Fraser** family castle still bears the family name; it's a weighty edifice with a secure-looking corner tower and a huge fireplace at one end of its Great Hall. And at **Inverurie**, halfway between them, the ubiquitous Andrew Carnegie left a memorial to his name in the form of the local **museum**. (Locals without family titles are more interested in the **Thainstone Agricultural Center**, one of Europe's largest, most modern auction venues.)

nanters were held prisoner here, "left to rot" in its doughty dungeons. Franco Zeffirelli chose this as a setting for his film *Macbeth*, eschewing sites historically associated with Shakespeare's hero, such as Glamis Castle to the south or Cawdor Castle to the northwest.

THE GRANITE CITY: ABERDEEN

Granite City or Garden City? **Aberdeen** is both. Scotland's third-largest city is as solid as the local rock from which it's built, and as blooming as the flowers which overflow its parks and help it win awards year after year. Seagulls wheel screaming in the ocean wind over the warm gray buildings of **Union Street**, the arrow-straight main artery of this prosperous port (which has flourished since the advent of North Sea oil). Towers and spires mark the skyline.

Above: Stonehaven in a peaceful mood.
Right: Patrolling the wares at Aberdeen's fish market.

Aberdeen has no fewer than three cathedrals – St. Andrew's, St. Mary's, and St. Machar's – but the tallest spire of all is that within **Marischal College**, a temple not of religion but of learning, and, after the Escorial, the second-largest granite building in Europe. Its finicky, ridged facade, turreted and towered, is as nervous as a pen-and-ink sketch, throwing shadows like thin black lines etched on its pale stone.

However, Marischal College isn't part of Aberdeen's original university: Old Aberdeen is in another area entirely. It grew up around the cathedral which St. Machar, following a divine injunction, had built at a place where the river made the shape of a shepherd's (or bishop's) crook; today, **St. Machar's Cathedral** is partly ruined, but with an intact nave dating from the early 1400s. Here are the buildings of **King's College**; and students walk the narrow cobbled streets, many closed to cars, that still exude the quiet aura of another age.

St. Machar's river was the Don; New Aberdeen, with its busy harbor, centers on the Dee. From the days of herring fishing to the present of North Sea oil – the discovery of Montrose Field in 1969 sparked Aberdeen's growth into the "supply center" for the offshore drilling rigs – the port has played a central role in Aberdeen's life. The city's maritime history is documented in a museum housed in the 16th-century **Provost Ross's House**, overlooking the modern harbor. Another 16th-century dwelling is **Provost Skene's House**, incongruous within a complex of modern buildings, and fitted out as a museum with rooms from every era of its history, from the 16th century to the Georgian age. Fascinating here is the Painted Room, a rare surviving example of early English Catholic art, with images of the Annunciation, the Crucifixion, and the like.

Aberdeen's oldest church isn't one of the cathedrals, but **St. Nicholas**, which sits darkly alongside Union Street, brooding over the wounds it received during the Reformation – much of it today dates from 18th and 19th century reconstruction – and protecting some interesting old tombs. Sleek **St. Andrew's Cathedral**, by contrast, is all sweetness and light; it's also the mother church of all Episcopalian churches in America. Not far from here, Union Street ends at the 17th-century **Mercat Cross**, a doughty pulpit-like structure topped with an improbably white unicorn, shining like ivory amid the city's elephantine gray, with portraits of the ten Stuart monarchs in medallion form set around his feet.

Another ten minutes on foot brings you across sweeping green lawns to the ocean, where the broad, clean **city beach** blithely ignores the presence of the nearby harbor. If it isn't warm enough to swim, there are other leisure pursuits at the year-round **amusement park**.

Gardeners and florists shouldn't neglect the city parks, among them extensive **Hazlehead Park**, with its topiary maze; **Duthie Park**, with roofed winter

gardens, exotic birds, and an aquarium; or the city-center **Union Terrace Gardens**, with a floral clock. An attraction of a different odor is the bustling early morning **Fish Market** at the harbor (off Market Street), Scotland's largest and also one of its oldest: it can be dated back to 1281.

Coasting Along

Scotland has been the source of much literary inspiration, but the inhabitants of **Cruden Bay**, north of Aberdeen, may not pride themselves on their claim to fictitious fame. A regular vacationer at Cruden Bay, Bram Stoker was inspired by the eerie ruins of Slains Castle to write a tale of the supernatural: the result was *Dracula*. In its prime, the castle wasn't as spooky as it seems in its ruined state; a century earlier, Boswell described it as "an excellent old house," with a picture gallery hung with Hogarths.

What impressed Boswell, and Dr. Johnson, was a nearby natural spectacle which you can still reach along a clifftop

path: the **Bullers of Buchan**. This is a kind of natural round chamber extending into the sea, completely surrounded by high cliff walls, with a small natural arch on the ocean side through which the water comes pounding in windy weather. Lining the inner walls of the basin are nesting seabirds, which whirl in the enclosed space below your feet, emitting a variety of throaty cries like wailing children, as you balance your way along the high, narrow cliff walls.

Up here, you've left tourist country altogether. **Peterhead**, the main town, is famous as the largest whitefish port in Europe; its oldest building is a still-working salmon smokery from 1585. Anyone who has time to play may retreat to the long stretch of beach by **St. Fergus**, where a massive gas terminal provides nearly half of the gas in the United Kingdom. Still farther north, the **Loch of**

Above and right: Lanterns of the north: the setting sun over the Moray Firth, and the ruined magnificence of Elgin Cathedral.

Strathbeg Nature Reserve is dubbed the "Heathrow of the bird world."

Fraserburgh claims to have the first lighthouse in Scotland, and proud they are of it. Built from part of the old castle in 1787, illuminated with 20 whale-oil lamps, the lighthouse at Kinnaird Head is now a **Lighthouse Museum**. Nearby is another tower, the 16th-century **Wine Tower**; no one knows why it was built, so, logically enough, it's reputed to be haunted. An even older monument is the town's **Mercat Cross**, dated 1736, but possibly as old as 1603; it's the only cross in Scotland to depict the arms both of the old Kingdom of Scotland and the new United Kingdom.

Not far from Fraserburgh is **Pitsligo Castle**, which the Frasers sold to the Forbeses in the mid-1500s. After Culloden, its Jacobite owner, Alexander Forbes, had to forfeit his lands; he was lucky enough to avoid arrest himself, dying in 1792, aged 84, after years on the run. Another Forbes later took it over: in 1989, American tycoon Malcolm Forbes bought

the old building. He managed to renovate it at least enough to shore up its structure before his death a few years later.

THE MORAY COAST

From Fraserburgh, the coast runs almost straight to Inverness, marking the northern border of the ancient Pictish province of Moray and the southern shore of the **Moray Firth** (which local accents turn into the "muddy" firth). This is a beautiful stretch of coastline. Broad bays scallop the shore, their silver waves washing beaches of golden sand, echoed in the duller metal of the low gray towns. Yet here these are functional, not ornamental, metals: the beauty is a by-product of a place where things get done, whether fishing, sailing, surfing, or eating seafood be the task at hand.

Macduff, Banff, Portsoy, Cullen: any and every one of these towns along the "Northeast Coastal Trail" would be a wonderful base for a holiday visit. At **Banff** stands **Duff House**, which William Adam built for William Duff, M.P., in 1735; rife with ornament in the stonework outside and the plasterwork within, this Baroque Georgian mansion is now an outpost of the National Gallery of Scotland, with a collection of Old Masters as well as rotating exhibitions. **Portsoy**'s showpiece is its green-toned marble, which even made it into Versailles; but its restored 18th-century harbor is also a treat. **Cullen**'s name is reproduced on countless Scottish menus as the soup *Cullen Skink* (see "Food," p. 226). The main street of this sloping town funnels into a striking view of the bay below, with the sandstone rocks of the "Three Kings of Cullen," framed by the arches of an abandoned railway viaduct that cuts dramatically across the panorama. Its 14th-century **Auld Kirk** holds some mortal remains of Elizabeth de Burgh, wife of Robert the Bruce; interred here were her "interior parts."

Crossing the Spey by **Fochabers**, a planned 18th-century village, and passing **Garmouth**, where Charles II first

201

set foot on the soil of his kingdom, you come to **Elgin**, where rise the ruins of the what was once one of the most beautiful medieval cathedrals in Scotland. Called "the lantern of the north" because of the spiritual light it shed over the area, it was unlucky from the start: consecrated in 1224, it was devastated by fire even before Alexander, the "Wolf of Badenoch," illegitimate son of Robert the Bruce, laid waste to Elgin and nearby Forres after quarrelling with the incumbent Bishop in 1390. This was only the first of several desecrations: local authorities had removed the lead from the roof to raise money to pay their soldiers a century before Cromwell's troops set about smashing things up. A bit north of town, ruined **Spynie Palace** was the bishops' residence until 1686. Farther north still, **Duffus Castle** is one of the best-preserved examples of Norman motte-and-bailey architecture (c. 1300).

Above: And all that jazz: in summer, floral sculptures adorn many coastal towns.

Despite all the destruction of religious war, Moray remained a center of Roman Catholicism. To the south, hidden in the Braes of Glenlivet, was the seminary of Scalan; at Clochan, near Fochabers, St. Gregory's was the first Roman Catholic church to be openly built after the Reformation. And this century has seen the revival of **Pluscarden Abbey**. Founded in 1230, the abbey took over the old Benedictine Urquhart Priory in 1454; almost 500 years later, Benedictines started restoring the old buildings. By 1948, some monks were able to move in; and the world's northernmost Christian monastery was elevated to an Abbey in 1974.

Floral Forres

Forres is a pendant to Aberdeen as far as flowers are concerned: this old Royal Burgh blossoms in every shop, window box, park, or garden, notably in the bright floral sculptures in **Grant Park**. The mapmaker Ptolemy noted Forres nearly 2,000 years ago; another old association is with Macbeth, as King Duncan held his court here. Still another extant sign of the past is **Sueno's Stone**, a 23-foot (7 m) standing stone some 1,000 years old, carved with a cross and scenes of warriors in battle. Relatively modern in comparison is **Brodie Castle**, mainly from the 16th century, extensively redone in Victorian days, with marvelous family furnishings from the resident family. And Brodie upholds the local floral theme: in spring, its gardens bloom with some 400 different species of daffodil.

The specialty of **Nairn** is – holidays: this is a popular and lovely little resort town with golf, beaches, and easy access to many highlights of the northeast as well as the Highlands. In fact, Dr. Johnson, also traveling from east to west, noted that, "At Nairn we may fix the verge of the Highlands, for here I first saw peat fires, and first heard the Erse language."

AVIEMORE AND SPEYSIDE
Accommodation
GRANTOWN-ON-SPEY: *MODERATE:* **Auchendean Lodge**, Dulnain Bridge, tel. (01479) 851347. Cozy lodge: fireplaces, scenic, good food. **CRAIGELLACHIE:** *MODERATE:* **Craigellachie Hotel**, tel. (01340) 881204. Good service.
Museums & Sights
Highland Folk Museum, Kingussie, open Mon-Sat 10 am-6 pm, Sun 2-6 pm, daily life in the Highlands, complete with "Black House," a day laborer's hut. **Speyside Cooperage**, Dufftown Road, Craigellachie, tel. (01340) 871108. One of last cooperages in Scotland, still making wooden barrels for the whiskey trade. **Cardhu Distillery**, Knockando, tel. (01340) 810204, Mar-Nov weekdays 9:30 am-4:30 pm, also Sat May-Sept, Dec-Feb by appointment.

ROYAL DEESIDE
Accommodation
BALLATER: *MODERATE:* **Balgonie**, Braemar Place, tel/fax (013397) 55482. Country house hotel with views of pine hillsides. Local seafood and Aberdeen Angus beef. *BUDGET:* **The Auld Kirk Hotel**, Braemar Road, tel. (013397) 55762, fax 55707. Actually in a former church: stained-glass, Gothic arches, comfortable rooms, good food.
BANCHORY: *MODERATE:* **Raemoir House Hotel**, 2.5 mi/4 km N of Banchory, tel. (01330) 824884, fax 822171. 18th-century manor with antiques, tapestries, fine dining.
Restaurants
BALLATER: *MODERATE:* **The Green Inn**, 9 Victoria Road, tel. (013397) 55701: best in town.
Museums & Sights
Balmoral, off A93 between Braemar and Ballater, open May-July, Mon-Sat, 10 am-5 pm. **Fyvie Castle**, off A947 SE of Turriff, tel. (01651) 891266, Apr-Sept 1:30-5:30 pm, Jul & Aug from 11 am, weekends in Oct. **Haddo House**, off B999 N of Pitmedden, tel. (01651) 851440, hours as Fyvie Castle. **Crathes Castle & Garden**, 3 mi E of Banchory (A93), tel. (01330) 844525. Easter-Oct, 11 am-5:30 pm. **Drum Castle**, Drumoak, tel. (01330) 811204. Open May-Sep & weekends in Oct, 1:30-5:30 pm.

ABERDEEN
Telephone area code (01224)
Accommodation
EXPENSIVE: **Marcliffe of Pitfodels**, North Deeside Road, tel. 861000. Small, personal luxury hotel; 2 fine restaurants. *MODERATE:* **Brentwood Hotel**, 101 Crown St, tel. 595440. Central, reasonably priced, with pub. **Atholl Hotel**, 54 King's Gate, tel. 323505, fax 321555. Pleasant granite building in residential neighborhood. *BUDGET:* **Mannofield Hotel**, 447 Great Western Rd., tel. 315888, homey, family-run, in Victorian house.

Restaurants
EXPENSIVE: **Silver Darlings**, Pocra Quay, North Pier, tel. 576229. Fine Scottish seafood restaurant, one of Aberdeen's best. **Faraday's**, 2 Kirk Brae, Cults, tel. 869666. Victorian ambience, Scottish-French cuisine. *MODERATE:* **The Courtyard on the Lane**, 1 Alford Lane (off Union St), tel. 213795. Two-level restaurant in old stone house.
Museums & Sights
Provost Skene's House, Guestrow (off Broad St), tel. 641086, open Mon-Sat 10 am-5 pm. **Aberdeen Maritime Museum**, Provost Ross's House, Shiprow, tel. 585788, Mon-Sat 10am-5 pm. **Aberdeen Art Gallery**, Schoolhill, tel. 646333, Mon-Sat 10 am-5 pm (Thu til 8 pm), Sun 2-5 pm; 18th-20th centuries, with portraits of (not by) 92 British artists. **Marischal Museum** in Marischal College, Broad St., tel. 273131, Mon-Fri 10 am-5 pm, Sun 2-5 pm.
Activities
His Majesty's Theatre hosts nationally-known stars and troupes in plays, musicals, dance, opera. Union Street, tel. 641122, fax 627353.
Tourist Information
Tourist Information Centre, St. Nicholas House, Broad Street, tel. 632727. **Aberdeen & Grampian Tourist Board**, 102 Migvie House, North Silver St., tel. 848848, fax 639836.

MORAY COAST
Accommodation
CULLEN: *MODERATE:* **Bayview Hotel**, Seafield St., tel. (01542) 841031. Family run, great food. **ELGIN:** *BUDGET:* **The Croft**, 10 Institution Road, tel. (01343) 546004. Friendly Victorian B&B. **NAIRN:** *MODERATE:* **The Links Hotel**, 1 Seafield St., tel. (01667) 453321. Pleasant, central.
Restaurants
BANFF: *BUDGET:* **Fagins**, Loch St., Whitehills, tel. (01261) 861321. Small, family-run.
BUCKIE: *EXPENSIVE:* **Old Monastery**, Drybridge, tel. (01542) 832660. Home fare, ex-church.
Museums & Sights
Scotland's Lighthouse Museum, Fraserburgh, tel. (01346) 511022, Apr-Sept Mon-Sat 10 am-6 pm, Sun 12:30-6 pm, Oct-Mar til 4 pm. **Duff House**, Banff, tel. (01261) 818181. Open Oct-Mar Thu-Sun 10 am-5 pm, May-Sep also Wed &Mon. **Elgin Museum**, 1 High St, tel. (01343) 543675. Includes some of earliest fossils in the world. Apr-Oct Mon-Fri 10 am-5 pm, Sat 11 am-4 pm, Sun 2-5 pm. **Pluscarden Abbey**, 6 mi SW of Elgin, tel. (01343) 890257. Daily 4:45 am-8:45 pm. **Brodie Castle**, 3 mi W of Forres, tel. (01309) 641371, open Apr-Sep Mon-Sat 11 am-5:30 pm, Sun 1:30-5:30 pm.
Tourist Information
Tourist Information Centre, 17 High Street, Elgin, tel. (01343) 542666, fax 552982.

CENTRAL
SCOTLAND
Heart Of The Kingdom

STIRLING
THE TROSSACHS
PERTH
FIFE / ST ANDREWS
DUNDEE

Scotland's central reaches form the core of Scottish identity. From rolling lowlands through Fife's sand beaches to pine-girt lochs, the central part of the country encompasses a spectrum of typically "Scottish" landscapes and locales. Here are located the Trossachs, birthplace of Scottish tourism; St Andrews, Scottish birthplace of golf; and Stirling, birthplace of a large chunk of Scottish history.

STIRLING

Scotland is rife with historic castles, but perhaps none has the special resonance of **Stirling**'s. Bound up with the country's history since the Middle Ages, Stirling Castle was a focal point of the rebellions, first, of "Braveheart" William Wallace (who captured it in 1296) and then, more successfully, of Robert the Bruce, who defeated Edward II at nearby Bannockburn in 1314. In troubled later days, it became a shelter for monarchs: James V was brought here for safety after his father's loss at Flodden Field, and his infant daughter Mary

Preceding pages: In the purple: heather glows across the hills by Dunkeld. Left: Some Scottish traditions are an acquired taste.

Queen of Scots was crowned here at the ripe old age of nine months.

Sitting atop a commanding rock, the castle is as impressive today as its wooden predecessor must have seemed in the 11th century. Approached from the Back Walk, its high walls seem impenetrable. Atop the rock, a drawbridge gives access through two levels of defenses to a sprawling complex that mingles legion architectural styles and various buildings with patent, and confusing, authenticity. Dominant are 15th-century elements, from the architecture of the **Palace** or the **Chapel Royal** (which was itself built in several stages) to the wooden coffers salvaged from the palace's original Renaissance ceiling, with marvelous portraits of men, women, and fabulous beasts. From the ramparts, you can look over the complex or out on a panoramic view of the surrounding area. Cannons are trained in every direction; one poses a welcome threat to the towering **monument to William Wallace**, put up in 1869, more than 500 years after Wallace's death: a relic of the Victorian Age's love for Scotland and often clumsy architecture.

A steep cobblestone street leads down to Stirling town, past the newly-restored 1630s mansion **Argyll's Lodging**, with characteristic period furnishings, and the

Gothic **Church of the Holy Rude**, with its 15th-century timber-beam ceiling and lovely stained glass. Here, James VI, Mary's son, followed his mother's precedent by being crowned King at the age of one. Further on, Broad Street sports the **Mercat Cross** and **Tolbooth**, built in 1701; on St. John Street, the restored **Old Town Jail** is now a museum of Victorian penal customs.

Battles raged around Stirling throughout the country's history. Most famous, or fondly remembered, is the Battle of **Bannockburn**, where Robert the Bruce routed King Edward II and his English troops in June, 1314; today, an equestrian statue of King Robert marks the site. Bonnie Prince Charlie tried to pick up some of Bruce's good fortune, briefly using Bannockburn House as his local headquarters in 1746. Another battle, at Sauchieburn (1488), was less auspicious; James III died there and was buried at **Cambuskenneth Abbey**. This abbey, built around 1140, saw the meeting of Bruce's Parliament in 1326; today, a partially restored bell tower rises above its ruined remains.

More peaceful, and more recent, is the spa town **Bridge of Allan**. Taking advantage of the tourists flocking to the nearby Trossachs, a local landlord "discovered" the curative powers of his waters in the 1820s; by mid-century, the town had developed into a full-fledged Victorian spa, an aspect which it retains today. Especially notable is the **Holy Trinity Church** (1860), less for its architecture than for the interior furnished in 1904 by Charles Rennie Mackintosh (see p. 111-2).

An older church lies to the north: **Dunblane Cathedral** dates from the 13th century. English art critic John Ruskin so loved its west facade that a window here is dubbed "Ruskin's Window." Inside, there's a stout Pictish cross predating even the cathedral; some notable stained-glass windows (south side of the choir),

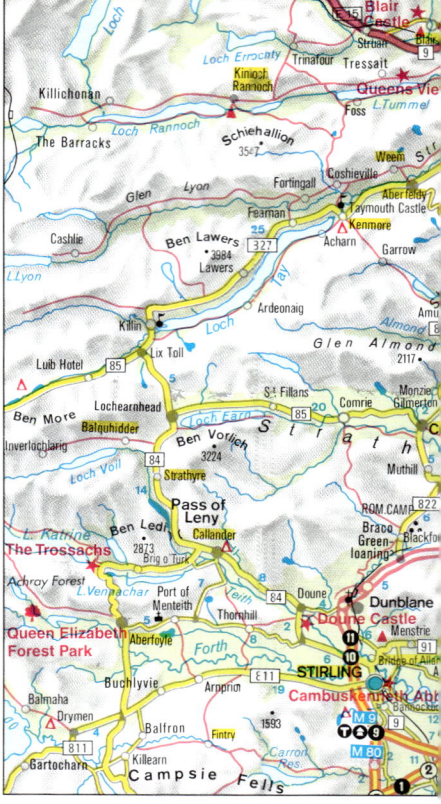

and a marvelous 15th-century choir screen and choir stalls carved with plant and animal motifs (including an evocative bat). Through the middle of town runs **Allan Water**, which brought Dunblane to prominence as a spa in the 19th century. Dunblane came unhappily to international attention in 1996, when a local ran amok and shot more than 20 young children in the town's elementary school.

Nestled between Stirling and Glasgow are the **Campsie Fells**, a gentle region of sweet little villages, rolling hills, and sheep-dotted meadows that seems light-years, rather than a mere hour's drive, from Glasgow. Center of the region is charming **Fintry**, guarded by 15th-cen-

tury **Culcreuch Castle** (now an elegant hotel).

THE TROSSACHS

Sir Walter Scott's epic poem *The Lady of the Lake* was more effective than any tourist brochure. For even before his (originally anonymous) *Waverley* novels, it won the author wide renown; and hordes of visitors came flocking to the region in which the poem was set to experience natural beauties which, in Scott's words, were "so wondrous wild the whole might seem/the scenery of a fairy dream."

One of the *Waverley* novels did its bit, as well: *Rob Roy*, the tale of local hero Rob Roy Macgregor, the Robin Hood of the north. The real "Red Rob" was not the noble freedom fighter into which literature and Hollywood have transformed him, but a plain cattle rustler. After absconding with money belonging to the Duke of Montrose, he withdrew to the hills and became his own master, switching allegiances with abandon to match his aliases (since the name Macgregor had been proscribed in 1603 after the clan had led one raid too many, Rob Roy often went by Campbell, his mother's maiden name), and possibly serving as a double agent in the first Jacobite Rebellion. Arrested and imprisoned in London, he was pardoned in 1727 and died a peaceful death on his home turf. A pretty

209

churchyard at **Balquhidder** contains his alleged grave, as well as that of his wife and two sons. There's also a **Rob Roy's Cave** on the east bank of Loch Lomond; and the region abounds with other memorials and visitors' centers bearing his name.

Near ruined **Inchmahome Priory**, on an island in the Lake of Menteith, **Aberfoyle** is the "gateway to the **Trossachs**." Although the term "Trossachs" is used for the whole region, the name actually applies only to the glen connecting Loch Katrine and Loch Achray. Known as the **Duke's Pass**, the road from Aberfoyle to **Brig o'Turk** leads through the glen, with plenty of scenic lookouts along the way. Offering more stunning views of the area is the 4-mile (7-km) **Achray Forest Drive**.

Loch Katrine was the Lake for Scott's *Lady*, Ellen Douglas; its name, however,

comes not from a woman but from *cateran*, Gaelic for robber, presumably describing the kind of company it once kept. The lake itself is as pure as can be; it's supplied Glasgow with drinking water since 1859. As a result, power boats are forbidden; the only vessel that plies its waters is the 1900-vintage steamer **S.S. Sir Walter Scott**. Located south of the loch is the **Queen Elizabeth Forest Park**.

Callander is another town with Queen Victoria associations, and often overcrowded, since many people follow Victoria's example and use it as a base for touring. Dominating the scenery is **Ben Ledi**, sacred to the Picts; the Druids celebrated the coming of spring by lighting a fire on its summit.

A detour along lovely **Loch Earn** leads into Perthshire and to **Crieff**. Crieff, too, saw its heyday under Queen Victoria, becoming a popular spa town where waters and walks were taken for the benefit of bourgeois health, and concerts heard in the evening at the band-

Above: Empty and breathtaking: Rannoch Moor (with Black Mount). Right: Britain's only private army: the Atholl Highlander.

stand in the town park. A literal overview of the town can be had from **The Knock**, a tree-covered hill rising north of town.

Tay for Two

Further north, long **Loch Tay** snakes toward the heart of Victoria country. Toward its northern end, at **Fortingall**, is a tree which claims to be the oldest yew in Europe, allegedly 3,000 years old. Legend, actively fostered by locals, has it that Pontius Pilate was born here, the son of a Roman legionary and a local woman; however, since the Romans didn't get this far north until 100 A.D., this is now held to be apocryphal (unless Mr. Pilate, Sr., was simply touring the area, like so many Europeans after him). Well worth touring is gorgeous **Glen Lyon**, which runs from here into the hills.

But it's fact, not fiction, that the River Tay, which wends its way from Loch Tay to the sea, is the source of the freshwater pearls that stud the throne in Edinburgh. At **Aberfeldy**, the river is crossed by one of the loveliest bridges built along General Wade's network of military roads in the 1730s (designed by William Adam). An oatmeal **water mill** shows another side of the past; while castle enthusiasts can explore nearby **Castle Menzies**.

Still farther north, Lochs **Rannoch** and **Tummel** run in a straight line from East to West, linking the wildness of Rannoch Moor (p. 137) with the greener, piney landscapes around Pitlochry. On the north bank of Loch Tummel is the most famous of several spots designated **Queen's View**. Victoria was enchanted with the outlook over Loch Tummel, with the silhouette of **Schiehallion**, the "fairy mountain," in the distance; but this particular Queen's View was supposedly so named even before she came here; the queen in question may have been Mary, Queen of Scots.

North of this is another view with decidedly aristocratic coloring: the white turrets of **Blair Castle**, stately home of the Dukes of Atholl and headquarters of

the only private army in Great Britain. Mary Queen of Scots visited here, as well; in fact, the castle, which houses collections of paintings, china, toys, and a natural history museum, has been receiving visitors for more than 720 years. **Blair Atholl** is also an agricultural center, which you can see in the local museum **Atholl Country Collection**, the still-working **Corn Mill**, and the international horse trials every fall.

Heading back to the Tay, you pass the **Pass of Killiecrankie**, site of the first conflict of the Jacobite cause in 1689. This conflict is fondly remembered because the Highlanders won, although they lost their leader, "Bonnie Dundee," in the process (see p. 33).

Pitlochry is literally, geographically, at the heart of Scotland; and it's one of the most-visited places in Scotland, as well, which can make it hard to find accommodation. Highlights here, besides

Above: The many moods of Central Scotland: skiing at Glenshee.

212

the general quaint Victorian ambience, are the **Fish Ladder**, built for the migrating salmon when the River Tummel was dammed as part of the Tummel Valley Hydro-Electric Scheme in the 1950s, and the **Pitlochry Festival Theatre**, with a summer season that draws theatergoers and performers from all over the world.

PERTH

The Tay meanders through Perthshire to empty into the Firth of Tay at **Perth** (where it's crossed by an elegant stone bridge dating from 1771). Perth can be accounted another cradle of Scottish history, for here was **Scone** (pronounced *scoon*), center of Kenneth Macalpine's kingdom after he brought the Stone of Destiny here from Dunstaffnage. Edward I removed the stone to Westminster in the 13th century (see "History," p. 20), and the 12th-century abbey that replaced Macalpine's original castle was destroyed in the Reformation. Today, stately **Scone Palace** stands on the site, behind a fragment of ancient gateway; it's been home to the Earls of Mansfield for 400 years.

Perth, founded as a royal burgh in the 13th century, boasts an older building: **St. John's Kirk** dates back to 1242, although it was so extensively restored in the 15th and 16th centuries that almost nothing remains of that early edifice. This church ensured its place in history in 1559, when an inflammatory sermon by John Knox effectively sparked off the Reformation. Some two centuries earlier, **North Inch**, today a public park, was the site of the 1396 Battle of the Clans, a conflict which pitted 30 champions of Clan Chattan against 30 of Clan Kay. The event is the backdrop for Scott's *The Fair Maid of Perth* (which Bizet later turned into an opera). Scott chose one of the oldest houses in town as his heroine's residence; you can still visit the **Fair Maid's House**. There's no physical memorial, however, to the year 1437, when in Blackfriar's Monastery James I was assassinated despite the attempt of a lady-in-waiting, Catherine Douglas, to keep his killers outside by using her arm in place of the bolt on the door. She was unsuccessful, but survived, and her name lives on in the expression "Katy bar the door."

FIFE

Between the Firth of Forth and the Firth of Tay, further separated from the mainland by the chain of the **Ochil Hills** between Stirling and Perth, is the stubby peninsula of **Fife**. Fife, folk wisdom has it, "is a beggar's mantle with a fringe of gold"; this poetic but obscure saying either indicates that the country's inland is poor while its coastlines are agriculturally rich, or refers to the fact that the salt-panning industry, a major source of income here, left a yellow tinge hanging in the air. Or, the "fringe of gold" could be a reference to the sun, said to shine more in Fife than in most of the rest of Great Britain, and the yellow sand of the beaches.

Fife was the southernmost of the Pictish kingdoms; its name derives from Fib, one of seven sons of a Pictish king. Its southern coast lies across the Firth of Forth from Edinburgh, today linked by the Forth Bridges from North to South Queensferry (see p. 69). Early inhabitants believed that Scotland was actually an island separate from England, cut off by a channel formed by the Firth of Forth and the Firth of Clyde. Stirling, which had a bridge, controlled access to the "mainland" to the south. Queen Margaret, wife of Malcolm Canmore, therefore set up a ferry near Dunfermline in the 11th century; and the Queens Ferry operated until the road bridge opened in 1964.

Margaret wasn't only a queen; she became a saint in 1250 (160 years after her death; see p. 49). Her piety is documented throughout **Dunfermline**, the "fort on the winding stream," where she established a priory later expanded and elevated to an abbey by her equally pious son, David I. The nave of the ponderous **Abbey Church** actually dates back to David's 1128 foundation; the architecture then travels through time (with some chunky, clumsy 16th-century buttresses) to a neo-Gothic choir from the last century over the tomb of Robert the Bruce (whose body was discovered during excavations in 1818 and re-buried with pomp). Margaret and Malcolm lie practically incognito in **St. Margaret's Chapel**, outside the church proper; but Dunfermline does have a **St. Margaret's Cave**, a **St. Margaret's Stone** (with prehistoric cup-and-ring markings), and other relevant reminders. Much Saint Margaret memorabilia, as well as Dunfermline relics from her day to the present, are well displayed in **Abbot House**, the oldest house in town.

Dunfermline was once a center of the linen industry; in fact, Queen Elizabeth II's wedding dress was made here. But the mills began to close even in the last century, which forced some local families to emigrate to America. Among them were the Carnegies, who departed in 1848 with their 13-year-old son, Andrew. Andrew, of course, became one of the richest men in America, and donated huge amounts of money to found libraries (2,810 of them), schools, and museums, both in his adopted country and in the place of his birth. His **birthplace** is today a museum revealing his humble beginnings. He also helped endow the upkeep of gorgeous, blossoming **Pittencrieff Park** (which encompasses 11th-century **Canmore's Tower**, the oldest building in town).

Many of the old burghs along the coast south of Dunfermline were falling into

Above: Flamingo-colored lions guard the town center of Falkland. Right: Crail, one of the loveliest of East Neuk's fishing villages.

disrepair before the National Trust stepped in. **Culross**, from the 17th and 18th centuries, was one of the NTS's first projects; today, you can inspect everything from the 16th-century palace to the carved lintels over the house doors. The Earl of Elgin built nearby **Charlestown**, where there are some well-preserved lime kilns, in the shape of the letter E. An even more striking rich man's folly is west of Culross and over the Kincardine Bridge: the famous 18th-century **Pineapple**.

But Fife proper lies further east, past **Inverkeithing**, by Queensferry, one of the oldest Royal Burghs in Scotland, with a splendid 16th-century **Mercat Cross**, and **Aberdour**, with its 14th-century castle (and doocot), an even older **St. Finian's Church**, and a marvelous beach with seal-spotting opportunities (from which you can also see **Incholm Island**, with its medieval abbey).

It's around shoreside **Kirkcaldy**, "the lang toun of Fife," that real holiday country begins. The beaches are as beautiful as the towns. At **East Wemyss**, **Wemyss Caves** contain a wealth of Pictish carvings. At **Dysart**, there are relics of later days in the restored 17th-century fishermen's houses of **Pan Ha'** (named for the nearby salt pans), or the distinctive church tower of **St. Serf's**. **Lower Largo** was the birthplace of Alexander Selkirk, whose experiences inspired Daniel Defoe to write his novel *Robinson Crusoe*.

Inland Pleasures

Inland Fife is a showplace of Stuart history. In **Loch Leven**, by **Kinross**, stand the ruins of the castle where Mary, Queen of Scots was imprisoned for 11 months after her abdication. Further east lies ancient **Falkland**, with **Falkland Palace**. Begun by James IV, this edifice served as sometime country house-cum-hunting lodge to eight Stuart monarchs,

including Mary. It was James V who built the bulk of the building, with its original **Chapel Royal** and a tennis court supposed to be the oldest in the world. He died here in despair, believing Scotland lost, in 1542. The news of the birth of his daughter was no consolation; "it came wi' a lass, and it will pass wi' a lass," he said, meaning that the Stuarts obtained the crown by marrying Marjory Bruce, and that his daughter would see the end of the line (neither observation was quite true). A centerpiece of the town's cobblestone streets around the palace is the stone **Bruce Fountain** with its flamingo-colored lions.

At **Cupar**, a monument to later wealth stands in the form of the **Hill of Tarvit Mansion House**, built in 1696 and remodeled in 1906 by architect Sir Robert Lorimer for Dundee industrialist F.B. Sharp. The building now displays Sharp's magnificent collection of antiques and tapestries, paintings and porcelain, and also houses a restored Edwardian laundry.

This Neuk of the Woods

"Neuk" is Old Scots for "corner," and the southeastern corner of Fife, **East Neuk**, has retained the flavor, and tranquility, of bygone days in its fishing harbors and villages of whitewashed stone houses. The stepped gables of some of these show that architectural styles, as well as goods, were imported during active trade with the Low Countries in the 17th century. Trade was followed by fishing; a **Scottish Fisheries Museum** at **Anstruther** (pronounced AIN-ster) documents an industry that was an important source of income until the herring departed these waters in the middle of this century.

Today, what draws money to the region are fine beaches, such as that at **Elie**, or castles, such as **Kellie Castle**, a few miles inland. Started in the 14th century, Kellie's main bulk dates from the 16th and 17th century, and it was rescued in the 19th century by the thorough renovation of James Lorimer. Its plasterwork

ceilings and painted panelling especially deserve attention; dating from the time of its renovation are a Victorian nursery, kitchen, and walled garden.

ST ANDREWS

While the apostle Andrew is the patron saint of Scotland, the story of how his relics got to these shores has been obscured by legend. But it's certain that they came here, some time between the 4th and 8th centuries A.D., and that a church was built to house them, and that pilgrims flocked to the church, which was subequently expanded into a **cathedral**, the largest church in Scotland before the Reformation left it in towering ruins.

Today, these ruins loom windowless at the end of **South Street**, turning empty eyes to the backdrop of the sea. St An-

Above: Net-mending is all in a day's work for a fisherman. Right: Stately Glamis Castle, childhood home of the Queen Mum.

drews's other defense between its smug stone houses and the elements is the **castle**, even more ruined than the cathedral, vainly holding a seaside rock with its shattered foundations.

Other venerable institutions here have had better luck. One survivor is the **university**, the oldest in Scotland, founded in 1412; you can see remnants of its early days in **St. Salvator's College**, where the church dates back to 1450. The theological faculty is housed in **St. Mary's College** on South Street (1538); in its courtyard is a tree planted by Mary, Queen of Scots.

St Andrews's other hallowed institution is, of course, golf. The town is home to the **Royal and Ancient Golf Club** which plays such a central role in Britain's golfing world, as well as to several famous courses, including the hallowed Old Course, a relic of the original Society of St Andrews Golfers, who began golfing here in 1754. (For more about the game of golf in St. Andrews, see "Golf," p. 236.)

DUNDEE

Crossing the Firth of Tay, the Tay Bridges link Fife with an erstwhile Scottish metropolis: **Dundee**. Long a busy harbor for trading, shipbuilding, and whaling, overshadowed by the (extinct) volcano of **Dundee Law**, the city was dubbed the "Naples of the North."

But today Dundee, perhaps like its Italian namesake, exudes an aura of decline. Shipping has departed, as it has from other parts of Scotland, and this southern city wasn't able to profit, as did Aberdeen, from North Sea oil: as a result, unemployment is fairly high. Furthermore, Dundee was anything but careful of its heritage: in the 19th and earlier 20th centuries, many of the city's noble old buildings were torn down to make room for new, less well-favored developments. Like a harbinger of ill

luck to come, the original Tay Bridge, built for the railroad, collapsed during a storm in 1879, plunging a train full of passengers into the waters of the firth: none survived.

Traditionally, Dundee has lived from the "three Js": jute, jam, and journalism. Dundee's marmelade is a city trademark (see p. 226); but it was jute, a fiber used in making ropes and sailcloth, that brought the city untold riches in the 19th century. One reason Dundee was so careless of its past was that it was a city of the *nouveau riche* in Victorian times: testimonial to these days are the jute barons' mansions, especially in nearby **Broughty Ferry**; while the city's newest visitor attraction is **Verdant Works**, a restored jute mill. As for the journalism: Dundee is home to two daily newspapers, and even more famously, the weekly *Sunday Post*. Once one of Scotland's leading press organs, known for its articles and its cartoons, it's today a rather conservative paper catering mainly to an older, more traditionally-minded readership.

Dundee prides itself on being a "City of Discovery," for it was from here, in Dundee-built ships, that Robert Scott, for one, set off on his first voyage for the South Pole in 1901. His ship, the *Discovery*, is now a floating museum; a nearby heritage center documents the city's maritime past. Another floating museum is the *Unicorn*, launched in 1824, the oldest British-built ship still afloat.

One attempt at retaining the past can be seen in the **City Churches**. The 15th-century church of St. Mary's was repeatedly destroyed by a number of factors ranging from English attacks to a devastating fire in 1841 (by which time three other churches were housed under the same roof); the building has been reconstructed, minus one church. Then, there's the **Howff**, once the garden of Greyfriars Monastery; later, after Mary, Queen of Scots gave it to the city, it was used as a graveyard as well as a meeting-point (*howff*) for the Nine Trades of Dundee (its gravestones are embellishedwith symbols of the various craft guilds).

North of Dundee

North of Dundee is stately **Glamis Castle**, traditionally the setting of *Macbeth*. Historically documented, at least, is that it's been a royal residence since 1372, and was the childhood home of Britain's beloved Queen Mum. Highlights include the plasterwork ceilings of the imposing Great Hall and the painted panels, of 17th-century Dutch origin, set into the ceiling of the church. Real castle fans can cut across country to the **House of Dun**, by Brechin (near Montrose), a William Adam house with marvelous plasterwork, entering which is not unlike walking into a Wedgwood teacup. Another Brechin highlight is a Celtic **round tower** from around 1000 A.D. (one of only two in Scotland; the other is in Abernethy). Nearby **Aberlemno** is worth a detour for its ornately carved Pictish stones.

Back on the coast, at **Arbroath**, there's yet another gorgeous ruined **abbey**. This is the spot where, in 1320, the Scottish aristocracy asserted their independence from England in the "Declaration of Arbroath." Anyone who knows Robert Southey's ballad "The Inchcape Rock" should note offshore **Bell Rock**, submerged at high tide. The story goes that a pirate, Sir Ralph the Rover, removed the warning bell which the local abbot had placed on the rock, hoping to profit from the cargos of wrecked ships; however, he received his just deserts when his own ship foundered on the rock and sank.

There are two further stops for literary pilgrims: inland **Kirriemuir**, by Glamis Castle, where *Peter Pan* creator **J. M. Barrie's birthplace** is now a museum; and **Arbuthnot**, by Inverbervie, where a **Grassic Gibbon Center** commemorates the author who immortalized this town as "Kinraddie" in the novel *Sunset Song* (see p. 231).

STIRLING
Telephone area code (01786)
Accommodation / Restaurants
MODERATE: **The Heritage Hotel**, 16 Allan Park, tel. 473660, fax 451291, Georgian town house, French-style interior, restaurant. **Castlecroft**, Ballengeich Rd., tel. 474933, friendly B&B. **39**, 39 Broad St., tel. 473929, small and popular restaurant.
Museums and Sights
Stirling Castle, tel. 450000, open daily Apr-Sept 9:30 am-6 pm, Oct-Mar 9:30 am-5 pm. Ranges from the 11th century to residential wings from the Renaissance. Includes the **Regimental Museum of the Argyll and Sutherland Highlanders**. A Visitor Centre presents a/v introduction. **Old Town Jail** (opened 1996, information not available yet). **National Wallace Monument**, Abbey Craig, Stirling, tel. 472140, open Feb & Nov Sat & Sun 10 am-4 pm, Mar-May & Oct daily 10 am-5 pm, June & Sept daily 10 am-6 pm, Jul-Aug 9:30 am-6:30 pm.
Tourist Information
Stirling Tourist Information Center, Dumbarton Road, tel. 475019.

TROSSACHS & SURROUNDINGS
Accommodation
FINTRY: *EXPENSIVE:* **Culcreuch Castle Hotel**, Stirlingshire, tel. (01360) 860228 or 860 555, fax 860556. 14th-century castle, now a country hotel with dungeon dining room, individually furnished bedrooms (one with hand-painted Chinese wallpaper that's been up since 1723). *BUDGET:* **Mrs. M. Mundell B & B**, Craigton Farm, Denny Road, tel. (01360) 860 426. Lovely farm B & B in new bungalow, with "lounge" for guests.
CALLANDER: *EXPENSIVE:* **The Roman Camp**, tel. (01877) 330003, fax 331533, 1625 mansion, gardens outside and cozy atmosphere within. *BUDGET:* **Brook Linn Country House**, tel. (01877) 330103, Victorian house, family-run.
Restaurants
MODERATE: **Creagan House**, Strathyre (near Balquhidder), tel. (01877) 384638, reasonably priced home cooking in pleasant surroundings. *BUDGET:* **Myrtle Inn**, Stirling Road, Callander, tel. (01877) 330919, old-style pub with solid grub.
Museums & Sights
Glengoyne Distillery, Dumgoyne, by Killearn, tel. (01360) 550254; smooth Highland malt distillery on the western edge of the Campsie Fells. Open Apr-Nov. **S.S. Sir Walter Scott**, Loch Katrine, tel. (0141) 9550128, daily cruises Apr-Sept.

PERTHSHIRE
Accommodation / Restaurants
BALQUHIDDER: *MODERATE:* **Monachyle Mhor**, Lochearnhead, tel. (01877) 384622, fax 384305. The dream getaway hotel, at the end of a

one-lane road 4 mi past Rob Roy's grave. Hotel/working farm with elegant dining room in full view of gorgeous Loch Voil. Award-winning food, individually furnished rooms, affordable. Bring walking gear and try the spiced bread ice cream if it's on the menu. **KENMORE:** *MODERATE:* **Kenmore Hotel**, tel. (01887) 830205, fax 830262. Located at one end of Loch Tay, this claims to be the oldest inn in Scotland and has a respectable restaurant. **KINLOCH RANNOCH:** *MODERATE:* **Bunrannoch Hotel**, tel. (01882) 367. Cozy ambiance with a hint of convivial British sloppiness in the hunting-lodge style lounge/dining room; large rooms; reliable pub-like food. **PITLOCHRY:** *EXPENSIVE:* **Pine Trees Hotel**, Strathview Terrace, tel. (01796) 472121, fax 472460. Beautiful Victorian country house in grounds with its own golf course. *BUDGET:* **Derrybeg Guest House**, 18 Lower Oakfield, tel. (01796) 472070, quiet private house with garden. **PERTH:** *MODERATE:* **Sunbank House Hotel**, 50 Dundee Rd., tel. (01738) 624882, fax 442515, refurbished Victorian house, with views and good restaurant. **Stakis Perth Hotel**, West Mill St., tel. (01738) 628281, fax 643423, in converted 15th-c mill in center of town.

Museums & Sights
Breadalbane Folklore Center, Falls of Dochart, Killin, tel. (01567) 820254, open Mar-Jun & Sept-Oct daily 10 am-5 pm, Jul-Aug 9 am-6 pm, Nov-Dec & Feb Sat & Sun 10 am-4 pm. Tales and legends of the region. **Aberfeldy Water Mill**, Mill St., tel. (01887) 820803, Apr-Oct Mon-Sat 10 am-5:30 pm, Sun 12-5:30 pm. **Castle Menzies**, Weem (W of Aberfeldy), Apr-Oct 10:30 am-5 pm, Sun 2-5 pm.
PERTH: Scone Palace, tel. (01738) 552300, open Good Friday-mid-Oct 9:30 am-5 pm. **Perth Museum & Art Gallery**, George St., tel. (01738) 632488, open Mon-Sat 10 am-5 pm; art, natural & local history. **Fergusson Gallery**, Marshall Place, tel. (01738) 441944, open Mon-Sat 10 am-5 pm, works of renowned Scottish artist. **Huntingtower Castle**, 3 mi from Perth on A85, open daily; 15th-c mansion with painted ceilings.

Tourist Information
Perthshire Tourist Board, 45 High St., Perth, tel. (01738) 638353, fax 444863.

FIFE
Accommodation / Restaurants
ST ANDREWS: *EXPENSIVE:* **Rufflets**, Strathkinness Low Road, tel. (01334) 472594, fax 478703. Manor house with great garden. *MODERATE:* **Glendarran Guest House**, 9 Murray Park, tel. (01334) 477951, fax 477908, pleasant row house. **ANSTRUTHER:** *MODERATE:* **The Hermitage Guest House**, Ladywalk, tel. (01333) 310909, attractive and simple. **CUPAR:** *EXPENSIVE:*

The Peat Inn, tel. (01334) 840206, area's leading restaurant, French/Scottish cuisine. *MODERATE:* **Ostler's Close**, tel. (01334) 655574, excellent bistro.

Museums & Sights
DUNFERMLINE: Andrew Carnegie Birthplace Museum, Moodie St., tel (01383) 724302. Open Nov-Mar daily 2-4 pm, Apr-Oct Mon-Sat 11 am-5 pm, Sun 2-5 pm. **Abbot House**, Maygate, tel. (01383) 733266, open daily 10 am-5 pm. **CUPAR: Hill of Tarvit Mansion House**, tel. (01334) 653127, open mid-Apr-mid-Oct, 1:30-5:30 pm, gardens open year round. **CRAIL: Crail Museum and Heritage Center**, 62/64 Marketgate, tel. (01333) 450869, open Apr-Sept 2:30-5 pm, Jun-mid-Sep also 10 am-12:30 pm. **ANSTRUTHER: Scottish Fisheries Museum**, St. Ayles, Harborhead, tel. (01333) 310628, open Nov-Mar Mon-Sat 10 am-4:30 pm, Sun 2-4:30 pm; Apr-Oct til 5:30 pm. **ST ANDREWS: Cathedral & Museum** open Oct-Mar Mon-Sat 9:30 am-4:30 pm, Sun 2-4:30 pm; Apr-Sept til 6:30 pm. **Castle & Visitor Center**, hours as cathedral. **Scotland's Secret Bunker**, Underground Nuclear War Command Center, Troywood, tel. (01333) 310301. Military and government HQ in the event of nuclear war, now a museum since the Cold War has defused. Open daily 10 am-5 pm.

Sports & Activities
GOLF: For advance reservation on all St Andrews courses, call (01334) 475757. The direct line for the Old Course is 473393.

Tourist Information
St Andrews Tourist Information Center, 70 Market St., tel. (01334) 472021.

DUNDEE
Telephone area code (01382)
Accommodation / Restaurants
MODERATE: **Shaftesbury Hotel**, 1 Hyndford St., tel. 669216, fax 641598. Former mansion of a jute baron, with nice, informal restaurant. **Hillside Guest House**, 43 Constitution St., tel. 223443. B&B-style, in Victorian villa. **Raffles Restaurant**, 18 Perth Rd., tel. 226344. Straightforward, decent cooking, with changing daily specials. *BUDGET:* **The Laurels**, 65 Camp-hill Rd. Broughty Ferry, tel. 776203. Simple, but friendly and cozy.

Museums & Sights
Discovery Point, Discovery Quay, tel. 201245, visitors' center, authentic old ship. **Broughty Castle Museum**, Broughty Ferry, tel. 776121, closed Fri. **Glamis Castle**, A94 (N of Dundee), tel. (01307) 840242, Apr-Oct 10:30 am-5:30 pm.

Activities
Dundee Rep Theatre, Tay Square, tel. 223530. Leading theater with wide range of performances.

Tourist Information
Dundee Tourist Board, 4 City Squ., tel. 434664.

WHISKY: THE WATER OF LIFE

Uisge beatha (oo-ISS-kay-bey-ah): in the Gaelic term for "water of life" lies the derivation of our word "whisky." The Latin cognate, *aquavitae*, lives on in Scandanavian aquavit. Call it aquavit, whisky (no e, please!), or by one of the names of Scotland's 100-odd distilleries (Glenfiddich, Oban): it's certainly one form of Scotland's life's blood.

The earliest recorded mention of "aquavitae" in Scotland dates from 1494, but the history of Scottish distilling probably goes back much farther. It's opined that the art of distilling arrived on Scottish shores with the Irish missionaries who brought Christianity to the country. Certainly it was a secular activity by the time the government, realizing what it had been missing in the way of revenues, started taxing it in the 17th century. With the laws unclear, and the pressure on to avoid excisemen and smugglers, illegal distilling boomed – one reason many distilleries seem to be tucked away in picturesque but out-of-the-way places. In 1823, the British Parliament stepped in to resolve things with the Distilleries Act. Most of the oldest operative distilleries officially date from the 19th century. There are several claimants to the title of "Scotland's oldest distillery;" one, Glenturret, has been going strong since 1775.

Whisky is divided into two categories: malt and grain. The beverage prized by whisky connoisseurs is single malt whisky, made with malted barley; grain whisky also contains unmalted barley and maize. While the famous distilleries pride themselves on their single malt, it represents a relatively small part of their output: 95% of their product goes into making better-known, mass-market blended whiskies, such as Dewar's. A blend like

Preceding pages: The national pastime. Right: Strathisla Distillery is one of Scotland's oldest.

J&B has between 35 and 45 single malts in its malt content – and the malt content represents only 40% of the finished product; the other 60% is grain.

Barley is "malted" by being soaked in water, spread on a concrete floor, and allowed to sprout. After this comes the first important step in producing a whisky's individual flavor: the sprouts are dried out by slowly roasting over a peat fire. Peat is used for flavor, rather than heat; here enters the smooth, smoky, peaty aroma of a good single malt. Each distillery uses its own blend of fuels; on the islands, seaweed is often used, whence the distinctive kick of Tallisker (Skye's only malt) or Laphroaig (a strong-flavored Islay malt). Some environmentalists protest the use of peat, a natural and limited resource; but in fact, whisky distilling uses only .5% of the country's total peat consumption.

After the barley has been roasted, it's ground, and the resulting grist is flushed with hot water. The point here is to get the sugar out of the mash; the mixture is sieved to extract the liquids (the husks that remain behind are used in animal feed). Yeast is added to the liquid in another vat, and the mixture ferments, after which it's pumped into a copper still and heated: the actual process of distilling. Heating kills the yeast; a signal difference between brewing beer and distilling whisky is that to make beer, you let the yeast live, whereas in whiskey it dies. After this, the whisky is cut with water. Water is another very important factor in a malt whisky's flavor, and its source is part of a distiller's mystique. Jura's only distillery, for example, boasts of the spring of Bhaille Mharghaidh; while Glenlivet conceals from the eyes of visitors its famous Josie's Well.

To mature, the whisky is put into barrels, which also play a role in the whisky's final flavor. Traditionally the best barrels for whisky are oak casks which have contained Spanish sherry; bourbon

barrels are even more common. These barrels also give the whisky its color (which is sometimes further enhanced with the addition of caramel). At the Speyside Cooperage, along the "Malt Whisky Trail," you can still watch the barrels being made. As they're paid per barrel, the men work extremely fast.

Malt whisky is usually aged for 12 years, but there are malts as young as 10 years, and as old as 18. Unlike wine, whisky knows no vintages; it stops aging once you get it out of the barrel and into the bottle. A 12-year-old whisky is always 12 years old, even if you hoard a bottle of it for years.

Opinions vary on the proper way to imbibe a single malt. Some prefer their "wee dram" with a "wee splash" of water, claiming that the water opens up the flavor; others hold that it must be taken straight. But it's a matter of general agreement that a good single malt should not be sullied with ice, or, God forbid, used in a mixed drink. Few places, even the Borestone Bar in Stirling, which ad-

vertises 850 different malts, will go so far as to offer you a *quaich*, the drinking bowl traditionally used for malt whiskies.

There are so many different malts and different flavors that finding your own is a matter of individual taste. To help get your bearings, you can orient yourself geographically. The four generally accepted malt whisky classifications are Highland, Lowland, Speyside, and Islay; Campbelltown, which used to be on the roster with some 40 distilleries, today has only one active one, and is therefore no longer counted. And each distillery has its own claim to fame, from Glenkinchnie and Auchentoshan in the Lowlands to Orkney's excellent Highland Park, Scotland's most northerly whisky.

Single malt whisky remains, for some, an acquired taste. During Prohibition, when alcohol was illegal in the United States, Laphroaig was the only alcohol that was allowed into the country. Customs officers took one whiff and simply couldn't believe that anyone would drink the stuff for pleasure. Or at least, so the story goes.

THE FOODS OF SCOTLAND

In ratings of international cuisines, Great Britain's food is generally placed at the bottom of the totem pole. This is an egregious injustice to the country's northernmost realm. Scotland has a distinct, age-old culinary tradition wholly separate from its southern neighbor. The fruits of its waters (salmon, herring, scallops), fields (Aberdeen Angus and Galloway beef), and forests (grouse, pheasant, and venison) provide a wealth of raw materials to gladden any chef's heart. And Scotland has had plenty of chefs: the "Auld Alliance" with France left its mark not only on the country's politics, but on its cooking. For a time, a French chef was the thing to have in Edinburgh's upper-class households; and a French flavor has remained, not least in cooking terms still in common use today. Lamb is called "jiggot" (*gigot*); a plate, an "ashet" (*assiette*); some soups are known as "pottages"; and small cuts of meat are not *escalopes*, but "collops."

Scotland's most famous culinary invention, the *haggis*, is a perfect symbol of the country's cuisine: beloved of Scots, much misunderstood, and maligned, by everyone else. The uninitiated balk at the idea of a sheep's stomach stuffed with a concoction of offal and oatmeal and boiled, although since nearly every country has its own offal specialty, from *boudin noir* to chitlings, it seems unfair to single out the haggis for ill repute. Haggis isn't just a meal: it's a piece of cultural heritage. Burns hailed it as the "great chieftain o' the puddin'-race," and one of the best introductions to the haggis experience is to participate in a Burns Night dinner (January 25). After being ceremoniously borne in from the kitchen, the haggis is split open, drenched with whisky, and formally greeted with a read-

ing of Burns's ode "To A Haggis." It's then taken back out to the kitchen, sliced, and served up with the traditional side dishes of *bashed neeps* and *chappit tatties* – mashed turnips and potatoes. Don't knock it 'til you've tried it.

Borrowings from French and Gaelic have given a poetic ring to the names of Scottish dishes. (Even the name haggis is thought to derive from the French *hachis*, to chop.) A meal might start with *feather fowlie*, a chicken soup with eggs and cream – its name is a corruption either of *oeufs filés* or *volaille* – or *cullen skink*, a delicious fish chowder made of smoked haddock with plenty of potato, named from the Gaelic word for "essence" (*skink*). Other names are more straightforward, such as *cock-a-leekie soup*, made of a chicken (cock), leeks (leekie), and – prunes. The French diplomat Talleyrand liked it, but thought the prunes should be taken out before serving.

In this country surrounded by water and perforated with rivers and lochs, fish and seafood have always been a dietary staple. Today, when Scottish salmon draws exorbitant prices in the world's capitals, it's hard to believe that the Scots used to regard it as food for the poor. Servants in upper-class households had clauses in their contracts stipulating that they didn't have to eat salmon more than three times a week; so common was the fish that it was even used as fertilizer.

Today, of course, fresh fish is more highly valued, whether it's salmon, Carnas na Ceardaich scallops (from the mouth of Loch Fyne), or cod served with a mustard sauce that reveals the influence the Vikings had on Scottish cookery (mustard sauces still feature on Scandinavian tables). In the days before refrigeration, however, fresh fish wasn't always available, and few countries can compete with Scotland's inventiveness in coming up with different ways to preserve it. Whether it's cod, haddock, or herring, there are more ways to cure a Scottish

Right: Charles MacSween presents the haggis in his Georgian kitchen.

fish than you can shake a fishing rod at. In Aberdeen, people started curing fish around the 13th century; here, too, the Vikings showed the way. Varieties include *Arbroath smokies*, small haddock smoked whole, in pairs, and the famous *Finnian Haddie*, smoked in burning seaweed. Kippered herring, *kippers*, are both salted and smoked; the finest of these come, appropriately, from Loch Fyne. Today, chemicals often stand in for genuine curing techniques; avoid fish that's too orangey or too uniformly colored.

The time to eat kippers, and many other fish, is the morning. Scottish breakfast menus often feature grilled kippers or even brown trout – a luxury which bears out Dr. Johnson's statement that "if an epicure could remove by a wish in quest of sensual gratification, wherever he had supped, he would breakfast in Scotland." Breakfasts are also enhanced by another staple food, oats. In days of yore, soldiers and students subsisted largely from bags of oats, generally used to make oatcakes. Today, the oat appears

in everything from soups to desserts. At breakfast, its most familiar form is *porridge*, although this is seldom served in the traditional communal wooden bowl, and people no longer eat it standing up.

Scotland's other best meal is tea. Afternoon tea was originally a Scottish institution: tea arrived in Edinburgh with James VII's wife, Mary of Modena, in 1681. Although both the church and the medical world were adamantly against it – some ministers felt it was worse than whisky – it rapidly became popular, a craze culminating in the tea-room fad that swept Glasgow in the late 19th century. For many people today, tea is an excuse to sample a variety of bakery products. Typical are *bannocks*, a name which applies to a variety of pancakes or soda breads, usually made with oatmeal or barley meal. There used to be a special bannock for virtually every occasion, from *Selkirk Bannock*, a preferred snack of Queen Victoria, to the ancient round *Yule Bannock*, with notched edges representing the rays of the sun. Out of this lat-

225

ter developed another famous Scottish edible: *shortbread*. *Petticoat tails*, a shortbread variant, supposedly got their name from French *petites gatelles*, little cakes; although some claim that they're so called because they're shaped like the full skirt of an Elizabethan petticoat.

Then there are the tea cakes: *Dundee cake*, its top studded with almonds; many varieties of gingerbread, such as *parkin* (which includes oatmeal); or, at Hogmanay (New Year's) the dark fruitcake called *Black Bun*. And then there are scones, from drop scones baked on a hot griddle, which look more like a pancake, to the more conventional soda variety. These are eaten with another Scottish invention: *marmalade*. Dundee's famous orange marmalade was supposedly the creation of an 18th-century housewife whose husband bought a load of oranges from a Spanish ship sheltering in the harbor; since the oranges were too bitter to

Above: The fruits of Loch Fyne. Right: True Harris tweed is still hand-loomed.

eat, she preserved them with ample quantities of sugar. Another story has it that marmalade was invented by the chef of Mary, Queen of Scots, to tempt her appetite when she was ill; the word's supposed derivation from *Marie malade* is, however, apocryphal.

After tea, not everyone has the appetite for a big supper of *howtowdie* with *drappit eggs* (that's chicken in a liver sauce served with spinach and poached eggs); *roastit beef* with *colcannon* (a side dish of mashed potatoes and cabbage, known, in the Borders, as *Rumbledethumps*); *grouse* with *skirlie* (made of oatmeal and drippings); or *cabbie-claw*, young cod in an egg sauce (from the French *cabillaud*, codling). And if one has mastered all that, there probably won't be room to tackle any "puddings," such as *clootie dumpling*, a pudding boiled in a cloth ("cloot") or *Tipsy Laird*, also called Scots Trifle.

The "Tipsy" ingredient in this "Laird" may be enough on its own: the Scottish liqueur *Drambuie*. When Bonnie Prince Charlie was fleeing Scotland by way of Skye after his Culloden rout, he thanked the Mackinnon family, his hosts, by giving them the recipe for his favorite liqueur. The same recipe has been used to make Drambuie ever since.

Another way to round off a good meal is *Atholl Brose*, a drink made of whisky, honey, and oatmeal. Some people may prefer to stick to oatcakes and a selection of mild Scots cheeses, from cheddars like *Orkney* or *Dunlop* (the first hard cheese in Scotland after Barbara Gilmour brought cheese-making back from Ireland in 1688) to *Caboc*, a cylindrical cream cheese rolled in oats.

Recent years have seen renewed interest in traditional Scottish recipes. Restaurants like Glasgow's Ubiquitous Chip spearheaded the Scottish culinary renaissance. Today, the "Taste of Scotland" scouts out restaurants with good Scottish food, and annually updates its results.

FROM TWEED TO TARTAN
Scottish Fabrics

On a cold, rainy day, it's easy to understand why Scotland has traditionally produced wool. From creating woollen shawls and sweaters to keep clansmen and fishermen warm through the dark winters, it was a short step to bringing it on the market; wool was one of the country's first exports, and the first to have duty charged on it. Originally, Lowlands regions were the leaders in wool production; but after the Highland Clearances, when sheep were introduced to land that had never supported sheep before, production began to spread.

Tweed is a perfect example. Now associated with famous Harris Tweed from the Outer Hebrides, this fabric was originally known as twill, and came from the Lowlands. Londoners misunderstood the funny accents of Scots vendors, hearing "tweel," which was corrupted to "tweed." Rather than correct the mistake, Scotsmen used it to advantage: a fabric that bore the name of a local river effectively advertised itself. (See p. 73.)

Harris Tweed became popular in the 1840s, when British aristocrats, bitten by the Scotland bug, all wanted to go shoot grouse in the Highlands. Lady Dunmore, wife of the islands' Laird, began pushing the fabric's merits as a material for hunting garments, hoping it could turn into the cash industry which the islanders desperately needed. She was right; Harris Tweed is still handwoven on the Isle of Harris today. Originally, the wool was colored with local dyes and hand-spun; today, the colors are at least inspired by the muted tones of the landscape. Once the wool is spun, it's delivered to weavers who operate treadle looms in their homes, as their forbears did 100 years ago.

Tartan

Tweed wasn't the only fabric to become popular during Britain's 19th-century Scotland craze. The fabric most associated with Scotland is tartan.

While the first reference to "tartan" *per se* dates from 1471, Roman sources already mention the Caledonians' "checkered garments." Still, woollen tartan was far from ubiquitous. Many Highlanders wore Irish-style linen tunics; when England invaded Ireland in the 16th century, the linen was no longer available, and woollen homespun became more widespread. Wool was certainly a better material for Highland weather. The word "plaid," the standard wool garment, described not a certain pattern, but a certain length: a rectangle of cloth up to 16 feet long, worn wrapped around the body, and doing double duty as a bedroll.

In his *Description of the Western Isles of Scotland*, published in 1703, Martin Martin wrote, "Every Isle differs from each other in their fancy of making Plads [sic], as to the Stripes in Breadth and Colours... They who have seen those Places,

Above: Aficionados can recognize a clan member by the stripe of his tartan. Right: Wool is cleaned before processing.

are able, at the first view of a Man's Plad, to guess the Place of his Residence..." Yet tartans may not originally have been associated with specific families. Observers have noted that tartan-clad Highlanders at Culloden wore cockades to identify which clan they belonged to.

Ironically, it was the English who made sure that tartan and clans were inseparably identified. After Culloden, seeking to control the rebel Highlanders, they outlawed the wearing of plaids altogether. Despite scattered defiance, the law was remarkable effective: by the time it was repealed in the 1780s, plaids had effectively died out. And it was an English king, George IV, who helped bring it back. When he visited Scotland in 1822, the first monarch to do so since the Stuarts, he not only donned a kilt, but asked people to wear their clan tartans to official functions. This started a scramble for clan tartans; those who didn't have them had tailors invent them, or adapted older patterns, as Sir Walter Scott did in 1826. The firm Brothers Sobieski Stuart published the *Vestiarum Scoticum*, an "official tartan catalogue" which included many of their own creations.

Purists struggle to weed out the spurious from the "original." The official registry lists more than 600 approved tartans. Many clans have several different patterns. There are dress tartans, mourning tartans, hunting tartans, chief's tartans, district tartans for various areas, down to the simple shepherd's tartan, of undyed brown and white checks, probably the oldest tartan of all. Royal tartans are still reserved exclusively for the use of the Royal Family; they include the Balmoral tartan, which Prince Albert designed himself.

Any Scot who wants to wear a tartan but doesn't belong to a clan can wear the "Jacobite" or "Caledonia" tartans, which Edinburgh ladies were sporting as an expression of their political sympathies as early as the 18th century.

Paisley's Pine Patterns

Another 19th-century development was the Paisley shawl. The town of Paisley was one of three Scottish shawl manufacturing centers in the mid-19th century. Paisley neither instigated the shawl fashion – the style came from Paris – nor began Scottish production of the shawls, but once the industry got underway, its shawls dominated the market.

It's ironic that Paisley shawls are now regarded as something luxurious: the point, originally, was to replicate expensive imports from India for a wide market, at lower prices. The shawls were woven of fine wool to emulate the softness, as well as design, of the originals from Kashmir, India (hence our word *cashmere*). In fact, there are a wide range of shawl designs, only some of which sport the "pine" pattern we call Paisley today.

The history of Paisley shawls echoes 19th-century social history. First, it follows the fluctuations of fashion: the shapes and designs of shawls reflect clothing trends, and the shawl fad received its death blow when the bustle arrived in the 1870s (no one wanted to cover their bustle with a shawl). Then, it traces the development of industry: the Jacquard loom, which enabled weavers to store patterns by means of a hole-punch card (the basic principle of early computers), revolutionized production.

Scotland is also known for knitwear, notably for Shetland's Fair Isle sweaters, with their distinctive patterned yoke. One theory is that these patterns were also specific to families, to make it easier to identify the bodies of drowned fishermen. Some claim that the designs can be traced back to the Balkans some 2,000 years ago. And there's a story that crew members of a ship from the Spanish Armada taught the patterns to the local inhabitants. The ship's presence on Fair Isle is documented, and one of its sailors is interred in St. Magnus's Cathedral on Orkney; the secret of whether or not he brought sweaters to Fair Isle lies buried with him.

THE BARDS OF ALBA
Scotland's Literature

Even Samuel Johnson, so grudging in his praise of Scotland, had to admit the extraordinarily high level of the country's literature – albeit, he felt, at the expense of other things. "I know not whether it be not peculiar to the Scots to have attained the liberal, without the manual arts, to have excelled in ornamental knowledge, and to have wanted not only the elegancies, but the conveniences of common life," he wrote. "The Latin poetry of *Deliciae Poetarum Scotorum* would have done honor to any nation; at least until the publication of May's Supplement the English had very little to oppose." Strong praise from one whose life centered on the literature and language of his own country.

Literature stems from literacy, and Scotland's was uncommonly high. As early as 1496, an Education Act required landowners to give their oldest sons university education. In the late 17th century, records show that 156 of Fife and the Lothians' 179 parishes had schools. The quality of education is reflected in the kinds of writers this small country has produced, and in the appreciation many of them have enjoyed among their countrymen. Robert Burns is a case in point: few countries are literate enough that a poet can become a popular hero of rock-star proportions.

What united readers and writers was a strong identification with their own country. Scotland's literature has centered on the country's heritage and history from the very beginning. Two of the earliest Scots literary works, epic poems both, are John Barbour's *Bruce* (around 1375) and *Wallace*, the work of the bard "Blind Harry" roughly a century later.

Right: The (fictitious) bard Ossian inspired 18th-century painters and poets throughout Europe (painting by F.B. Gerard).

Obviously, bards used to fulfill a role Hollywood has taken over; today's epic Wallace work is known as *Braveheart*.

Then as now, choosing Scottish subject matter was a way to assert the individuality of Scotland and its freedom from the influence of England. For Scotland's neighbor to the south has been a philosophical and linguistic, as well as a political, threat; and the printed word was a defense against that threat. Printing was introduced to Scotland in 1507 with the publication of the *Aberdeen Breviary*, meant to safeguard the Scottish liturgy against the English one. And the next significant printed work was a *History of Scotland*, published in Latin in 1526, and in English a decade later.

But linguistically, England has won out. Most of Scotland's literature is in English. The occasional Gaelic writers, like poet Duncan Ban Macintyre, "the Burns of the Highlands," remain, owing to the language barrier, historical curiosities rather than strong influences. The only Gaelic writer to have achieved real renown was the 3rd-century bard Ossian, supposedly born in a cave by Glencoe. In the 1760s, a writer named James MacPherson presented to the public new translations of Ossian, including the epic poem *Fingal*, based on thereto-unknown manuscripts. He sparked off an Ossian fad which lasted until his inability to produce any proof of the manuscripts' existence led to the realization that he had written the works himself; and the utterances of a primitive mind became less fascinating when that mind was found to exist in an 18th-century cranium.

Scots is distinct from Gaelic; vocabulary, not grammar, sets it apart from English. The greatest champion of Scots is Robert Burns (see p. 87). Burns anthologies usually include glossaries explaining words like *brae* (slope) and *muckle* (big, great). In Burns's day, however, to use Scots was to turn to the vernacular; one reason Burns was so beloved was

that he wrote in the idiom of the popular audience, which few poets had done.

In the 20th century, on the other hand, authors have used Scots in an effort to keep a fading heritage alive. One ardent modern advocate was poet Hugh Mac-Diarmid (1872-1978), born Christopher Grieve in the Borders town of Langholm (where there's a hilltop monument to him in the form of an open book). MacDiarmid's use of Lallans (Lowlands) Scots was a political as well as a literary statement; he passionately supported Scottish independence. The unfamiliar words in poems like *A Drunk Man Looks at the Thistle* may have scared off readers and kept him from taking a larger place in the 20th-century canon, which is a shame, because MacDiarmid is a very good poet.

Another modern author who used Scots dialect words was Lewis Grassic Gibbon (1901-34), the pen name of northeastern writer James Leslie Mitchell. Gibbon's greatest work is the trilogy of novels *A Scots Quair*, and the best of those is *Sunset Song*. Surely the

only reason this isn't more widely read today is that the first chapter is filled with unfamiliar Scots words – a difficulty the writer himself acknowledged. But this beautiful story of a young woman's coming of age in a small village, in the shadow of World War I, has the vivid characters and lyrical beauty of a great novel. Gibbon never quite matched it again, although not for lack of trying; he'd published 17 books by his early death at the age of 33.

But even the most English of Scottish writers have something uniquely Scottish about them. In the 18th century, Scotland produced two historians whose writing has retained its colorful, offbeat flavor to the present day: Thomas Carlyle (1795-1881), whose seminal work is his strikingly emotional *History of the French Revolution*; and James Boswell (1740-95), chronicler of the life of Samuel Johnson. Johnson and Boswell's journals of their trip to Scotland make entertaining reading, and demonstrate that Boswell was the better *raconteur* of the two.

Equally colorful and offbeat are the novels of ship's surgeon Tobias Smollett (1721-71). Irreverent, satiric, with intricate plots and memorable characters, *Roderick Random*, *Humphrey Clinker* and *Peregrine Pickle* influenced the novels of Dickens, George Eliot, and Trollope. (Smollett also did an excellent translation of *Don Quixote*.)

The Scottish specialty wasn't just novels, but *historical* novels. In Scotland, the historical novel played a role it never did in England: writing about the past is essential to the identity of a country which no longer exists as a country per se. No surprise, then, that many people feel the historical novel was invented in Scotland, with the publication of the book *Waverley* (1814) by Sir Walter Scott (1771-1832).

Scott is the first in a line that continues down to John Jakes. He invented not only

Above: Reading is no joke among the highly literate Scots. Right: Inventor of the historical best-seller: Sir Walter Scott.

the historical novel, but also the international bestseller. Everyone, everywhere, read Scott. The Trossachs became one of the first mass tourist destinations as people thronged to see the settings of *Rob Roy* or *The Lady of the Lake*. If he had lived today, Hollywood would have filmed everything; in the 19th century, the popular medium was opera, and more than 50 of them were based on his books, including works by Bizet, Rossini, and Donizetti (*Lucia di Lammermoor*).

Yet Scott didn't actually want to be a novelist. He was a lawyer and a poet. In fact, he kept his authorship of *Waverley* a secret for 15 years, through the publication of eight more successful novels (there are 27 Waverley novels in all). Respected as a serious literary figure for works like *The Lady of the Lake*, and knighted for his services to literature in 1820, he was worried that admitting to writing more low-brow best-sellers might tarnish his reputation; later, he enjoyed the sense of having a "hidden treasure," watching all the speculation about the Waverley novels' still-anonymous author. Not all of the Waverley novels are set in Scotland; but Scott was adamantly Scottish all his life, and not only in his books. It was he who helped set the wheels in motion for George IV's epic 1822 visit; he who instigated the search for the missing Scottish Regalia. He spent the last years of his life working off his publisher's debts.

In this century, Scott's torch was taken up by authors like John Buchan (1875-1940) and Neil M. Gunn (1891-1973). For Buchan (see p. 74) was a prolific writer of historical novels about Scotland, which he found superior to his more popular Richard Hannay books, like *The 39 Steps* (which Hitchcock filmed) or *Greenmantle*. Neil Gunn's territory was the eastern Highlands, where he set novels about daily life in the past, like *The Silver Darlings*, the story of crofters learning to be herring fisherman after being displaced in the Clearances.

Another historical novelist often pigeonholed as a children's author is Robert Louis Stevenson (1850-94). *Kidnapped* is certainly a contender for the title of Greatest Scottish Novel. Yet the best-known children's book from Scotland is *Peter Pan*, by J. M. Barrie (1860-1937), whose many novels and plays for adults are now largely forgotten.

Even Scottish novels that are not historical *per se* have a profound sense of place. The events of Muriel Spark's *The Prime of Miss Jean Brodie* are intimately bound up with Edinburgh: one senses on every page the coolness of its stone facades, the doors closing on the families within the tidy Georgian houses. And George Mackay Brown's compact stories, crafted so water-tight that no word could slip from any sentence, are permeated with the textures of Orkney, its green meadows and the omnipresent water. Mackay Brown hardly left Orkney himself; after studying with another local poet, Edwin Muir, and doing post-grad-

uate work at Edinburgh University, he returned to his islands to write for the local paper and spin his craft at his own pace until his death in 1996. In the larger, mainland scale of the novel, Mackay Brown seemed less at ease; although the novel *Greenvoe* stands out, his best works are the archipelagoes of stories in *A Calendar of Love* or *A Time to Keep*.

In 1996, the term "modern Scottish literature" became synonymous with *Trainspotting* when the movie based on Irvine Welsh's book became an international success; the tale of directionless youth on drugs seemed to tap into some vital element of the age. Another talented and prolific young writer is Iain Banks, who shot to attention with *The Wasp Factory* in 1982 and has stayed there ever since, also writing science fiction under the deceptive alias of Iain M. Banks. And for all the hip, contemporary tone of a novel like *Complicity*, the tale of a burned-out Glasgow journalist, the book is entirely bound up with Scotland – a land rich in literary potential.

233

SCOTLAND ON FOOT

For hiker, walker, rambler, or pedestrian by any other name, Scotland's countryside has to be one of the world's prime destinations. Stunning landscapes enfold foot travelers in 360-degree panoramas, views that are filtered and distanced through the windows of a car. And the compact scale of the place means that you can cover significant stretches of territory on foot – even, if you choose, going from one coast to the other along the Southern Upland Way.

Walking isn't a new fad: Scotland's first mountaineering club, the "Cobbler Club," was formed in 1865, named after the nickname of Loch Lomond's Ben Arthur. Many of the highest mountains here are called Ben, a short form not of Benjamin, but of Beann or Beinn, alternate forms of the Gaelic for "mountain."

Above: Crossing from Glen Doll into Glen Clova. Right: Another way to conquer Scotland's hills.

The most significant figure in Scotland's mountain history is Sir Hugh Munro. In 1891, he published a list of 538 peaks with altitudes of more than 3,000 feet (917 m); many of these were adjacent peaks of one large mountain, so he considered that the list included 283 distinct mountains. The list has been emended to 277 mountains, known as the Munros. Many walkers aspire to climb them all, a pursuit known as "Munro-bagging." No technical climbing is required to "bag" most of the Munros; just good shoes and plenty of stamina.

The second-ever person to bag all the Munros was John Rooke Corbett, who completed the task in 1930. Corbett proceeded to compile a list of mountains of between 2,500 and 3,000 feet (765 and 917 m). His list of "Corbetts" was distinct from Munros in that he only counted elevations with at least 500 feet between them and the next significant peak: thus, where Munro would list several of a mountain's peaks as individual Munros, Corbett perceived a mountain with several summits as a single Corbett. The "Corbetts" are not as widely recognized as the Munros, but some of them provide equally beautiful hikes.

What hillwalker A. Wainwright is to the Lake District, William Poucher is to Skye: the definitive chronicler of local peaks. Poucher's guides are illustrated not with pen-and-ink drawings, but with black and white photographs; Poucher was an able photographer, even in days before cameras had reached the level of technical proficiency they have today.

Nowhere in Britain are more tall peaks more closely concentrated than in the Cuillin Hills on Skye. To the east are the tamer Red Cuillins; it's the wild Black Cuillins, to the west, that include the "inaccessible pinnacle" of Sgurr Dearg and other challenging peaks. Scotland's other major mountain mass are the Cairngorms by the river Spey in Grampian: this chain includes six peaks more than 4,000 feet (1,223 m) high.

The most famous Munro is Ben Nevis, the highest peak in the British Isles. Surprisingly, the ascent of this isn't all that difficult; the easiest route is a simple walk some 6-8 hours up and back. Don't be too overconfident, however; failure to check the weather forecast, or forgetting a trail map, can have dire consequences.

Walking doesn't have to mean scaling peaks; Scotland's long-distance walks are a way to immerse oneself in the landscape and get to know a section of the country intimately. The two most famous are the abovementioned Southern Upland Way and the West Highland Way. The former extends some 215 miles (350 km) from Portpatrick on the southwestern Rhins of Galloway all the way to Cockburnspath on Pease Bay, not far from Dunbar, on the east coast of the Borders. Perhaps even more spectacular – certainly including a number of Scotland's "greatest hits" – is the 95-mile (150 km) West Highland Way, which starts a bit north of Glasgow and takes you past

Loch Lomond and through the Trossachs to Rannoch Moor and Glencoe before ending at Fort William. Shorter and simpler is the Speyside Way, a 45-mile (73 km) ramble from Tugnet to Tomintoul.

Walkers in Scotland are asked to observe the Country Code, basically a codified form of general hiking etiquette. It includes injunctions to guard against fire and, in a country where many public footpaths lead over private lands, to keep to paths across farmland, fasten all gates securely behind you, and avoid damaging fences, hedges, or drystone walls. An additional Mountain Code specifies the need for maps and compasses, as well as familiarity with mountain distress signals, and stipulates that walkers not travel alone and always leave written word of their route behind them. If you see snow, bring an ice axe, and learn to recognize dangerous snow slopes. Another useful tip is to note the main hunting seasons; most of them fall between August 12 and October. And it's not a bad idea to wear bright clothing. Better safe than sorry.

235

THE NATIONAL PASTIME

Could any nation other than the Scots possess a golf museum? Golf is a Scottish passion, and the British Golf Museum, opposite the Royal and Ancient Golf Club in St. Andrews, sets out five hundred years of the game's history. Since it opened in 1990, with visual and touch-screen displays visitors have been able to relive golden moments of great matches.

And yet it may be that golf, the Scottish national sport, isn't really from Scotland at all. There are records of a similar game, played with a club and ball, in the days of the Romans. And the very name of the game may come from the Continent; it's been linked to the Dutch *kolven*, cognate to the German *Kolben*, "club."

That club was originally made of wood; not until some time in the late 1700s were iron plates, called "cleeks,"

Above and right: The mother of all golf links: the Old Course at St Andrews (laid out in 1754).

first added to the heads of golf clubs, and steel shafts weren't introduced until the 20th century. Similarly, the wooden ball evolved into a creation of sewn leather stuffed with boiled feathers before the more familiar gutta-percha form was introduced in the middle of the last century.

Another kind of golf club, of course, is a venue where the sport can be played. The oldest official golf club in the world is the Honorable Company of Edinburgh Golfers, founded in 1774. It originally played in Musselburgh, where golf dates back at least to the 17th century, before moving to its current championship course of Muirfield on West Links Road, Gullane, East Lothian.

Informal associations date even farther back. In 1754, the Society of St. Andrews Golfers, 22 aristocrats and gentlemen, laid out the Old Course on the raised beach by the town. William IV conferred upon them the official title of Royal and Ancient Golf Club, which underlined royal interest in the sport, and gave the club its enduring status as the effective

governing body of British golf. Its head-quarters are in a 19th-century classical building, which also houses a collection of ancient mementoes of the game.

St. Andrews, the Mecca of golfing, has five 18-hole courses. Most famous is the Old Course, its bunkers initially created simply by the weather. This is a traditional "links" course: comprised, that is, of sand and heathland, located directly on the coast. Fear, loathing, and awe characterize golfers' approaches to this course, especially the 11th hole (the Sea Hole) and the 17th (or Road Hole). Other courses include the New Course, the Eden, and the Jubilee.

Other celebrated courses and golfing fraternities proliferate throughout Scotland. No account of golfing would be complete without mentioning Gleneagles in Perthshire, which has three major courses: the King's Course, the Queen's Course, and the Monarch's Course (designed by Jack Nicklaus in 1992).

The coast southwest of Glasgow is another golfing center: Prestwick, in fact,

hosted the first British Open in 1860. Today, Troon may have pride of place, and often does the Open honors. All in all, there are some 30 courses along this stretch of the Atlantic.

At Carnoustie in Angus are two championship links, one of them lengthy and strenuous, golfing at times stopped by a mist wafting in from the sea.

Aberdeenshire is also a golfer's haven. Golf has been played on the Queen's Links at Aberdeen since 1625. Ballater has a course from which you can relish views of splendid cones and rocks, such as Craig Cailleach (which means "hill of the old woman" because of what can be read into the profile). Another celebrated golf course here is that of Cruden Bay. And golf continues up into the Highlands, to the northerly Royal Dornoch, which aficionados account one of the finest in the British Isles.

And since golf in Scotland generates romantic legends, West Lothian claims that Mary, Queen of Scots first played golf in the Peel, Linlithgow's royal park.

PREPARING FOR YOUR TRIP

What to Pack

The information that it's likely to be cool and rainy will come as no surprise to anyone who knows the British Isles. Bring sweaters, a couple of pairs of long pants or jeans, and adequate rain gear: an unlined windbreaker or parka is handy winter or summer. That said, summer can be lovely and warm, even hot (relatively speaking), and summer clothing can come in handy. And don't forget your bathing suit; even if it's too cold to swim, there are legion hotel pools and leisure centers.

Good walking shoes are a necessity: sturdy rubber-soled ones for daily travel, and hiking boots if you plan any longer walks. Walkers should also bring a day pack, a canteen, a pocket knife for picnics and emergencies, moleskin and band-aids for blisters the first few days, sun lotion, and a hat or kerchief. You can get great maps at bookstores and tourist offices, so don't bother to bring any. Insect repellent should be writ large on everyone's packing list, particularly if you're going to the west coast or the Highlands, whence the midges flock in summer.

Buying film and camera equipment is no problem, although slide film can be harder to find.

Chemists' shops (pharmacies) are generally well stocked with the usual Western complement of aspirin and other light "drugs" as well as prescription pharmaceuticals. Of course, if you're taking prescription medication, make sure to bring plenty with you, because pharmaceuticals may differ slightly (certainly in name) from one country to another. But you won't be stranded if you run out of something.

When to Go

The best times to see Scotland are late spring and early summer (May and June) or early fall (September-early October).

At these times, you improve your chances for good weather while missing the worst of the crowds. Spring sees wildflowers in the meadows, the first bloom of Scotland's many luxuriant gardens, and baby lambs; in fall, you get the benefit of the heather blooming across the hills. Scottish ski resorts are also on the rise, ushering in winter as a new tourist season.

Visas and Customs

The same visa regulations apply to Scotland as to the rest of Great Britain. Citizens of European Union countries may enter Scotland simply with their identity cards; Swiss citizens also need a pink visitor's card. Non-EU citizens need a valid passport. Tourists can stay in the country for up to six months.

Anyone bringing a car should make sure to have his driver's license, vehicle registration papers, and a green international insurance card.

Since the introduction of the EU common market, visitors from EU countries can export larger amounts for personal use. The highest limit is 800 cigarettes, 400 cigarillos, 20 cigars, 1 kilo of tobacco, 10 liters of alcohol, 90 liters of wine (no more than 60 liters of which can be sparkling wine), and 110 liters of beer. For non-EU residents, as well as shoppers in duty-free shops (which will continue to operate until 1999), the limits are 200 cigarettes, 100 cigarillos or 50 cigars or 250 grams of tobacco, 2 liters of wine plus 1 liter of alcoholic beverage (less than 22%), or 2 liters of alcoholic beverage of less than 22% (such as sparkling wine), 60 ml of perfume, and 250 ml of eau de toilette.

Any animal that is brought into Great Britain is subject to the country's strict quarantine regulations. There's no rabies in Great Britain, and the British are determined to keep it that way. Animals therefore have to spend six months in quarantine; birds, 35 days. For further information, contact the Ministry of Agriculture,

Fisheries and Food, Government Bldgs., Hook Rise South, Tolworth, Surbiton, Surrey KT6 7NF, tel. (0181) 3304411.

Anyone wanting to bring in a firearm must declare it upon entering the country. You also need a visitor's firearm permit; for this, a sponsor in Scotland has to apply for you to the local authorities.

For further information about customs regulations, contact HM Customs and Excise, New King's Beam House, 22 Upper Ground, London SE1 9PJ, tel. (0171) 6201313.

Currency

While officially a part of the United Kingdom, Scotland prints its own money. In fact the Scottish one-pound note is not technically legal tender (i.e. government-supported), but rather backed by the country's banks (and three of Scotland's five major banks issue their own banknotes). However, the Scottish pound is identical in value to the English pound, and English pounds are also universally accepted.

The pound is divided into 100 pennies, or pence; Scottish coins come in denominations of 1, 2, 10, 20, and 50 p, as well as 1 pound. Banknotes come in denominations of £1, 5, 10, 20, 50, and 100.

Note that some credit card companies, especially in the United States, automatically lower your credit limit when you travel overseas. Check before your departure, and take travelers' checks. (See also "Banks and Money Exchange," p. 244.)

Tourist Offices Abroad

Information on Scotland is generally dispensed tby the British Tourist Authority.
Australia: BTA, 8th Floor, University Centre, 210 Clarence Street, Sydney, NSW 2000, tel. (2) 261607, fax 2674442.
Canada: BTA: 111 Avenue Road, Suite 450, Toronto, Ontario M5R 3J8, tel. (416) 925 6326, fax 9612175.
Ireland: BTA, 18-19 College Green, Dublin 2, tel. (1) 670 8000, fax 670 8244.
New Zealand: BTA, Suite 305, 3rd Floor, Dilworth Building (corner Queen/Customs Street), Auckland 1, tel. (9) 303 1446, fax 377 6965.
South Africa: BTA, Lancaster Gate, Hyde Lane, Hyde Park, Sandton 2196, or P.O. Box 41896, Craighall 2024, tel. (11) 325 0343.
U.S.A.: New York: BTA, 551 Fifth Avenue, New York, NY, 10176-0799, tel (1 800) GO2 BRITAIN, fax (212) 986 1188. Chicago: BTA, 625 North Michigan Ave., Suite 1510, Chicago, IL 60611.

TRAVELING TO SCOTLAND

By Plane

Glasgow is Scotland's main international airport; Edinburgh's airport is more demure. There are frequent direct flights to and from both, on a number of carriers. British Airways, for example, flies direct to Glasgow from Boston, Düsseldorf, Frankfurt, Hanover, Milan, Munich, New York, and Paris, and to Edinburgh from Düsseldorf, Munich, Paris, and Zürich; British Midland has flights to and from Copenhagen from both airports. Most other international carriers offer at least some direct flights: Sabena, for instance, has direct service from Brussels; Air France, from Paris.

Many travelers arrive from England or elsewhere in Great Britain, at least through having to change planes in London or Manchester. The main hub is, of course, London. British Airways has a regular air shuttle service from London to both Glasgow and Edinburgh, with 12 flights a day leaving almost (though not quite) hourly.

By Train

Since Britain's rail service was privatized on January 1, 1997, British Rail no longer holds the monopoly on train travel. New train lines, such as Virgin Cross Country, are appearing with new offers for travel in the British Isles. But for the time being, British Rail still has the largest concession.

Trains depart London for Scotland from Euston Station: with an Intercity train, the trip to Glasgow takes about 5 hours; the trip to Edinburgh, about 4. Intercity's "Caledonian Sleeper" runs nightly (except Saturdays) from London to Glasgow, Edinburgh, Aberdeen, Inverness, and Fort William. A BritRail pass allows unlimited travel within Great Britain for up to 4 weeks.

With a credit card, you can reserve British Rail tickets by phone from abroad by calling (44 131) 2468765 (Mon-Fri 9 am-6 pm, Sat 9 am-4 pm, Scottish time).

By Boat

Most ferries to the British Isles from mainland Europe stop at one of the English ports – Portsmouth, Dover, Felixstowe, Hull, or Newcastle – from which travelers can continue on to Scotland by train or car. But **P&O Scottish Ferries** does operate car ferry service from Bergen, Norway to the Shetland Isles and Aberdeen. Reservations can be made through local travel agencies or by contacting **P&O Scottish Ferries**, PO Box 5, Jamieson's Quay, Aberdeen, AB9 8DL, tel. (01224) 572615, fax 574411.

By Car

In addition to the Channel ferries or ferries directly to Scotland, drivers can take advantage of the Eurotunnel from Calais to Folkstone, opened in 1994: the train *Le Shuttle* transports buses, cars and passengers every 35 minutes from 7 am-11 pm, every 75 minutes from 11 pm-7 am (tel. 44 990/353535). The drive from southern England to Scotland takes at least a day. British Rail also runs an Auto Shuttle Express train from London to Edinburgh, Glasgow and Inverness (information at travel agents or from British Rail, tel. 44 194/643355, fax 611896).

TRAVELING IN SCOTLAND

By Plane

Anyone who wants to visit a number of the islands has the option of a British Airways Express "Highland Rover" fare, which offers a special rate for a maximum of five, a maximum of 12 flights to the islands.

For its domestic Scottish service, British Airways teams up with the small carrier LoganAir, which operates smaller planes and goes to virtually every island that can physically support a landing strip, from Benbecula (Outer Hebrides) to Papa Westray (Orkney). The mainland airports that serve as points of departure are Glasgow, Edinburgh, Inverness, Dundee, Perth, and Aberdeen.

British Airways, 50 Waterloo St., Glasgow, tel. (0345) 222111.

By Train

Privatization of Britain's rail services (see "Traveling to Scotland," above) will also affect train services in Scotland; but BritRail's local arm ScotRail still has the largest concession.

ScotRail offers a "Freedom of Scotland Travel Pass" which entitles you to unlimited travel on Scotland's trains, as well as ferry service to most of the islands and discounts on buses. Passes range from 8 consecutive days for around £100 to 22 consecutive days; the latter must be purchased abroad. There are also ScotRail Rovers passes, which are valid for train travel only; you can either get one for all of Scotland (£115 for 12 out of 15 consecutive days of travel) or for specific regions, such as the West Highlands.

Tickets can be purchased with a credit card by phone. In Scotland, you can call toll-free: (0800) 450450. If you're calling from overseas, see "Traveling to Scotland," above.

For information in Scotland, contact ScotRail, Caldonian Chambers, 87 Union

Street, **Glasgow** G1 3TA, tel. (0345) 212282. In **Edinburgh**, tel. (0131) 5562451; in **Inverness**, tel. (01463) 242124; in **Aberdeen**, tel. (01224) 582005.
ScotRail offices overseas (BritRail): **Belgium**: Rue de la Montagne 50, 1000 Bruxelles, tel. (2) 548 0040. **Ireland**: 123 Lower Baggot Street, Dublin 2, tel. (1) 6620293. **U.S.A.**: 1500 Broadway, New York, NY 10036-4015, tel. (212) 575 2667.

By Bus

The extensive network of bus routes means you can travel by bus to virtually every corner of Scotland. The two largest bus lines are **Scottish Citylink Coaches** (tel. 0990/505050) and **National Express** (tel. 0990/808080). The long-distance buses travel overnight. Both lines offer various discounts and travel packages.

In most areas, there are also local bus lines; regional tourist offices can provide detailed information. In addition, post buses, which deliver mail to even the remotest parts of the country, also have limited room for passengers: contact **Royal Mail Communications**, West Port House, 102 West Port, Edinburgh EH3 9HS, tel. (0131) 2287407, or **Post Bus Controller**, Royal Mail, 7 Strothers Lane, Inverness IV1 1AA, tel. (01463) 256273.

By Boat

All of the islands along Scotland's west coast are serviced by Caledonian MacBrayne ferries – from the Clyde islands near Glasgow to the Outer Hebrides. The company offers a range of special prices for people wishing to visit several islands (such as *Island Rovers*, for 8 to 15 consecutive days, or *Island Hopscotch*, for 3 months), and teams up with other organizers to offer package weekends to golfers and other special-interest vacationers. For timetables, price information, or a general brochure, contact **Caledonian MacBrayne**'s head of-

fice at the Ferry Terminal, Gourock, PA19 1QP, tel. (01475) 650100, fax 637607. To make reservations, call (0990) 650000 (Mon-Sat 8:30 am-5 pm).

The largest ferry line serving Orkney and Shetland is **P&O Scottish Ferries**, whose mainland ports are Scrabster and Aberdeen. For addresses, see "Traveling to Scotland," p. 249. There are also smaller ferry companies providing service to individual islands; for more information, see "Guidepost" sections of the individual chapters.

By Car

With a plethora of small towns linked by narrow single-track roads through stunning landscape, Scotland is perhaps best explored by car. Once you've gotten used to driving on the "wrong" side of the road, the advantages of having a car, in terms of mobility and sight-seeing, will quickly make themselves felt.

The standard large car rental ("car hire") firms such as Hertz and Avis are represented throughout Scotland. **Avis**, for example, has offices at 100 Dalry Road, Edinburgh, tel. (0131) 3376363, as well as at Edinburgh Airport, and at 161 North St., Glasgow, tel. (0141) 2212827. **Hertz** has offices at both Edinburgh and Glasgow Airports, at 10 Picardy Place and at Waverly Station in Edinburgh (tel. (0131) 5568311 and 5575272), and at Central Station and 106 Waterloo St., Glasgow (tel. (0141) 204 3373 and 2487736). **Budget** also has offices in Edinburgh (The Royal Scot Hotel, 111 Glasgow Rd., tel. (0131) 3347739) and Glasgow (101 Waterloo St., tel. (0141) 2264141). Sometimes lower prices can be had from smaller companies, such as the national firm **Woods Car Rental** (in Glasgow: Unit 9, Airlink Industrial Estate, Inchinnan Road, Paisley, tel. (0141) 8481559; in Edinburgh: Hilton National Hotel, Belford Road, Edinburgh, or at Edinburgh Airport, Unit 16, Tartraven Place, East Mains Industrial Estate,

Broxburn, both tel. (01506) 858660). Aberdeen, Dundee, and Inverness also have plenty of car rental agencies.

If you're not used to driving on the left, give yourself some practice time, and pay extra attention on the legion roundabouts (traffic circles), where traffic comes zooming around at you from the right.

Distance indications and speed limits are still posted in miles, not kilometers; 1 km is .62 miles. The official speed limit on motorways is 70 miles an hour (112 kilometers per hour); in practice, this is generally exceeded. In towns, the speed limit is 30 or 40 m.p.h.; speed limits are always posted.

In the country, especially in the Highlands, many roads are one-lane or single-track roads with passing places provided at intervals to allow two cars to squeeze past each other. Slower drivers are legally obliged to pull over and let cars behind them pass them; this, very sensibly, keeps vacationers who are taking in the scenery from blocking the somewhat faster local traffic.

If you're driving in rural areas, keep an eye on your gas tank. In the Highlands and Islands, especially, gas (or petrol) stations are few and far between; what's more, they're often closed on Sundays.

PRACTICAL TIPS

Accommodation

Prices for hotel rooms are quoted per person rather than per room, so a £30-a-night room may not be quite the bargain you think if you're travelling as a couple. Prices usually include a full English breakfast. The term "en-suite" denotes that a room has a private bathroom and toilet. In the Guidepost sections of this book, £50 per person is the approximate cut-off between "Moderate" and "Expensive"; anything below about £25 qualifies as "Budget."

Theubiquitous Scottish Tourist Board seems to have evaluated every form of overnight accommodation in Scotland. From the doors of luxury hotels to the gateposts of isolated farmhouse B&Bs, the blue thistle sticker signifies that an establishment has been subject to the STB's ratings system. The STB puts out four separate guides with listings of Hotels, Bed & Breakfast, Self-Catering Cottages, and Camping & Caravan Parks; these can be ordered from the Scottish Tourist Board (see "Addresses," below).

Hotels: The STB's rating system is most thorough for hotels, with two separate marks: one for quality, ranging from "Deluxe" to merely "Approved," and one that evaluates the services available, from the most basic amenities ("Listed") to the height of luxury (five crowns). Considerations like charm and ambience don't figure largely in this rating system, however; many "Highly Commended" four-crown establishments turn out to be soulless – albeit luxurious – concrete blocks. The present guide attempts to steer clear of these.

A number of private hotels join hotel associations. One good organization, featuring privately-owned and run hotels in the moderate-to-expensive price class, is **Scotland's Commended** (33 Craiglockhart Drive South, Edinburgh EH14 1JA, tel. 01786/825550, fax 824440). This group also has foreign representation: in **Australia**, Vizit International Pty Ltd, 16 Indra Rd., Tascott, NSW 2250, tel. (01061) 43 234443, fax 4322; in **New Zealand**, Gullivers Pacific Ltd., P.O. Box 3839, Auckland, tel. 0 9 3770660, fax 3078873; in the **U.S.A.**, McFarlands Ltd., 5720 Buford Highway, Norcross, GA 30071, tel. (770) 4480049, fax 4478475.

B&B: Bed and Breakfasts, universally known as B&Bs, are a very attractive feature of travel in the British Isles. No farmhouse in Scotland is too remote to sport a blue-and-white B&B (or BB) sign. Generally private homes with an extra room or two for guests, B&Bs are cheaper than hotels (around £15-£20 a night), and can even exceed them in comfort and cleanliness. Most B&Bs these days have a lounge with sofas, tables, and a TV. Another advantage is contact with locals, affording more insight into everyday life than you can get in most hotels.

Scottish Farmhouse Holidays, Drumtenant, Ladybank, Fife, KY15 7UG, tel. (01337) 830451, fax 831301. This organization arranges in advance for B&B-type accommodation with families on working farms. In general, the set-up is B&B-like, one difference being that people often stay for periods of several days, another being that dinner is generally included as well as breakfast. Don't expect your room to be made up for you; these are private homes, not hotels.

Signs for **Self-Catering Cottages** dot the roadsides; these are detached vacation homes with kitchens and bathrooms, rented by the day, week, or even month to visitors. Cleaning is not provided, nor is cooking. Some B&B owners or farmers have built small self-catering cottages in addition to their in-house accommodations. The Scottish Tourist Board rates self-catering cottages on the same scale they use for hotels and B&B, and there are listings in most of their local accommodation brochures.

Campus Hotels Scotland: Eight of Scotland's universities have formed this loose association, which offers student accommodation during holiday periods and, on a more limited scale, year-round. This is a great option for reasonably-priced city accommodation. To reserve, contact the individual universities. **Edinburgh**: Alan H. Bruce, St. Leonard's Hall, Pollock Halls of Residence, 18 Holyrood Park Rd., Edinburgh EH16 5AY, tel. (0131) 6671971, fax 6683217. **Glasgow**: Ishbel Duncan, Conference and Vacation Officer, University of Glasgow (Kelvingrove), 52 Hillhead St., Glasgow G12 8PZ, tel. (0141) 3305385, fax 3345465; or Linda Brownlie, Residence and Catering Services, University of Strathclyde (by the cathedral), 50 Richmond St., Glasgow G1 1XP, tel. (0141) 5534148, fax 5534149. **Aberdeen**: Ian M. Pirie,

Conference Officer, University of Aberdeen, Regent Walk, Aberdeen AB9 1FX, tel. (01224) 272664, fax 276246. **St Andrews**: John Horobin, Conference and Group Services, 79 North St., St Andrews, Fife KY16 9AJ, tel. (01334) 463000, fax 462500. **Stirling**: Elaine O'-Hare, Conference Campus, University of Stirling, FK9 4LA, tel. (01786) 467140, fax 467143. **Dundee**: Graham Anderson, Residences Office, University of Dundee, DD1 4HN, tel. (01382) 23181, ext. 4038, fax 202605.

Camping and Caravaning sites ("caravan" being the British word for what Americans call a "camper") are also charted out and evaluated by the STB.

Youth Hostels: An extensive network of youth hostels is administered by the **Scottish Youth Hostel Association**, 7 Glebe Crescent, Stirling FK8 2JA, tel. (01786) 451181, fax 450198. You can get a list of independent hostels and budget accommodations from the **Independent Backpackers' Hostels Scotland**, Croft Bunkhouse & Bothy, Portnalong, Isle of Skye IV47 8SL, tel. (01487) 640257.

Automobile Clubs / Breakdowns

Automobile Association (AA), 18-22 Fanum House, Melville St., Edinburgh EH3 7PD, tel. (0131) 2253562; 269 Argyll St., Glasgow, G2 8DW, tel. (0141) 2212240. **AA Information** (and emergencies), tel. (0990) 500600, daily 7 am-7 pm (except December 25 and 26). **Royal Automobile Club (RAC)**, 200 Sinnieston St., Glasgow G3 8NZ, tel. (0141) 2484444. **Royal Scottish Automobile Club (RSAC)**, 11 Blythswood Square, Glasgow G2 4AG, tel. (0141) 2213850, fax 2213805.

Breakdown Assistance: **AA**, tel. (0800) 887766. **RAC**, tel. (0800) 828282.

Banks and Money Exchange

There are five main Scottish banks: the Bank of Scotland, Royal Bank of Scotland, Clydesdale Bank, TSB Scotland, and Girobank. Three of these issue their own bank notes (see "Currency," p. 238). Each bank has its own opening hours; in general, however, banks are open Monday-Friday from around 9:15 am to 4 or 4:30 pm. Some TSB branches in the cities are also open on Saturday mornings. Smaller branches may close for lunch.

Banks offer the best exchange rates. Thomas Cook also operates money exchange offices in international aiports and major cities; and there are other money exchange offices, as well as the large hotels. Automatic teller machines displaying the appopriate symbols sometimes accept Visa or Cirrus cards; most will take standard EC cards.

There are also three **American Express** offices, with the standard range of cardholder services (including client mail), open Mon-Fri 9 am-5 pm, Sat 9 am-noon. **Edinburgh:** 139 Princes St., tel. (0131) 225 7881; **Glasgow:** 115 Hope St., tel. (0141) 221 4366; **Aberdeen:** 4/5 Union Terrace, 2nd Floor, tel. (0224) 641050.

Business Hours

Post offices are generally open Mon-Fri 9 am-5:30 pm, Sat 9 am-12:30 or 1 pm. Smaller branches may close for lunch. For banking hours, see above.

Many towns, especially in rural areas, have a weekly "Early Closing Day," when shops stay shut in the afternoon. This varies from town to town; local tourist offices can give you details.

Disabled Travelers

The Scottish Tourist Board issues a booklet of "Practical Information for Visitors with Disabilities." Another useful source of information is **Disability Scotland Information Department**, Princes House, 5 Shandwick Place, Edinburgh EH2 4RG, tel. (0131) 2298632.

Doctors

Britain's National Health plan is available to residents of the EU or any other country which has a reciprocal health agreement with the U.K., making them eligible for emergency medical treatment at any National Health Service hospital's Accident and Emergency Department. Residents of other countries should make sure that their policies cover them abroad, or take out travel medical insurance, before they go.

Electricity

Scotland's electrical current is 240 volts, 50 Hz. You can use standard European 220-volt appliances with no problem. However, British sockets differ from their Continental counterparts, so you'll need an adaptor if you're bringing any electrical appliances with you. If you're coming from overseas, you'll need a transformer and an adaptor.

Emergency

The emergency telephone number for police, ambulance or fire brigade is 999.

Festivals and Holidays

While all of England closes down for "Bank Holidays," Scotland doesn't regard these dates as national holidays: banks and some offices are closed, but otherwise it's business as usual. Still, most offices will be closed at Christmas (December 25 and 26), New Year's (January 1), and Easter.

Most places in Scotland observe a spring and an autumn holiday, but these tend to vary from region to region, place to place (although they're usually on a Monday). The Glasgow Chamber of Commerce puts out a booklet detailing all of the public holidays on a town-by-town basis.

New Year's in Scotland is a particularly big event: dubbed "Hogmanay," it's celebrated with festivities, special meals, and children going from door to door asking for presents. Other days dear to Scottish hearts are Burns Night (January 25, the poet's birthday) and St. Andrew's Day (November 30).

Food

The quality of food in Scotland seems to be improving all the time (see "The Foods of Scotland," p. 222). If you're unfamiliar with British restaurants, this general rule of thumb may help you avoid mediocre establishments: If dishes like lasagne, chili, gammon steak, jacket potato and breaded plaice predominate, the food is likely to be run-of-the-mill, with overcooked veg to boot ("breaded plaice" is a fancy way to say fish'n'chips). Look, instead, for fresh seafood, local ingredients, and more creative combinations.

A handy restaurant guide is the **Taste of Scotland**, issued annually. This organization covers the whole country, seeking out the best eateries, be it a visitors' center cafeteria with surprisingly good fare or a five-star gourmet temple in Edinburgh, and listing some 400 restaurants. The book also includes recipes and brief introductions to things like salmon or Scottish cheeses. In addition, the organization confers annual awards for Restaurant of the Year, Hotel of the Year, etc. To order, write, call or fax Taste of Scotland, 33 Melville St., Edinburgh EH3 7JF, tel. (0131) 2201900, fax 2206102.

Gaelic

In the drive to reclaim old traditions which has captured much of the western world, Scotland's Gaelic roots are bearing new fruit. Unlike Scots, which was spoken throughout the country, Gaelic was mainly confined to the Highlands and Islands, where it was a living lan-

guage until reprisals for the Jacobite Rebellion and, later, the Clearances contributed to its decline. As early as the 19th century, however, people began to fight for its survival: in 1891, the society **An Comunn Gaidhealach** was founded to preserve the traditions and language of the Scottish Gael. The society is alive and well today (109 Church St., Inverness, IV1 1EY, tel. 01463/231226, fax 715557), but now it's only one of a host of organizations dedicated to Gaelic heritage. Although only about 2% of Scotland's population actually speaks Gaelic, thousands are learning it; BBC even has a Gaelic radio station, and there are other local radio and television stations. There are legion opportunities for Gaelic study vacations. You can get a free informational brochure from Fàilte, **Comunn na Gàidhlig**, 5 Mitchell's Lane, Inverness IV2 3HQ, tel. (01463) 234138, fax 237470. There's also information at a Web page at http://www. smo.uhi.ac.uk/cnag/failte/.

One way to get a taste of Gaelic is at the annual **Royal National Mod**. Mod, meaning gathering, is now the term for a competitive Gaelic music festival; the national one is organized by An Comunn Gaidhealdach (see above). Smaller mods held in various places throughout the country. Another popular kind of meeting is the *ceilidh* (pronounced KAYlay), meaning "visit." These visits have always meant impromptu entertainment: originally in small hamlets where people would gather to listen to a local bard or singer; today, often in hotels or restaurants with paid musicians. What they have in common is the chance to have a good time with plenty of liquid refreshment.

Nature Reserves and Gardens

There are 70 nature reserves in Scotland. The majority of them, such as the Cairngorms or the island of Rhum, are run by **Scottish Natural Heritage**, 12 Hope Terrace, Edinburgh EH9 2AS, tel.

(0131) 4474784, fax 4462277. The **Scottish Wildlife Trust**, Cramond House, Kirck Cramond, Cramond Glebe Road, Edinburgh EH4 5BN, tel. (0131) 3127765, fax 3128705, administers the Lochnagar Reserve. A number of bird reserves are under the aegis of the **Royal Society for the Protection of Birds** (RSPB), 17 Regent Terrace, Edinburgh EH7 5BN, tel. (0131) 5573136, fax 5576275.

Scotland's Garden Scheme, 31 Castle Terrace, Edinburgh EH1 2EL, tel. (0131) 2291870, fax 2290443, offers a listing of more than 300 gardens open to the public, from castle grounds to lovingly tended private gardens.

Newspapers, Radio, and Television

Scotland's glorious literary tradition is reflected in its host of newspapers. The two major "national" newspapers, the *Herald* (out of Glasgow) and the *Scotsman* (out of Edinburgh), are both reliable broadsheets in the general style of British newspapers (with, that is to say, a certain elegance of style), covering international and Scottish news. A larger circulation than either of these, however, is enjoyed by the *Dundee Courier*, the local paper of Scotland's densely-populated central regions. Dundee has long been associated with journalism, one of the city's "three Js" (see p. 217): it also produces another traditional national paper, the *Sunday Post*. Another leading local organ, farther north, is the *Aberdeen Press and Journal*, whose territory extends to the Highlands and Islands. You can also buy national British papers (the *Times*, the *Guardian*, the *Independent*, and a motley range of dreadful tabloids) throughout Scotland.

In radio and television stations, there's also a certain overlap with England: BBC, after all, is the *British* (not English) Broadcasting Corporation. BBC operates a special Scottish radio station, as well as one in Gaelic. On television, too, BBC Scotland (channel 3) broadcasts a mixture of programs from BBC 1 and 2 as well as some Scottish programming (nationwide news is shown at 6 pm; Scottish news at 6:30). In addition, there's STV, Scottish Television, the country's independent network. There are also two large independent regional networks, Grampian and the Borders.

Recommended Reading

The feature on "Scotland's Literature" (p. 230) can be taken as a reading list for fiction and poetry. Some general non-fiction titles of interest to travelers:
Mary, Queen of Scots, by Antonia Fraser.
A History of Scotland, by J. D. Mackie.
Culloden; *Glencoe*; *The Clearances*; and other titles by John Preeble.
Scenes and Legends of the North of Scotland, by Hugh Miller.
The Orkneyinga Saga, by Viking bards (Penguin prints an English translation).
A Journey to the Western Isles, by Samuel Johnson and James Boswell.
And some light travel reading:
Eminent Dogs, Dangerous Men: Searching Through Scotland for a Border Collie, by Donald McCaig: an American learns the insider world of Scottish sheepdogs and their owners.
Five Red Herrings, by Dorothy L. Sayers: Lord Peter Wimsey unravels a murder among the artists of Kirkcudbright.
Whisky Galore, by Compton Mackenzie: World War II rationing hits the Hebrideans hard, until the shipwreck of a boat carrying whisky restores their well-being.
Ring of Bright Water, by Gavin Maxwell: the true story of a writer's life on the west coast with his pet otters.

Shopping

Many of Scotland's souvenirs are edible. The tidy tartan-patterned tins of Walker's shortbread are familiar the world over; similarly, attractive jars of Dundee marmalade or packages of fudge are prominent in airport duty-free shops. The latter are a fine place to stock up on another souvenir, single malt whisky – a better option than buying a bottle in a whisky distillery and then lugging it around with you for the rest of your trip. Glasgow Airport and Manchester Airport, in England, deserve special mention.

Woolen mills offer wide selections of tartan articles, from kilts to coasters (see "From Tartan to Tweed," p. 248). In the Highlands, away from the press of tourists, you find more individual items; Brora Woolen Mills is one good outlet. The Highlands also has local stoneware and pottery at, for example, the Anta shop near Tain (tartan, but tasteful, ceramics) or Highland Stoneware at Ullapool. Glass and crystal fans should check out Caithness glass or Edinburgh crystal (especially at Penicuik).

Sports and Activities

Cycling: Many Scotland travelers arrive with their own bikes; you can also rent them for anywhere from £8-20 a day, depending on quality (addresses of some rental outlets appear in the "Guideposts" at the end of many chapters). The STB's brochure Scotland - Cycling includes a number of tour suggestions. One organization that will arrange tours for you is **Scottish Cycling Holidays**, Ballintuim Post Office, Blairgowrie PH10 7NJ, tel. (01250) 886201, fax (01382) 202507.

Golf: Individual tourist boards can provide detailed information on area clubs; some information is contained in the Guidepost sections of the individual chapters. The magazine *Golf Monthly* puts out a golf map of Scotland, which can be ordered from the STB.

Hunting and Fishing: Since at least the 19th century, many vacationers to Scotland have come primarily to hunt and fish. Grouse on the moors, red deer in the woods, or salmon in the streams were all as much lures for Victorian-era shooting

parties as they are for sportsmen today.

In a field of experts, terminology is important. "Shooting" means to bag an animal with a shotgun: quarry for "game shooters" include grouse, partridge, pheasant, and other game birds. Deer, by contrast, are "stalked" rather than "shot"; the weapon used for this purpose is a rifle. By the same token, fishing is hardly ever called anything but "angling," and of course, there's a world of difference between "coarse fishing" in a river or loch and "sea angling" on a chartered boat off the country's coasts.

Anyone who comes to Scotland to shoot grouse or deer, hare or pheasant, has to obtain a Game Licence from the Post Office; licenses are available for the whole year, half a year, or fourteen days. However, rabbit, duck, geese, and pigeons are free game – provided you have permission from the owner of the land you're shooting on.

Make sure that you know when the season is for the animal you want to hunt (the grouse season, for example, begins August 12). Note, too, that it is not customary to shoot game birds on a Sunday.

If you want to bring a gun into Scotland or buy one there, you'll need to get a visitors' firearm or shotgun permit. For laws about importing firearms into Great Britain, see "Customs," p. 239.

A number of agencies and estates arrange shooting and stalking excursions for visitors. The Scottish Tourist Board will send a comprehensive listing on request. For further information, contact the British Association for Shooting and Conservation headquarters at Marford Mill, Rossett, Wrexham, Clwyd, LL12 0HL.

Fishing is perhaps even more popular, and certainly tamer, than hunting. You need a fishing permit for salmon and trout. Permits are available at a range of places, from post offices to local hotels; check at local tourist offices for specific information. Prices vary depending on the popularity of the river or loch. The Tweed, for example, can run you several hundred pounds; while in the lochs of Orkney Mainland, you don't need a permit at all. Note that you can't fish for salmon and sea trout on Sundays, although fishing for brown trout on that day is fine.

The dates of the salmon season vary regionally, but run approximately from November to mid-February. Brown trout season is fixed: Oct 7-March 14. Coarse fishing – angling for perch, pike, eel, and about anything else you can find in a loch or river – has no season at all; still, it's wise to get permission before settling in. In some areas, anglers are restricted to one rod only. Local fishing clubs are generally happy to welcome visitors.

Sea anglers can get information on boat charter from local tourist offices or directly in the harbors; most have a couple of boats for visiting anglers. The catch ranges from mackerel to shark; the latter is particularly plentiful in the cold northern waters around Orkney and Shetland.

The authority for fishing in Scotland is the Department of Agriculture and Fisheries for Scotland, Pentland House, 47 Robb's Loan, Edinburgh EH14 1TY, tel. (0131) 556 8400.

Riding: An unforgettable way to see Scotland is on horseback. Local tourist offices can give information about regional riding centers, such as Argyll's Castle Riding Centre (see also the "Guidepost" for "The West Coast").

Walking: For information about routes for long walks, contact **Scottish Natural Heritage**, 12 Hope Terrace, Edinburgh, EH9 2AS, tel. (0131) 4474784.

The STB booklet *Walking in Scotland* gives 20 routes at all levels of difficulty.

Anyone planning serious walking should look at the Scottish Mountain Safety Group's "Safety on Scotland's Hills," which you can get by sending a stamped, self-addressed envelope to the **Scottish Sports Council**, Caledonia House, South Gyle, Edinburgh EH12 9DQ. Another source of information is the **Mountaineering Council of Scotland**, 71 King St., Crieff, PH7 3HB, tel. (01764) 4962.

From Tartan to Tweed

Scotland's stores offer a huge amount of wool fabrics, both spurious and genuine. There is information available to help tell the difference. Since Comrie's Tartan Museum has closed, and the Tartan Society is searching for new premises, the leading tartan centers, apart from the official Register Office in Edinburgh, are affiliated with shops. The **Scotch House** on Princes Street, Edinburgh, has a small museum, and there's a **Clan Tartan Centre** (basically a computer to help people locate family tartans) in Bangor Road, Leith, Edinburgh. Most woolen mills also have information on the tartans they sell, mainly geared toward tourists. The **Harris Tweed Association** is represented on Lewis (6 Garden Road, Stornoway) and in Inverness (Ballantyne House, 84 Academy St., IV1 1LU).

Telephones

While British Telecom has introduced a telephone card, not all phone booths (telephone boxes) take these cards. Equally common are phones that take regular credit cards, such as Visa; while coin phones prevail. A local call costs 10 p. For an operator, dial 100. For directory information within Scotland, call 192. 155 will put you through to an international operator for dialling assistance; 153 gives you international directory information.

The country code for Scotland is the same as that for England and Wales: 44 (0044 from continental Europe; 011 44 from the United States). In 1995, the prefix "1" was added to all local area codes (Edinburgh's went from 031 to 0131). Some older tourist brochures may not include this 1.

To place international calls from Scotland, dial 00 before the country code prefix, as in the rest of Europe (to call the United States, for example, dial 001; to Germany, 0049).

Time

Scotland's time zone is Greenwich Mean Time; Daylight Savings Time turns clocks ahead an hour at the end of March (often a week or two before the start of Daylight Savings Time in the United States). This means that when it's midnight in Edinburgh, it's 7 pm in New York, 4 pm in Los Angeles, 8 am in Melbourne, and, of course, midnight in London.

Whisky

Scotch Whisky Association, 20 Atholl Crescent, Edinburgh, EH3 8HF, tel. (0131) 2294383. There's another office at 17 Half Moon St., London W1Y 7RB. A *Whisky Map of Scotland* is available in bookstores.

ADDRESSES

The Scottish Tourist Board, 23 Ravelston Terrace, Edinburgh EH4 3EU, tel. (0131) 332 2433, fax 3154545.

Diplomatic Representation in Scotland

U.K.: Glasgow Passport Office, 3 Northgate, 96 Milton St., Cowcaddens, Glasgow, G4 0BT, tel. (0141) 332 0271.
U.S.A.: Consulate General, 3 Regent Terrace, Edinburgh, EH7 5BW, tel. (0131) 566 8315.

GLOSSARY

The people of Scotland, of course, speak English; in fact, it's claimed that the inhabitants of Inverness speak the purest form of British English to be found anywhere in the world. The older Scots dialect, made most familiar through the poetry of Burns, persists in some areas.

quean . . . . woman
childe . . . . man
bairn . . . . child
bap . . . . roll
eldritch . . . . frightful, strange
meikle . . . . great, much
muckle . . . . large
keek . . . . to peep, peek
vennel . . . . alley
douce . . . . quiet, sensible
forbye . . . . besides
howff . . . . meeting place
lift . . . . sky
links . . . . sand dunes
cutty . . . . short
sark . . . . shirt
sonsie . . . . attractive
soutar . . . . cobbler

On the Outer Hebrides, and in parts of the Highlands, you encounter Gaelic, but its use is not yet widespread on the mainland. Gaelic is most evident in place names.

aber, inver . . . . river mouth
beag . . . . little
ben, beann . . . . mountain
kil . . . . church
killie, coillie . . . . wood
eilean, ey, inch . . . . island
mhor . . . . large
strath . . . . broad valley
oban, uig . . . . bay
uachdar, auchter . . . . high

AUTHORS

Anne Midgette is a freelance writer on music, art and travel who writes for *The Wall Street Journal*, *Opera News*, *Newsday, Town & Country*, and other publications. Author of a travel guide to Bavaria, and contributor to travel guides on Germany and the *Nelles Guides USA East and West*, she was co-Project Editor of the *Nelles Guide New York*. A graduate of Yale University with a degree in Classical Civilization, she divides her time between Munich and New York. She wrote the chapters on History, the Southwest, Glasgow, the West Coast, the Highlands, the Northeast, and Central Scotland; the section on Orkney; and the features on whisky, food, fabric, literature, and hiking.

James Bentley is a prize-winning author who broadcasts regularly on radio and television, writes television scripts, and is a journalist for *The Times*, *The Daily Telegraph*, and *Hello! Magazine*. His 24 travel books include works on France, Italy, and Germany. He has also written books on history and biographies. He became a full-time writer after a career as an Anglican clergyman, vicar of Oldham and senior chaplain at Eton College, Windsor. As well as Oxford degrees in modern history and theology, he holds a Ph.D. in central European history. He divides his time between England and France. He wrote the chapters on Edinburgh, the Borders, and the Outer Hebrides; the sections on Islay, Jura, Mull, and Shetland, and the feature on golf (with Anne Midgette).

Special thanks to **Judith Sleigh**, as well as **Stephanie Lewis** and other staff members of the Scottish Tourist Board, for great help in the writing of this book.

PHOTOGRAPHERS

Explore the World

AVAILABLE TITLES

Australia
Bali / Lombok
Berlin and Potsdam
Brittany
California
  Las Vegas, Reno,
  Baja California
Cambodia / Laos
Canada
  Ontario, Québec,
  Atlantic Provinces
Caribbean
  The Greater Antilles,
  Bermuda, Bahamas
Caribbean
  The Lesser Antilles
China – Hong Kong
Corsica
Crete
Cyprus
Egypt
Florida
Greece - *The Mainland*
Hawaii
Hungary
India
  Northern, Northeastern
  and Central India

India - *Southern India*
Indonesia
  Sumatra, Java, Bali,
  Lombok, Sulawesi
Ireland
Israel - *with Excursions*
  to Jordan
Kenya
London, England and
  Wales
Malaysia
Mexico
Morocco
Moscow / St Petersburg
Munich
  Excursions to Castels,
  Lakes & Mountains
Nepal
New York - *City and State*
New Zealand
Paris
Philippines
Portugal
Prague / Czech Republic
Provence
Rome
Scotland
South Africa

Spain - *Pyrenees, Atlantic*
  Coast, Central Spain
Spain
  Mediterranean Coast,
  Southern Spain,
  Balearic Islands
Sri Lanka
Thailand
Turkey
Tuscany
U.S.A.
  The East, Midwest and
  South
U.S.A.
  The West, Rockies and
  Texas
Vietnam

Nelles Guides – authorative, informed and informative.
Always up-to-date, extensivley illustrated, and with first-rate relief maps.
256 pages, appr. 150 color photos, appr. 25 maps